Appalachian Trail Guide to North Carolina–Georgia

Appalachian Trail Guide to
North Carolina–Georgia

including the
Great Smoky Mountains National Park

Richard H. Ketelle
Don O'Neal
Lisa Williams
Field Editors

THIRTEENTH EDITION

APPALACHIAN TRAIL
CONSERVANCY

Harpers Ferry, West Virginia

Cover photo: Looking toward North Carolina from the A.T. near Clingmans Dome in
Great Smoky Mountains National Park. © Mark Carroll
Half-title page photo: Aphrodite Fritillary on Powell Mountain, Georgia.
   © Phillip Jordan.
Title-page photo: Long Creek Falls, Georgia. © Phillip Jordan
Please see page 281 for additional photography credits.

ISBN 978-1-889386-56-0

Printed in the United States of America on recycled paper.

Contents

The Appalachian Trail

Welcome to America's best-known long-distance footpath, the Appalachian Trail. If you've never visited it before, you're in for a memorable time, and we hope this official guidebook will help you make the most of it. If you know the Trail, but not this part of it, we hope this book will help you discover new aspects of an experience that changes from state to state, mile to mile, and season to season.

Not long after the end of World War I, a Massachusetts forester and regional planner named Benton MacKaye envisioned a footpath running along the crests of the eastern mountains, from New England to the southern Appalachians. The work of, at first, scores of volunteers helped that dream become the Appalachian Trail, which extends more than 2,175 miles between Katahdin, in central Maine, and Springer Mountain, in northern Georgia. Its terrain ranges from swampland bog bridges to near-vertical rock scrambles that challenge the fittest

Silers Bald

wilderness trekker; its white "blazes" lead from busy small-town streets to remote mountain ridges, days from the nearest road crossing.

The "A.T.," as it's called by hikers, is a linear trail that can be enjoyed in small pieces or large chunks. Hikers follow its blazes on round-trip day-hikes, on loop-hikes (where side trails connect with it and form a loop), on one-way "section-hikes" or overnight back-packing trips that cover short or long segments, or on end-to-end "thru-hikes" that cover the entire Trail. It is continuously marked, using a standard system of paint blazes and signs, and is cleared of undergrowth and maintained to permit single-file hiking. (Bicycles, horses, and motorized vehicles are not permitted along most of the route.) Many campsites and more than 250 primitive woodland shelters are located along the Trail, typically about a day's hike apart. The path itself is usually dirt, or rock, or grass, and only very short segments are paved or wheelchair-accessible.

This remarkable footpath is much more than just a walk through the woods. When it was first begun in the 1920s and completed in the 1930s, it was little-known and rarely traveled. Large parts of it were on private property. Since 1968, it has been a part of the same national park system that includes Yellowstone, Yosemite, and the Great Smoky Mountains. Its official name today is the Appalachian National Scenic Trail, and 99.6 percent of it runs over public lands. Hundreds of roads cross it, and scores of side trails intersect with it. In some parts, the Trail "corridor" is only a few hundred feet wide; in other parts, entire mountains are protected by it.

Unlike other well-known national parks, there's no "main entrance" to the A.T., with a gate and a ranger collecting tickets. You can begin or end your hike at hundreds of places between its north-ern and southern ends. As the longest, skinniest part of America's national park system, the A.T. stretches across fourteen different states and passes through more than sixty federal, state, and local parks and forests. Maybe the most important difference between the A.T. and other national-park units is that it was built by volunteers, and volunteers still are responsible for keeping it up. The A.T. relies on a system known as "cooperative management" rather than on a large, paid federal staff. Yes, there are a handful of National Park Service staff members and a ranger assigned to the Appalachian Trail Park

Volunteer Trail maintainers

Office in Harpers Ferry, West Virginia, but thousands of the people who maintain, patrol, and monitor the footpath and its surrounding lands are outdoor lovers like you. Each year, as members of thirty "maintaining clubs" up and down the Appalachians, they volunteer almost two hundred thousand hours of their time looking after this public treasure. They would welcome your help.

About the Appalachian Trail Conservancy—We are the volunteer-based organization that teaches people about the Trail, coordinates the work of the maintaining clubs, and works with the government agencies, individuals, and companies that own the land that the Trail passes over. The membership of the Appalachian Trail Conservancy (ATC) includes hikers and Trail enthusiasts who elect a volunteer Board of Directors every two years. Members' dues and contributions help support a paid staff of about forty-five people at the ATC head-quarters in Harpers Ferry; at regional offices in New England, Pennsylvania, Virginia, and North Carolina; and at a sales distribution center, also in West Virginia. Our Web site, <www.appalachiantrail. org>, is a good source of information about the Trail. Information about contacting the Conservancy is at the back of this book.

Maine Appalachian Trail Club—www.matc.org

Appalachian Mountain Club—www.outdoors.org

Dartmouth Outing Club—www.dartmouth.edu/~doc

Green Mountain Club—www.greenmountainclub.org

AMC Berkshire Chapter—www.amcberkshire.org

AMC Connecticut Chapter—www.ct-amc.org

New York–New Jersey Trail Conference—www.nynjtc.org

Wilmington Trail Club—www.wilmingtontrailclub.org

Batona Hiking Club—members.aol.com/Batona

AMC Delaware Valley Chapter—www.amcdv.org

Philadelphia Trail Club—m.zanger.tripod.com

Blue Mountain Eagle Climbing Club—www.bmecc.org

Allentown Hiking Club—www.allentownhikingclub.org

Susquehanna Appalachian Trail Club—www.satc-hike.org

York Hiking Club—www.yorkhikingclub.com

Cumberland Valley A.T. Club—geocities.com/cvatclub

Mountain Club of Maryland—www.mcomd.org

Potomac Appalachian Trail Club—www.potomacappalachian.org

Old Dominion Appalachian Trail Club—www.odatc.org

Tidewater Appalachian Trail Club—www.tidewateratc.org

Natural Bridge Appalachian Trail Club—www.nbatc.org

Roanoke Appalachian Trail Club—www.ratc.org

Outdoor Club at Virginia Tech—www.outdoor.org.vt.edu

Piedmont Appalachian Trail Hikers—www.path-at.org

Mount Rogers Appalachian Trail Club—www.mratc.org

Tennessee Eastman Hiking Club—www.tehcc.org

Carolina Mountain Club—www.carolinamtnclub.com

Smoky Mountains Hiking Club—www.smhclub.org

Nantahala Hiking Club—www.maconcommunity.org/nhc

Georgia Appalachian Trail Club—www.georgia-atclub.org

Tips for enjoying the Appalachian Trail

Follow the blazes—The Appalachian Trail is marked for daylight travel in both directions, using a system of paint "blazes" on trees, posts, and rocks. There are some local variations, but most hikers grasp the system quickly. Above treeline, and where snow or fog may obscure paint marks, posts and rock piles called "cairns" are used to identify the route.

A blaze is a rectangle of paint in a prominent place along a trail. White-paint blazes two inches wide and six inches high mark the A.T. itself. Side trails and shelter trails use blue blazes; blazes of other colors and shapes mark other intersecting trails. Two white blazes, one above the other, signal an obscure turn, route change, incoming side trail, or other situation that requires you to be especially alert to changes in direction. In some states, one of the two blazes will be offset in the direction of the turn.

If you have gone a quarter-mile without seeing a blaze, stop. Retrace your steps until you locate a blaze. Then, check to ensure that you haven't missed a turn. Often a glance backward will reveal blazes meant for hikers traveling in the opposite direction.

White blaze

Double blaze

Volunteer Trail maintainers regularly relocate small sections of the path around hazards or undesirable features or off private property. When your map or guidebook indicates one route, and the blazes show another, follow the blazes.

A few cautions—The A.T. is a scenic trail through the forests of the Appalachian Mountains. It is full of natural splendors and is fun to hike, and parts of it run near roads and across fairly level ground. But, most of the Trail is very steep and runs deep in the woods, along the crests of rocky mountain ridges, miles from the nearest houses or paved roads. It will test your physical conditioning and skills. Plan your hike, and prepare sensibly.

Before you set out to hike the Trail, take a few minutes to review the information in this guidebook. It is as current as possible, but conditions and footpath locations sometimes change in between guidebook editions. On the Trail, please pay close attention to—and follow—the blazes and any directional signs that mark the route, even if the book describes a different route.

Although we have included some basic tips for preparing for an A.T. hike in the back of this guidebook (see page 226), this is not a "how-to" guide to backpacking. Many good books of that sort are available in your local bookstore and library. If you've never hiked before, we recommend that you take the time to read one or two and to research equipment, camping techniques, and trip planning.

Post

Cairn

If your only hiking and camping experience is in local parks and forests, be aware that hiking and camping in the mountains can be extremely strenuous and disorienting and has its own particular challenges. You will sometimes encounter wildlife and will have to make do with primitive (or nonexistent) sanitary facilities. Remember that water in the backcountry, even at water sources mentioned in this guidebook, needs to be treated for microorganisms before you drink it.

Responsibility for safety—Finally, know that you are responsible for your own safety and for the safety of those with you and for making sure that your food and water are safe for consumption. Hiking the A.T. is no more dangerous than many other popular outdoor activities, but, although the Trail is part of the national park system, it is not the proverbial "walk in the park." The Appalachian Trail Conservancy and its member clubs cannot ensure the safety of any hiker on the Trail. As a hiker, you assume the risk for any accident, illness, or injury that might occur there.

Leave No Trace—As more and more people use the Trail and other backcountry areas, it becomes more important to learn to enjoy wild places without ruining them. The best way to do this is to understand and practice the principles of Leave No Trace (shown at right), a seven-point ethic for enjoying the backcountry that applies to everything from a picnic outing to a long-distance expedition. Leave No Trace is also a non-profit organization dedicated to teaching the principles of low-impact use. For more information, contact Leave No Trace at <www.lnt.org> or call (800) 332-4100.

1. **Plan ahead and prepare**. Evaluate the risks associated with your outing, identify campsites and destinations in advance, use maps and guides, and be ready for bad weather. When people don't plan ahead, they're more likely to damage the backcountry.

2. **Travel and camp on durable surfaces.** Stay on trails and don't bushwhack short-cuts across switchbacks or other bends in the path. Keep off fragile trailside areas, such as bogs or alpine zones. Camp in designated spots, such as shelters and existing campsites, so that unspoiled areas aren't trampled and denuded.

3. **Dispose of waste properly.** Bury or pack out excrement, including pet droppings. Pack out all trash and food waste, including that left behind by others. Don't bury trash or food, and don't try to burn packaging materials in campfires.

4. **Leave what you find.** Don't take flowers or other sensitive natural resources. Don't disturb artifacts, such as native American arrowheads or the stone walls and cellar holes of historical woodland homesteads.

5. **Minimize campfire impacts.** Campfires are enjoyable, but they also create the worst visual and ecological impact of any backcountry camping practice. If possible, cook on a backpacking stove instead of a fire. Where fires are permitted, build them only in established fire rings, and don't add rocks to an existing ring. Keep fires small. Burn only dead and downed wood that can be broken by hand—leave axes and saws at home. Never leave your campfire unattended, and drown it when you leave.

6. **Respect wildlife.** Don't feed or disturb wildlife. Store food properly to avoid attracting bears, varmints, and rodents. If you bring a pet, keep it leashed.

7. **Be considerate of other visitors.** Limit overnight groups to ten or fewer, twenty-five on day trips. Minimize noise and intrusive behavior. Share shelters and other facilities. Be considerate of Trail neighbors.

How to use this book

We suggest that you use this book in conjunction with the waterproof Trail maps that were sold with it. Information about services available in towns near the Trail is updated annually in the *Appalachian Trail Thru-Hikers' Companion*. Mileage and shelter information for the entire Trail is updated annually in the *Appalachian Trail Data Book*.

Although the Trail is usually well marked and experienced hikers may be able to follow it without either guidebook or map, using the book and the maps will not only help you keep from getting lost or disoriented, but will also help you get more out of your hike.

Before you start your hike:

■ *Decide where you want to go and which Trail features you hope to see.* Use the book to help you plan your trip. The chapter on Loop Hikes (page 220) lists a number of popular day-hikes and short trips that have proven popular with hikers along this part of the Trail. The introductions to each section give more detail, summarizing scenic and cultural highlights along the route that you may wish to visit.

■ *Calculate mileage for linear or loop hikes.* Each chapter lists mileage between landmarks on the route, along with details to help you follow the path. Use the mileage and descriptions to determine how far you must hike, how long it will take you, and where you can camp if you're taking an overnight or long-distance hike.

■ *Find the Trail.* Use the section maps included in the guidebook to locate parking areas near the A.T. and the "Trailheads" or road crossings where the footpath crosses the highway. In some cases, the guidebook includes directions to nearby towns and commercial areas where you can find food, supplies, and lodging.

After you begin hiking:

- *Identify landmarks.* Deduce where you are along the Trail by comparing the descriptions in the guidebook and the features on the waterproof maps to the landscape you're hiking through. Much of the time, the Trail's blazes will lead you through seemingly featureless woodlands, where the only thing you can see in most directions is trees, but you will be able to check your progress periodically at viewpoints, meadows, mountain tops, stream crossings, road crossings, and Trailside structures.

- *Learn about the route.* Native Americans, colonial-era settlers, Civil War soldiers, nineteenth-century farmers, pioneering railroaders, and early industrial entrepreneurs explored these hills long before the A.T. was built. Although much of what they left behind has long since been overgrown and abandoned, your guidebook will point out old settlements and forest roads and put the landscape in its historical context. It will touch on the geology, natural history, and modern-day ecosystems of the eastern mountains.

- *Find campsites and side trails.* The guidebook includes directions to other trails, as well as creeks, mountain springs, and established tenting and shelter sites.

Areas covered

Each of the eleven official Appalachian Trail guidebooks describes several hundred miles of the Trail. In some cases, that includes a single state, such as Maine or Pennsylvania. In other cases, the guidebook may include several states, such as the one covering northern Virginia, West Virginia, and Maryland. Because so much of the Trail is in Virginia (more than 500 miles of it), a hiker needs to use four different guidebooks to cover that entire state.

The eleven guidebooks are:

Maine
New Hampshire–Vermont
Massachusetts–Connecticut
New York–New Jersey
Pennsylvania
Maryland and Northern Virginia
Shenandoah National Park
Central Virginia
Southwest Virginia
Tennessee–North Carolina
North Carolina–Georgia

How the guidebook is divided

Rather than trying to keep track of several hundred miles of the Trail from beginning to end, the Trail's maintainers break it down into smaller "sections." Each section covers the area between important road crossings or natural features and can vary from three to thirty miles in length. A typical section is from five to fifteen miles long. This guidebook is organized according to those sections, beginning with the northernmost in the coverage area and ending with the southernmost. Each section makes up a chapter. A summary of distances for the entire guidebook appears at the end of the book.

How sections are organized

Brief description of section—Each section begins with a brief description of the route. The description mentions highlights and prominent features and gives a sense of what it's like to hike the section as a whole.

Section map and profile—The map shows how to find the Trail from your vehicle (it is not a detailed map and should not be relied on for navigating the Trail) and includes notable roads along with a rough depiction of the Trail route, showing shelter locations. A schematic profile of the high and low points in the section gives you an idea of how much climbing or descending is ahead.

Shelters and campsites—Each chapter also includes an overview of shelters and campsites for the section, including the distances between shelters and information about water supplies. Along some parts of the Trail, particularly north of the Mason-Dixon Line, the designated sites are the only areas in which camping is permitted. In other parts of the Trail, even where "dispersed camping" is allowed, we recommend that hikers "Leave No Trace" (see page 9) and reduce their impact on the Trail's resources by using established campsites. If camping is restricted in a section, it will be noted here.

Trail description—Trail descriptions appear on the right-hand pages of each chapter. Although the description reads from north to south, it is organized for both northbound and southbound hikers. Northbound hikers should start at the end of the chapter and read up, using the mileages in the right-hand column. Southbound hikers should read down, using the mileages in the left-hand column. The descrip-

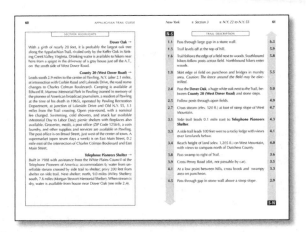

tion includes obvious landmarks you will pass, although it may not include all stream crossings, summits, or side trails. Where the Trail route becomes confusing, the guide will provide both north- and southbound directions from the landmark. When a feature appears in **bold** type, it means that you should see the section highlights for more detail.

Section highlights—On the left-hand pages of each chapter, you will find cultural, historical, natural, and practical information about the **bold** items in the Trail description. That includes detailed information about Trailheads, shelters, and campsites, along with notes on the historical and cultural resources of the route, notes on landforms and natural history, and descriptions of side trails.

End of section—The northern and southern ends of each section are noted in **bold** in the Trail description and detailed in the section highlights at the beginning and ending of each chapter of the book, respectively. The information includes brief directions about how to find the Trailhead from the highway; information about where to park, if parking is available; distances to nearby towns and facilities; and notes on the services available near the Trail, such as grocery stores and restaurants.

Guidebook conventions

North or "compass-north"?—For the sake of convenience, the directions *north, south, east* and *west* in the guide refer to the general north–south orientation of the Trail, rather than the true north or magnetic north of maps and charts. In other words, when a hiker is northbound on the Trail, whatever is to his left will be referred to as "west" and whatever is to the right will be "east." For southbounders, the opposite is true.

Although this is instinctively the way A.T. hikers orient themselves, it can be slightly confusing for the first-time A.T. hiker, since the Trail does not always follow an actual north–south orientation. For example, you might be "northbound" along the Trail (headed toward Maine), but, because of a sharp turn or a switchback up the side of a mountain, your compass will tell you you're actually pointed south for a while. Nevertheless, in this guide, a trail or road intersecting on the left side of the A.T. for the northbound hiker will always be referred to as "intersecting on the west side of the A.T.," even where the compass says otherwise.

When the compass direction of an object is important, as when directing attention to a certain feature seen from a viewpoint, the guidebook will refer to "compass-north," "compass-west," and so forth.

Undocumented features—The separate waterproof hiking maps meant to accompany this guide generally reflect all the landmarks discussed here. Because the maps are extremely detailed, some features that appear on them, such as streams and old woods roads, may not be mentioned in the guidebook if they are not important landmarks. Other side trails that the hiker encounters may not be mentioned or mapped at all; in general, this is because the unmarked trails lead onto private property, and Trail managers wish to discourage their use.

Public transportation and shuttle services—Many sections of the Trail are served by persons providing shuttles to hikers, and some sections are reachable by public transportation. For the most up-to-date list of those services, please visit the Hike the Trail section of the ATC Web site, <www.appalachiantrail.org>.

Using the Trail in Southwest North Carolina and Georgia

Between Tenn. 32/N.C. 284 at Davenport Gap, at the northern end of the Great Smoky Mountains National Park, and Springer Mountain, at the southern end of the Blue Ridge, the Trail leads almost 236 miles over a route that includes the highest and most remote parts of the entire Maine-to-Georgia footpath. Practically speaking, the route breaks down into three parts: the Great Smoky Mountains, the Nantahala Range, and the eastern Blue Ridge Mountains.

In those three parts, volunteers from three Appalachian Trail Conference maintaining clubs keep the Trail open and passable to hikers: the Smoky Mountains Hiking Club (SMHC), the Nantahala Hiking Club (NHC), and the Georgia Appalachian Trail Club (GATC).

 Smoky Mountains Hiking Club—The Smoky Mountains Hiking Club, which dates to 1924, is a group of people of all ages who enjoy the outdoors together. Members maintain the Appalachian Trail and promote conservation for nearly 100 miles of the Appalachian Trail from the Nantahala River to the northeast end of Great Smoky Mountains National Park. The club sponsors several trips every year to work on the Trail, removing the trees and branches that fell on it during the winter, repainting the white blazes, repairing the places where the footpath has been damaged by the weather, building new sections of Trail, and building and repairing shelters. The club works to protect wildlife and promote good state and national park and forest management, recognizing that whatever its members do today will affect the enjoyment of wilderness areas by future generations. It works with the National Park Service and the U.S. Forest Service to develop management plans for the Trail and surrounding areas, and club representatives work with regional conservation groups, such as the Tennessee Citizens for Wilderness Planning, and with national conservation organizations, such as the Sierra Club and the Wilderness Society. Members also work to keep state and national representatives informed about conservation issues and work with them to preserve wild areas.

Prospective members should be at least 16 years of age and should participate in at least three scheduled club hikes before applying for membership. Visitors automatically receive a membership application upon the completion of three hikes, although this does not imply an obligation to become a member. Dues for "regular membership" are $14 a year; dues for additional "family members" are $1. A copy of the current *SMHC Handbook* and the monthly *Club Newsletter* are sent to regular members. Two additional classes of membership have been established to augment the funds available for conservation work: "supporting membership" at $20 covers an entire family, as does "life membership" at $250. Nonmembers may subscribe to the *Club Newsletter* by sending $10 to P.O. Box 1454, Knoxville, TN 37901. Subscriptions ordered before September 1 will expire at the end of the year. Subscriptions ordered after September 1 will expire at the end of the following year. A current *SMHC Handbook* may be obtained for an additional $4. Both costs may be deducted from membership dues if the application for membership is submitted before the end of the subscription year. For more information, see the club's World Wide Web site at <www.smhclub.org>.

 Nantahala Hiking Club—In 1940, after the Appalachian Trail had been blazed through the mountains of southwestern North Carolina, the Rev. A. Rufus Morgan, an Episcopal priest, returned to his family's home place in Macon County and took responsibility for keeping up 55 miles in the Nantahala Mountains. Morgan applied himself to brushing, blazing, and small-tree removal for twenty-seven years and was called "the one-man hiking club" as he did trail maintenance with friends and Boy Scouts. He was an ATC board member for almost thirty years and was awarded honorary life membership in 1964. He worked in the early 1960s to establish the Nantahala Hiking Club, which was recognized formally by ATC as a Trail-maintaining club in 1968.

The club's A.T. responsibilities take in the 58.5 miles between Bly Gap near the Georgia/North Carolina border and the Nantahala River at Wesser. Both the Nantahala and the Tusquitee districts of the Nantahala National Forest are crossed, as well as designated wilderness areas. The club has about 300 members, most of whom are retired and can work on the Trail at any time. Wednesday is set aside as the Trail-maintenance day for the club crew. Short sections have individual maintainers who work on "their" section as time permits, but at least four times a year. Membership is open to anyone interested. A newsletter goes out every two months, telling of coming events and listing the hiking schedule for Saturdays and Sundays. Annual membership dues are $10 (family or single). For more information, write to: NHC Membership Chairman, 173 Carl Slagle Road, Franklin, NC 28734, or see the club's World Wide Web site, <www. maconcommunity.org/nhc>.

 Georgia Appalachian Trail Club—The 76.4 miles of the Trail in Georgia and into North Carolina to Bly Gap, along with its shelters and campsites, are managed and maintained by the more than 600 members of the Georgia Appalachian Trail Club. The club also maintains the Amicalola Falls approach trail and trails to the Len Foote Hike Inn, which it helps to manage. The club was organized in 1930, largely due to the efforts of Everett B. ("Eddie") Stone, assistant state forester in Georgia, with the help of his assistant, Charles Elliott. While leaders of the then-Appalachian Trail Conference, based in New England and the mid-Atlantic, were debating the route of the A.T. in Georgia, Stone was busy building the Trail and marking where he thought it should go. His efforts to have it located along the Blue Ridge were successful, and he immediately began forming a club to support the new route. Elliott rounded up a number of influential people in the state, as well as enthusiastic outdoors folks, and, at the organizational meeting in November 1930, twenty-five joined the new club. Most were mainly interested in hiking, but Stone slowly convinced them to take on responsibilities

Appalachian Trail Conservancy: Regional Office, Asheville, N.C., (828) 254-3708; main office, Harpers Ferry, W.Va., (304) 535-6331; <www.appalachiantrail.org>

NATIONAL PARK SERVICE

Great Smoky Mountains National Park—Gatlinburg, Tenn., (865) 436-1294; (865) 436-1230; <www.nps.gov/grsm>

Appalachian Trail Park Office—Harpers Ferry, W.Va., (304) 535-6278; <www.nps.gov/appa>

USDA FOREST SERVICE

<www.fs.fed.us>

Nantahala National Forest, National Forests in North Carolina—(828) 257-4200
    Cheoah District, Robbinsville, N.C., (828) 479-6431
    Nantahala District, Franklin, N.C., (828) 524-6441
    Tusquitee District, Murphy, N.C., (828) 837-5152
Chattahoochee and Oconee National Forests—(770) 297-3000
    Blue Ridge District, Blairsville, Ga., (706) 745-6928
    Chattooga River District, Clayton, Ga., (706) 782-3320

Local police, fire, and emergency

Dial 911; if 911 is not available, dial the following local numbers:

Tennessee—Blount County, (865) 983-3620; Sevier County, (865) 453-4668; Cocke County, (423) 623-3064

North Carolina—Clay County, (828) 389-6354; Macon County, (828) 369-9116; Swain County, (828) 488-2197; Graham County, (828) 479-3352; Haywood County, (828) 452-6666.

Georgia—Dawson County, (706) 265-3333; Lumpkin County, (706) 864-3633; Gilmer County, (706) 635-4162 (*Sheriff*), (706) 635-4652 (*fire/rescue*); Fannin County, (706) 632-2043; Union County, (706) 439-6038; White County, (706) 865-5177; Towns County, (706) 896-7460; Habersham County, (706) 778-3911; Rabun County, (706) 782-3612

State Police

Tennessee—Knoxville District, (865) 594-5800
North Carolina—Asheville District, (828) 298-4252
Georgia—Atlanta, (404) 624-6077

as Trail maintainers and advocates.

The Georgia club grew gradually in numbers and purpose. Today, members can look with pride on the club's rich heritage and long tradition of Trail stewardship, one that it has shared over the years with the U.S. Forest Service, originally in the Cherokee and later in the Chattahoochee national forests. You may see GATC members on the Trail at any time, constructing erosion-control devices, building shelters and bridges, painting blazes, cutting weeds, and generally improving the quality of corridor and footpath. For a detailed history of the club, see the two-volume *Friendships of the Trail,* published by the GATC.

Anyone who desires to be involved in Trail maintenance or the club itself is invited to contact the GATC and to participate in any of its Trail-maintenance or other outings. Write Georgia Appalachian Trail Club, Inc., P.O. Box 654, Atlanta, GA 30301; or visit the club's Web site at <www.georgia-atclub.org>.

Public Transportation and Shuttles—Information on public transportation to and from the Trail (scarce in these states) and current shuttle providers can be obtained from ATC's Web site at <www.appalachiantrail.org/shuttles> or by calling the information center at (304) 535-6331.

Camping in the Great Smoky Mountains National Park—Our second most-visited national-park unit, <www.nps.gov/grsm>, officially begins for northbounders on the northern side of Fontana Dam; for southbounders, Davenport Gap is the beginning. In recent years, the park has hosted more than nine million visitors annually. Backcountry permits must be obtained before entering the park. "Thru-hikers" (which the park defines as anyone beginning *and* ending an A.T. hike at least 50 miles north *and* south of the park boundaries) may self-register. A self-registration facility is located at the Fontana Dam Shelter for northbound hikers. Southbound hikers can get a permit at the Forest Service office in Hot Springs, N.C. At Davenport Gap, the park's Big Creek Ranger Station is 1.3 miles away, and permits are available there. Thru-hikers are permitted to tent outside A.T. shelters, but only if they are full. Section-hikers (considered to be anyone *not* beginning *and* ending a hike 50 miles outside the park) must make reservations by calling the park reservations office at (865) 436-1231. Anyone caught without a permit will be fined.

In the 1990s, a privy-building campaign, underwritten by ATC and the Smoky Mountains Hiking Club, resulted in new facilities at the more heavily used shelters. Spence Field, Double Spring Gap, Tri-Corner Knob, Pecks Corner, Mt. Collins, Cosby Knob, and Ice-water Spring shelters now have "moldering privies." All shelters have been rebuilt in recent years (or are scheduled for 2008 rebuilding), with the "bear fencing" removed from the fronts. Elsewhere in the park, hikers should bury their wastes in accordance with accepted backcountry-sanitation practices.

Dogs are *not permitted* on trails in the park. Hikers violating this rule will be fined and escorted from the park.

Camping in the Nantahala and Chattahoochee national forests— Most of the Appalachian Trail corridor south of the Smokies lies within broad tracts of national forest lands purchased by the federal government prior to and during the Great Depression, after loggers extracted much of the timber value, or as a result of the A.T. protection effort since 1968. Three-quarters of a century after being stripped nearly barren, deep, mature forests now cover most of the mountainsides, sometimes for miles on either side of the Trail. Unlike many parts farther north, where the A.T. corridor follows a narrow strip of land in which camping is strictly regulated, the national forests of North Carolina and Georgia offer hikers the chance to find their own "dispersed" campsites away from the beaten path.

With the freedom to pick one's own campsite, however, comes the increased responsibility of adhering faithfully to the practices of Leave No Trace (LNT) wilderness ethics (page 9). Few hikers enjoy seeing trampled, denuded clearings near creeks or springs or blackened fire rings near every good viewpoint and every couple of hundred yards along the path, but that's what happens when campers don't employ LNT principles. The more that we abuse the freedom that these woodlands offer, the more likely it becomes that government land managers will impose restrictions on where (and how) we camp. Please do your part. Either concentrate use by camping at sites

Tentsite in Chattahoochee National Forest

that are already firmly established, leaving surrounding areas untouched, or apply all your art and woodcraft to making sure that the pristine glade where you spend the night looks equally pristine to the next person who comes along.

Campfires—In keeping with Leave No Trace principles, we encourage hikers and campers to use portable backpacking stoves for cooking, rather than campfires. In the Great Smokies, campfires are permitted only at designated sites. Campfires are permitted on most national forest lands, except where posted otherwise. Only downed and dead trees may be used for firewood. To prevent forest fires, follow these steps:

- Keep fires away from overhanging branches.
- Use an existing fire ring if possible.
- Avoid building campfires on dry, windy days.
- Keep water nearby in case of an emergency.
- Stack firewood upwind and well away from any campfire.

- Never leave a campfire unattended.

- Drown the fire and surrounding area with water before you leave, stirring until the ashes are cold to the touch.

- Do not bury coals, which can smolder for hours, even days, and surface again to start a forest fire.

Groups—Please limit day-hiking groups to twenty-five or fewer members (ten or fewer in designated wilderness areas). If you're part of an organized group, such as a Scout troop, church excursion, or college outdoor program, please carry tents, and do not monopolize shelters, on which solo hikers often depend. Keep overnight groups small (eight to ten people, including leaders), and keep noise to a minimum at shelters and campgrounds between 9 p.m. and 7 a.m. for the sake of those attempting to sleep. Please cooperate and consider the needs of others.

Shelters—Shelters (sometimes called lean-tos in New England) are generally three-sided, with open fronts and a sloping roof, and usually are spaced less than a day's hike apart. They often have pads around them on which you can pitch a tent. They may be fitted with bunks or have a wooden floor for sleeping. Water, a privy, and a table or benches may be nearby; some have fireplaces, and most have a fire ring in front. If a shelter has a register, please sign it. Except in the Smokies, where reservations are required for all hikers not thru-hiking, A.T. shelters are available on a first-come, first-served basis, for overnight stays only, and may be crowded during weekends in hiking season. Except in the case of bad weather, injury, or emergency, they are not intended for stays longer than one or two nights. Hunters, fishermen, and other nonhikers should not use the shelters as bases of operation.

On the following pages is a north-to-south list of shelters and campsites along the A.T. south of Davenport Gap.

Shelters, including two on the approach trail to Springer Mountain, are typically situated at intervals permitting easy day-hikes between them. Some are closer together to accommodate hikers in popular areas. All but two of those shelters are three-sided, open-front types.

Shelters and Campsites

Trail Section	Miles from Davenport Gap	Miles from Springer	Shelter or Campsite
GREAT SMOKY MOUNTAINS			
N.C. 1	0.0	235.9	**Davenport Gap**
N.C. 1	0.9	235.0	**Davenport Gap Shelter**
N.C. 1	8.0	227.9	**Cosby Knob Shelter**
N.C. 1	15.7	220.2	**Tri-Corner Knob Shelter**
N.C. 1	20.9	215.0	**Pecks Corner Shelter** (0.5m E)
N.C. 1	28.3	207.6	**Icewater Spring Shelter**
N.C. 2	35.8	200.1	**Mt. Collins Shelter** (0.5m W)
N.C. 2	42.1	193.8	**Double Spring Gap Shelter**
N.C. 2	43.8	192.1	**Silers Bald Shelter**
N.C. 2	49.3	186.6	**Derrick Knob Shelter**
N.C. 2	55.6	180.3	**Spence Field Shelter** (0.2m E)
N.C. 2	58.5	177.4	**Russell Field Shelter**
N.C. 2	61.0	174.9	**Mollies Ridge Shelter**
N.C. 2	66.4	169.5	**Birch Spring Gap Campsite**
NANTAHALA MOUNTAINS			
N.C. 3	72.3	163.6	**Fontana Dam Shelter**
N.C. 3	75.9	160.0	**Campsite**
N.C. 3	78.9	157.0	**Cable Gap Shelter**
N.C. 4	85.0	150.9	**Brown Fork Gap Shelter**
N.C. 5	94.1	141.8	**Sassafras Gap Shelter**
N.C. 6	101.8	134.1	**A. Rufus Morgan Shelter**
N.C. 6	106.7	129.2	**Wesser Bald Shelter**
N.C. 7	112.5	123.4	**Cold Spring Shelter**
N.C. 7	117.3	118.6	**Wayah Shelter**

Trail Section	Miles from Davenport Gap	Miles from Springer	Shelter or Campsite
N.C. 8	124.6	111.3	**Siler Bald Shelter** (0.5m E)
N.C. 9	132.1	103.8	**Rock Gap Shelter**
N.C. 9	137.4	98.5	**Big Spring Shelter**
N.C. 9	144.2	91.7	**Carter Gap Shelter**
N.C. 9	151.8	84.1	**Standing Indian Shelter**
N.C. 10	156.7	79.2	**Muskrat Creek Shelter** (4,600')

BLUE RIDGE MOUNTAINS

Trail Section	Miles from Davenport Gap	Miles from Springer	Shelter or Campsite
N.C. 11	161.6	74.3	**Campsite**
N.C. 11	163.9	72.0	**Plumorchard Gap Shelter** (0.2m E)
N.C. 11	167.3	68.6	**Campsite**
Ga. 12	171.9	64.0	**Deep Gap Shelter** (0.3m E)
Ga. 12	179.4	56.5	**Tray Mountain Shelter** (0.2m W)
Ga. 12	181.4	54.5	**Cheese Factory Campsite**
Ga. 13	187.2	48.7	**Blue Mountain Shelter**
Ga. 13	188.1	47.8	**Campsite**
Ga. 13	194.4	41.5	**Low Gap Shelter**
Ga. 13	199.0	36.9	**Whitley Gap Shelter** (1.2m E)
Ga. 15	207.6	28.3	**Blood Mountain Shelter**
Ga. 15	208.4	27.5	**Slaughter Creek Campsite**
Ga. 15	208.9	27.0	**Woods Hole Shelter** (0.4m W)
Ga. 16	220.8	15.1	**Gooch Mountain Shelter** (0.1m W)
Ga. 17	228.1	7.8	**Hawk Mountain Shelter** (0.2m W)
Ga. 17	233.1	2.8	**Stover Creek Shelter**
Ga. 17	235.7	0.2	**Springer Mountain Shelter**

The exceptions are a four-walled, two-room stone structure on top of Blood Mountain and the Fontana Dam Shelter, at which two shelters face each other, connected by a "breezeway." All of the shelters have floors, and most have springs close by. Some have "bear cables" for hanging food. Most have privies, and five have lofts.

Bears and other campsite raiders—Skunks, possums, raccoons, squirrels, and mice are common along the A.T. in the Smokies, North Carolina, and Georgia. They sometimes visit shelters and well-established camping areas—usually after dark. If they smell your food, they'll eat it if they can! Mice inhabit most Trail shelters.

A healthy black-bear population lives in the Smokies and the southern forests, too. The fact that bears are hunted each fall in Georgia and North Carolina makes them somewhat more timid than in the Smokies, where they are protected from hunting; they will generally retreat when they encounter people, unless a mother bear thinks her cubs are threatened. That doesn't mean they won't steal your food from camp, if given the chance, or that an especially aggressive bear won't try to intimidate you into dropping your pack. Always remember that bears are powerful and unpredictable animals that should be treated with caution and respect.

The best defense against bears and other campsite raiders is preparing and storing food properly. Cook and eat your meals away from your tent or shelter, so food odors do not linger. Bear cables for hanging food are being installed at many shelters and campsites along the A.T. in the Smokies, Nantahalas, and Georgia Blue Ridge, but some sites still lack them. Where cables are not available, plan to hang your food, cookware, toothpaste, personal hygiene items, and even water bottles (if you use flavored drinks in them) in a sturdy bag from a strong tree branch at least ten feet off the ground and well away from your campsite. Make sure the bag does not dangle too close to the trunk of the tree; black bears are crafty climbers and good reachers. Never feed bears or leave food behind for them. That simply increases the risks to you and the hikers who follow you.

Hiking During Hunting Season

Most of the Appalachian Trail in southwest North Carolina and Georgia is on national-forest land where hunting is legal, subject to state laws. Deer season, typically in the months of October, November, December, and January, should be a time for special caution by hikers. In some areas, hunting is legal on the Trail itself. In sections where hunting is prohibited, hunters on nearby properties may wander near the Trail, not knowing that they are near the Trail.

Take this seriously. When the national forests were formed in the mid-1930s from smaller forests and new lands, overhunting and habitat destruction had nearly wiped out most large and small game. Seven decades of habitat and game management mean not only that hikers have an array of many special places but also that hunters today are harvesting record numbers of deer, turkey, and bear on the lands covered in this guide.

Hikers should call ATC or check state Web sites or ATC's site, <www.appalachiantrail.org>, for detailed information about hunting seasons. ATC recommends that hikers wear plenty of highly visible "blaze orange" clothing when hunters are sharing the woods.

A walk south along the Appalachian Trail

The Appalachian Trail in east-central Tennessee, southwestern North Carolina, and northern Georgia takes hikers high into remote southern Appalachian forests, across the Trail's loftiest summits, and through some of its wildest areas. The northern end, at Davenport Gap, is near where the Pigeon River flows west toward the Tennessee Valley, cutting through the master ridge of the Appalachians. The southern end of the section, the southern terminus of the Trail at Georgia's Springer Mountain, is near the southern end of the Appalachians, where high ridges give way to the rolling Piedmont in northern Georgia.

In between, the Trail follows mountain ridges through a region rich in biological diversity and American history. The northern third of the Trail described in this guidebook leads through the Great Smoky Mountains National Park, a vast forest preserve that includes the Trail's highest point and longest roadless sections. In the middle third, the Trail threads through the ridges and balds of the Nantahala range in the Nantahala National Forest, a transverse line of mountains linking the Smokies, on the western side of the southern highlands, with the Blue Ridge, on the eastern side, like the cross-stroke of a capital "H." The southern third follows the less lofty escarpment of the Blue Ridge from North Carolina into Georgia through the deep woods of the Chattahoochee National Forest.

As you hike through the Trail sections covered in this guidebook, you will repeatedly encounter odd and interesting place names that hark back to the time when Euroamerican settlers were pushing west and north into lands occupied by native Americans—the Cherokee nation, in particular—and displacing them. One of the persistent (though incorrect) rumors about the Appalachian Trail is that it follows the route of traditional Indian footpaths along the mountain ridges. That story isn't true. The Trail was built in the 1920s and 1930s over existing roads and newly scouted footpaths. Nonetheless, the portion

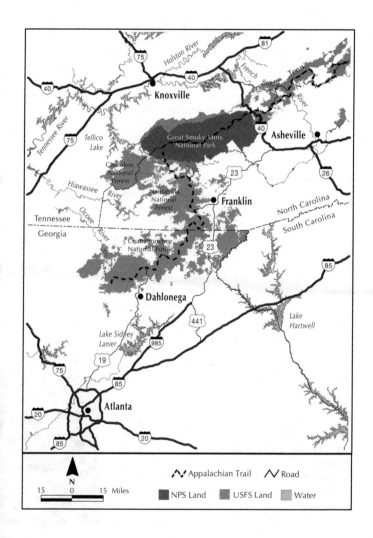

of the Trail described here passes through lands that were "Indian Territory" within living memory of the Trail's construction, and where that heartbreaking chapter of American history is perhaps closer to the surface than almost anywhere else along the A.T.'s 2,176 miles. Cherokee culture has been established here since at least 8,000 B.C.E., as Spanish explorer Hernando de Soto discovered in 1539. More than a century later, Ulster-Scots emigrating from British repression arrived in these mountains and were embraced by the Cherokee, with whom they traded tools, crafts, music, and dance (mountain clogging being a mixture of the two traditions). All that ended with the wars of the late-eighteenth and early-nineteenth centuries.

The Smokies—The Great Smoky Mountains are central to eastern Appalachian culture, as a corner of America that Horace Kephart documented in his 1913 book, *Our Southern Highlanders*. Kephart, an early blazer of the A.T., offered his readers a detailed look at the landscape and culture of the Smokies—bear hunters, moonshiners, hardscrabble farmers, and hermits—in the years before World War I and before the states started condemning land for the national park, forcing the remaining mountain folks out. Geologically speaking, the Smokies are the heart of the Appalachians, too. They form the western side of what geologists call the "Blue Ridge Province"(see page 239). But, while the Blue Ridge for most of the Appalachians is just that—a narrow ridge of mountains—here the geological region spreads out broadly, like the blade of a canoe paddle below the long, narrow handle. West of the Smokies is the fertile Tennessee Valley. To the east lie the narrow, twisting mountain valleys and hollows of the North Carolina highlands, the mountain plateau between the Smokies and the eastern escarpment of the Blue Ridge.

For much of its length, the Trail in the Smokies is about a mile high, and, at its highest point, at Clingmans Dome, it's well over that. The steep, inhospitable slopes of these formidable mountains have long discouraged development, and even today you can find corners of the national park that have never been logged or settled—virgin forest that has grown there since the last Ice Age. As a result, the Great Smoky Mountains National Park is among the most biologically diverse habitats in all of North America. According to the National Park Service, more than eighty-five inches of rain falls on

Observation tower on Clingmans Dome

the high ridges each year, draining into 2,100 miles of streams. Five different types of forest (see page 247) here are home to more than 1,500 species of flowering plants and at least 4,000 nonflowering varieties, not to mention a wide range of wildlife.

Hiking southwest, you will climb the ridge of the Smokies out of Davenport Gap, treading a footpath built by the Civilian Conservation Corps during the Great Depression, and follow the ridgeline on or past a series of 5,000- and 6,000-foot summits. At Newfound Gap, the Trail descends to its only road crossing in the park, then ascends again to Clingmans Dome, the roof of the range. From there, hikers cross a series of balds and alpine meadows that date back to times when Indians and settlers cleared the high ridges and cattle grazed there. At the southern end of the park, the Trail leaves the main ridge of the Smokies, and the North Carolina–Tennessee boundary line, to descend along a side ridge to the valley of the Little Tennessee River, flooded by Fontana Lake, where you will cross the park's southern boundary.

The Nantahalas—The Nantahalas were inhabited by the Cherokees when explorer Hernando de Soto traveled from Nikwasi (the present-day Franklin, N.C.) across the Nantahalas to Murphy. He must have passed through one of the gaps along the route of the Appalachian Trail. In 1775, naturalist William Bartram traveled an Indian trail from Nikwasi to the Nantahala River, hoping to reach the "overhill towns" of the Cherokees. The following year, General Griffith Rutherford and Col. Andrew Williamson, on a punitive search-and-destroy mission against the Cherokees, led troops across the Nantahalas, fighting skirmishes and burning native villages as they went, to discourage them from siding with the British in the Revolutionary War.

Between the Smokies and the eastern Blue Ridge, the A.T. crosses two steep river valleys—the Little Tennessee and Nantahala—and various tributaries of those rivers. Above the valleys, the footpath ascends a series of 5,000-foot summits (heath balds typical of the southern Appalachians) and 4,000-foot gaps. Road crossings are rare, but regularly spaced. A 3,000-foot descent into and ascent out of the Nantahala Gorge are among the most physically challenging

View from Wayah Bald

sections of the A.T., certainly in the South. (For northbound hikers, the Nantahala is the first river crossing north of Springer Mountain.) From Winding Stair and Wallace gaps near Franklin, the Trail ascends the eastern escarpment of the Blue Ridge at Standing Indian Mountain, just north of the Georgia line, which hikers cross just south of Bly Gap.

The Blue Ridge—Between Bly Gap and Springer Mountain, hikers generally follow a line of mountains that falls off steeply to the east and is famously known as the Blue Ridge. The eastern ridge runs from Springer Mountain north into Pennsylvania (the A.T. follows it in Georgia, parts of Virginia, Maryland, and Pennsylvania). Although, from a geologist's point of view, the Smokies and Nantahalas are technically part of the Blue Ridge Mountains, this part of the Trail follows the Blue Ridge proper—the escarpment that marks the boundary between the populous Piedmont region and the high country.

The mountains west of the Trail were the last unfettered home of the Cherokees, part of a once-vast territory that settlers gradually whittled away until the native inhabitants were rounded up and forcibly marched to "Indian Territory" in Oklahoma along the notorious "Trail of Tears" in 1838—less than a century before the Appalachian Trail was first blazed here. (A remnant of the tribe hid in North Carolina, and eventually a reservation was established for them there.) A gold rush and homesteading followed, after which the mountains became an important strategic consideration to Union forces advancing into Georgia from the Tennessee Valley during the last months of the Civil War. In the impoverished postwar era, the highlands were stripped of timber and minerals; large portions were sold in the early-twentieth century to the federal government for national forests. Like most of the mountain region, northern Georgia remained sparsely populated and isolated until the mid-twentieth century. Now, the high country is much prized for vacation homes and resorts and is a magnet for refugees from the fast-growing Piedmont cities, who seek

scenic areas for hiking, camping, fishing, hunting, and boating.

From roadless Bly Gap, the Trail mostly follows the ridgeline, descending frequently into gaps and ascending over 3,000- to 4,000-foot knobs, knolls, and summits, but not gaining or losing much net elevation. It is crossed by several highways and numerous county roads. Streams north and west of the Georgia Blue Ridge generally flow northwest and west to the Mississippi River. Those on the south and east flow south and west, either to the Chattahoochee River or, on the southern end of the ridge, to the Coosa and Alabama rivers to the Gulf of Mexico. North of the ridge, leading east from Tray Mountain, streams flow into the Tallulah River, then south and east to the Atlantic Ocean. The southern terminus of the A.T., at Springer Mountain, is near the southernmost point of the Blue Ridge. An "approach trail" leading to Springer from Amicalola Falls State Park is one of several access routes to the southern terminus.

View from Blood Mountain

Great Smoky Mountains National Park

Most of the seventy-two miles of the A.T. between the Pigeon River and the Little Tennessee River lies within the Great Smoky Mountains National Park, along the crest of the master range of the southern Appalachians. With the exception of the Black Mountains in North Carolina, the Smokies are the loftiest mountains in the East. The highlights of the route through the park can be found on page 30.

Although the first serious proposal to establish a national park in the Smoky Mountains was made before 1900, the efforts that were ultimately successful began in 1923. Private and public efforts to acquire land began in 1925. In 1928, John D. Rockefeller, Jr., contributed $5 million to match contributions of states and private citizens, and purchasing of land began in earnest. By 1930, 158,000 acres had been bought; by 1935, 400,000 acres. The park was formally dedicated in 1940 by President Franklin D. Roosevelt.

The original route of the A.T. extended the length of the Great Smokies to Deals Gap. Beyond, the Trail traversed 3.3 miles of privately owned land to Tapoco, where it crossed the Little Tennessee and Cheoah rivers on a highway bridge and then led back east along the crest of the Yellow Creek Mountains. This route was necessary because there was no other crossing of the Little Tennessee River. The TVA dam at Fontana on the Little Tennessee River made possible a Trail relocation that not only

eliminated a difficult and circuitous route but added several unusual features to the Trail system: Fontana Dam, which serves as a crossing of the Little Tennessee; a 29-mile-long lake that forms the southern boundary of the Great Smokies; and Fontana Village, now a recreational center.

At the suggestion of the Smoky Mountains Hiking Club (SMHC), the Trail was relocated in 1946 and 1947 to leave the crest of the Smokies at Doe Knob, the point of most direct access to Fontana Dam. This change in route eliminated from the Trail two outstanding features, Gregory Bald and Parson Bald, now accessible on side trails.

Half of the A.T. within the park is open to horseback riding and horse-camping under a compromise incorporated in the 1968 National Trails System Act that brought the A.T. into the national park system. Horse users may also share A.T. shelters. SMHC and ATC have made a concerted effort to resolve issues with the horse users, who are now helping with A.T. maintenance within the park.

Air pollution is one of the Smokies' most aggravating problems. Pollution can drop visibility from 93 to 22 miles on an otherwise clear day. Along with sulfur, nitrogen provides the basis for acid deposition, which includes acid rain. Ozone can make breathing difficult and causes visible damage to sensitive plants, including black cherry, milkweed, and 30 other species in the park. The park's ozone, nitrogen, and sulfur levels are among the nation's highest and often remain high longer than in nearby urban communities. Much of this pollution comes from power plants and highways to the west. Hikers with asthma and other respiratory problems should be particularly careful on hazy days, park officials say.

Silers Bald

Davenport Gap (Tenn. 32/S.R. 1397) to Newfound Gap (Tenn. 71/ U.S. 441)

31.3 MILES

This section, also identified as Tennessee–North Carolina Section Seventeen, traverses the wildest portion of the Great Smokies. At its northern end is a steep ascent from (or descent to) Davenport Gap (elev. 1,975 feet) of 3,025 feet over a distance of 5.2 miles. At its southern end is a 955-foot descent to (or ascent from) Newfound Gap (elev. 5,045 feet). In between are many deep gaps and high peaks, with eleven major climbs and descents. Those include Mt. Cammerer, the northernmost peak in the Smokies range; Cosby Knob; Mt. Guyot, just below its 6,621-foot summit; Tri-Corner Knob; Mt. Chapman; Mt. Sequoyah; Pecks Corner; Porters Mountain; Charlies Bunion; and Mt. Kephart, above Newfound Gap. The route through the section is graded, never steeper than 15 percent. Davenport Gap to Pecks Corner is open to horse use. The section is easier to hike south to north, from Newfound Gap to Davenport Gap, with ascents totaling 4,608 feet and descents totaling 7,678 feet (the reverse is true from north to south). The section's many deep gaps and high peaks involve considerably more climbing than a casual inspection of the route would indicate. Allow for extra time and exertion. See the introductory section (pages 16–27) for advice about campfires, water sources and scarcity, wildlife protection, bears, and camping permits. Please note that the actual compass orientation of the Trail through the Smokies is along a generally southwest–northeast axis, described as north–south in this guide; see page 14 for information on how compass directions are used in the A.T. guides.

Mt. Cammerer

Road Access—Both the northern (Tenn. 32/S.R. 1397 or old N.C. 284) and southern (Tenn. 71/U.S. 441) ends are accessible by vehicle.

Maps—Refer to National Geographic Maps *Great Smoky Mountains National Park Map* for route navigation. For additional area detail, refer to USGS Clingmans Dome, Mt. LeConte, Mt. Guyot, Luftee Knob, Hartford, and Waterville quadrangles.

Shelters and Campsites—This section has five shelters: Davenport Gap Shelter (mile 0.9/30.4), Cosby Knob Shelter (mile 8.0/23.3), Tri-Corner Knob (mile 15.7/15.6), Pecks Corner (mile 20.9/10.4, 0.4 mile from A.T.), and Icewater Spring (mile 28.3/3.0). The entire section is within the Great Smoky Mountains National Park. Overnight use along the A.T. is by permit only. Tent camping is not allowed, except by thru-hikers and then only when the shelter is full. Campfires are allowed only in campfire rings or shelter fireplaces. Campfires should be attended at all times and completely extinguished when you leave a shelter. Be sure to pack out all food and trash.

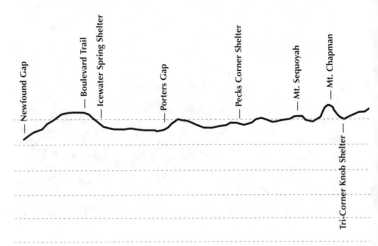

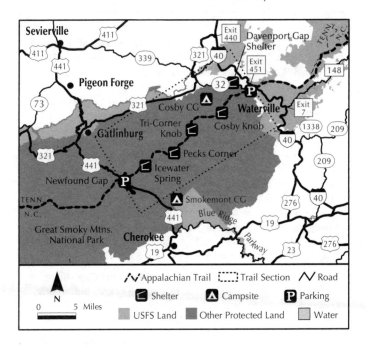

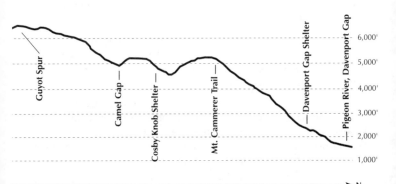

31.3 MILES

SECTION HIGHLIGHTS

Northern end of section →

At Davenport Gap, Tenn./N.C., 27 miles south of Newport, Tenn., *via* U.S. 321 and Tenn. 32, and 31 miles east of Gatlinburg, Tenn., *via* U.S. 321 and Tenn. 32. It is 55 miles northwest of Asheville, N.C., *via* I-40. The simplest access is I-40, exit 451 (Waterville), 1.3 miles through Waterville, N.C., on S.R. 1332 and west on S.R. 1397 (Old N.C. 284) to Davenport Gap. Big Creek Ranger Station and primitive campground is a short distance from the intersection of S.R. 1332 and S.R. 1397, at Mt. Sterling Village. Public transportation is not available to Davenport Gap. Because of vandalism, it is not advisable to leave cars overnight near the Trail crossing; park at the Big Creek Ranger Station. Public accommodations, supplies, stores, post offices, restaurants, and lodging are available at Newport, Cosby, and Gatlinburg, Tenn.; and Cherokee, N.C. A country store with supplies, bunkrooms, and a grill is located 1.3 miles east of the Trailhead in Waterville *via* S.R. 1397 and S.R. 1332.

Davenport Gap Shelter →

Built-in bunks accommodate 12, with spring nearby but no privy. Shelter is fenced to keep out bears. Next shelter: south, 7.1 miles (Cosby Knob); north, 10.7 miles (Groundhog Creek).

Chestnut Branch Trail →

Leads east 2.0 miles to Big Creek Ranger Station, 0.5 mile from NPS campground.

Lower Mt. Cammerer Trail →

Leads west 7.8 miles to public road at NPS Cosby Campground in Tennessee on easy grade, going around northern side of Mt. Cammerer through younger forest growth.

Rock construction →

The spectacular rock work on the Trail below Mt. Cammerer was done by the Civilian Conservation Corps (CCC) during the Great Depression, in the early days of the park. The corps assigned crews of unemployed men to public-works projects throughout the United

N-S	TRAIL DESCRIPTION	

0.0	**Northern end of section** at Davenport Gap (elev. 1,975 feet), at a winding road on the Tennessee–North Carolina state line. To the west, the road is Tenn. 32; to the east, it is S.R. 1397 (Old N.C. 284/Cove Creek Road). Between here and Pecks Corner (mile 20.9/10.4 below), hikers share the Trail with horseback riders. ■ SOUTHBOUND hikers enter Great Smoky Mountains National Park, beginning steady, five-mile, 3,025-foot ascent to Mt. Cammerer along a graded trail. ■ NORTHBOUND hikers, follow S.R. 1397 20 yards east (right), cross road, and ascend briefly on steps before continuing the descent toward the Pigeon River and Interstate 40 crossing (See *Appalachian Trail Guide to Tennessee–North Carolina*).	31.3
0.9	Pass **Davenport Gap Shelter**, 200 yards west of A.T.	30.4
1.9	Pass Trail junction with **Chestnut Branch Trail** to east. Pass through gap.	29.4
2.8	**Lower Mt. Cammerer Trail** intersects to west.	28.5
3.1	Pass side trail leading 50 yards east to spring.	28.2
3.2	Cross spur on North Carolina side of Mt. Cammerer. Make a sharp turn.	28.1
4.2	Make very sharp turn at ridgecrest with view west toward Hartford, Tenn. Trail remains on east side of ridge.	27.1
4.4	Reach large rock that provides great view to east and north. Note considerable **rock construction** in retaining walls on the A.T. north of here.	26.9
4.7	Pass spring to west of Trail, near site used as a camp by the CCC in construction of Mt. Cammerer fire tower.	26.6

SECTION HIGHLIGHTS

States during the 1930s; the A.T. was a grateful beneficiary of their labor here and in other states. Many of the trails and structures of the park were built by CCC crews, including major parts of the Appalachian Trail route.

Mt. Cammerer →

Originally called White Rocks, or Sharp Top, the 4,928-foot summit was renamed to honor Arno B. Cammerer, director of the National Park Service from 1933 to 1940, the time of the establishment of the park. The stone lookout tower there was built between 1937 and 1939 by the CCC to provide a vantage point for fire control. It was refurbished in 1995 by the Friends of the Smokies.

Sunup Knob →

Shows examples of two types of rock prominent along the Trail in this area. Most common is a massive, medium- to coarse-grained gray rock called *graywacke*, composed of sand and chalky-looking feldspar grains formed when they settled with fine material from an undersea landslide, probably about 700 million years ago. The other rock is a black slate, which is thin-bedded and may break into flat plates. This was formed by intense pressure on beds of mud, which settled out in the sea during periods between continental collisions. The black color indicates that carbon is present and that the sea water had little oxygen content. Some slate layers are straight, and others are curved.

Low Gap Trail →

Leads east to reservation-only wilderness campsites at Walnut Bottoms, following Low Gap Branch, and west 2.5 miles to developed NPS Cosby Campground and 2.9 miles to hiker parking, following Cosby Creek.

Cosby Knob Shelter →

Built-in bunks accommodate 12, with spring nearby; bear cables (no fence); privy. Next shelter: south, 7.7 miles (Tri-Corner Knob); north, 7.1 miles (Davenport Gap).

N-S

| TRAIL DESCRIPTION |

Lichen north of Cosby Knob Shelter

5.2	Pass junction with graded side trail, which leads 0.6 mile west to **Mt. Cammerer**.	**26.1**
5.4	Cross high point (elev. 4,928 feet) on ridgecrest at Tennessee–North Carolina border.	**25.9**
6.3	Skirt west side of **Sunup Knob** (elev. 5,050 feet).	**25.0**
6.7	Cross crest of ridge west of summit of Rocky Face Mountain.	**24.6**
7.3	Low Gap (elev. 4,242 feet) and intersection of **Low Gap Trail**.	**24.0**
7.9	Pass area where water crosses Trail.	**23.4**
8.0	Pass side trail to **Cosby Knob Shelter**, which is 150 feet to east.	**23.3**

S-N

Hell Ridge →

Between Cosby Knob and Pinnacle Lead (mile 13.4/17.9 below), the Trail follows "Hell Ridge," named because of devastation resulting from a forest fire on the North Carolina side along a four-mile section, after logging early in the twentieth century stripped away the forest "roof" that kept fast-burning undergrowth in check.

Camel Gap Trail →

Leads east and south 5.1 miles to Walnut Bottoms and Big Creek and 5.1 miles farther to NPS Big Creek primitive campground near Mt. Sterling and Davenport Gap area *via* Big Creek Trail.

Snake Den Ridge Trail →

Leads west through eastern-hemlock forest down Snake Den Mountain to Cosby Campground in 5.3 miles. A spring is about 0.8 mile down this trail. Maddron Bald Trail branches from Snake Den Ridge Trail in 0.7 mile, crosses Maddron Bald, and leads 7.2 miles to Laurel Springs Road and, ultimately, to U.S. 321.

Inadu Knob →

Inadu means "snake" in Cherokee and refers to snake dens on the mountainside. On January 4, 1984, an Air Force F-4 Phantom jet smashed into Inadu Knob south of the intersection of the A.T. and Snake Den Ridge Trail. The explosion was heard as far away as Newport, Tenn. Both crewmen were killed. Fragments of the plane can still be seen from the Trail. Since 1920, more than 55 planes have crashed in what is now Great Smoky Mountains National Park.

Deer Creek Gap →

Fantastic views from here of Mt. Guyot, Luftee Knob, Balsam Corner, and Mt. Sterling, with their sharply defined ridges reaching down to Big Creek. Mt. Sterling is the northernmost prominent summit of the Benton MacKaye Trail, the southern terminus of which is on Springer Mountain. For northbounders, the Trail will not ascend above 6,000 feet again until Roan Mountain in Tennessee, 150 miles farther.

N-S

| | TRAIL DESCRIPTION | |

8.6 Cross spur on west side of ridge, near Cosby Knob (elev. **22.7**
5,145 feet), which is to east. ■ SOUTHBOUND hikers enter
"**Hell Ridge**" area. ■ NORTHBOUND hikers descending from
the higher ridges may notice that the forest growth on
Tennessee side changes near here from coniferous to deciduous, largely oaks, beeches, maples, and a few chestnuts
that survived an early twentieth-century blight.

9.0 Pass around forested Tennessee side of Ross Knob (elev. **22.3**
5,025 feet).

9.5 Camel Gap (elev. 4,645 feet). **Camel Gap Trail** intersects **21.8**
to east, with good views of Big Creek watershed.

10.5 Reach wooded side of Camel Hump Knob (elev. 5,250 **20.8**
feet).

11.9 **Snake Den Ridge Trail** intersects to west. Just south of **19.4**
the junction, the A.T. crosses the eastern slope of **Inadu
Knob** (elev. 5,941 feet).

12.2 Pass Yellow Creek Gap. **19.1**

12.8 Reach **Deer Creek Gap** (elev. 6,020 feet). **18.5**

13.3 Pass good view of English Mountain in the valley area on **18.0**
the Tennessee side.

S-N

SECTION HIGHLIGHTS

Pinnacle Lead →

This ridge forms the boundary between Sevier and Cocke counties of Tennessee.

Hell Ridge →

See mile 8.6/22.7.

Mt. Guyot →

The second-highest peak (elev. 6,621 feet) in the Great Smokies. Along with another Mt. Guyot near the A.T. in New Hampshire, it is named for Princeton University geographer Arnold Guyot (1807–1884), Swiss-born geologist and educator, who provided accurate measurements for many of the peaks of the Smokies. Guyot's name now also describes a common kind of flat-topped submarine volcanic mountains. He measured and mapped the height of many of the mountains along the Appalachian Trail.

Guyot Spur →

At 261 feet below the summit of nearby Mt. Guyot, the spur is higher than any summit on the A.T. north of here, including New Hampshire's Mt. Washington.

Tri-Corner Knob →

Balsam Mountain leads from Tri-Corner Knob (elev. 6,120 feet) to form the boundary between Swain and Haywood counties of North Carolina. Tri-Corner Knob is the junction of two major Appalachian ranges, the Great Smoky Mountains range (followed by the Appalachian Trail) and the Balsam range (followed by the Blue Ridge Parkway). It was given its name by geographer Arnold Guyot.

Balsam Mountain Trail →

Leads 10.1 miles compass-southeast along the ridge of the Balsam Mountains to Pin Oak Gap and Balsam Mountain Road (closed in winter). Laurel Gap Shelter is 7.0 miles away *via* this trail (accommodates 14, spring nearby). Balsam Mountain Road leads east 8.5 miles to Balsam Mountain Campground and west 5.0 miles to Round Bottom.

N-S

TRAIL DESCRIPTION

13.4	Cross **Pinnacle Lead**, a spur off Tennessee side of Old Black, with a pleasing view of English Mountain in Tennessee and valley sections at the foot of the Great Smokies range. ■ NORTHBOUND hikers enter "**Hell Ridge**" section of the Smokies; from here to Davenport Gap, the Trail primarily descends.	**17.9**
13.6	Gap between Mt. Guyot and Old Black.	**17.7**
13.8	Faint trail, obstructed by blowdowns, leads east to **Mt. Guyot**.	**17.5**
13.9	Pass Guyot Spring.	**17.4**
14.5	Cross **Guyot Spur** (elev. 6,360 feet), high point of the section.	**16.8**
15.1	Reach sharp-ridged gap between **Tri-Corner Knob** and Mt. Guyot, with fine views into North Carolina, particularly of Mt. Sterling and North Carolina side of Hell Ridge.	**16.2**
15.5	Pass junction with **Balsam Mountain Trail,** which leads east.	**15.8**

S-N

SECTION HIGHLIGHTS

Tri-Corner Knob Shelter →

Built-in bunks accommodate 12; privy and spring nearby. Bear cables (no fence). Next shelter: south, 5.6 miles (Pecks Corner); north, 7.7 miles (Cosby Knob).

Mt. Chapman →

Named for Colonel David C. Chapman, chairman of the Great Smoky Mountain Conservation Organization; he has been called the "Father of the Park." Summit elevation is 6,417 feet.

Mt. Sequoyah →

Named for a Cherokee leader, Sequoyah (also called George Gist; c. 1760–1843), probably the son of a British trader and the Cherokee mother who raised him. He was an accomplished artisan and fighter who served with the U.S. Army in the Creek War in 1813–14. Although he could not read English, he saw the value to Euroamericans of writing and devised the "Talking Leaves," an 86-character syllabic alphabet for the Cherokee language, which most Cherokees could read after a short time. The civilization, farms, housing, and literacy of the Cherokee people did not prevent their forcible removal to Oklahoma on the "Trail of Tears" in 1838. Sequoyah, whose name was also given to the giant trees of the American West, subsequently died in Mexico.

Hughes Ridge Trail →

Leads compass-southeast 12.6 miles to NPS Smokemont Campground, passing through 1.5 miles of the Cherokee Reservation (not maintained by the park) through a northern hardwood forest, with exceptional forest views near Bradley Fork and sections of azalea.

Pecks Corner Shelter →

Pecks Corner is the junction of Hughes Ridge and the state line. Go 0.4 mile east on Hughes Ridge Trail to gap, and then turn left, downhill, 100 yards in beech woods. Built-in bunks (not fenced) accommodate 12; bear cables; spring, privy nearby. Next shelter: south, 7.8 miles (Icewater Spring); north, 5.6 miles (Tri-Corner Knob).

N-S	TRAIL DESCRIPTION	

15.7	Pass junction on east side of A.T. with trail that leads 100 yards to **Tri-Corner Knob Shelter.**	**15.6**
15.8	Pass through Big Cove Gap (elev. 5,825 feet) between Tri-Corner Knob and Mt. Chapman.	**15.5**
16.7	Reach high point (elev. 6,218 feet) on side of **Mt. Chapman**.	**14.6**
17.5	Reach Chapman Gap (elev. 5,801 feet).	**13.8**
18.2	Reach summit of **Mt. Sequoyah** (elev. 6,003 feet).	**13.1**
18.9	Reach Old Troublesome, a spur off Tennessee side of Mt. Sequoyah.	**12.4**
19.2	Pass Copper Gap (elev. 5,478 feet).	**12.1**
19.9	Reach northern end of Eagle Rocks.	**11.4**
20.0	Arrive at spectacular view of precipitous slopes and sharp gorges in headwaters of Eagle Rocks Creek.	**11.3**
20.4	Swing around western peak of Eagle Rocks (elev. 5,900 feet).	**10.9**
20.9	Reach junction with **Hughes Ridge Trail**, which leads east to **Pecks Corner Shelter** and on to Smokemont Campground, near the **Qualla Boundary** (see next page). About 100 feet beyond junction of Hughes Ridge Trail is intermittent spring on the west side of A.T. Between here and Davenport Gap (mile 0.0/31.3), hikers share the Trail with horseback riders.	**10.4**

Qualla Boundary →

A few hundred members of the Cherokee tribe escaped the ordeal of the "Trail of Tears" by becoming citizens of North Carolina and thus were exempted from the purge that forced 16,000 of their fellow Cherokees to walk west to Oklahoma, "Indian Territory," at the cost of about 4,000 lives. The remaining tribesmen and others who hid out in the mountains settled in the Qualla Boundary, in the Oconaluftee Valley east of the Smokies. They were officially recognized as a tribe after the Civil War, and the land was protected in the 1973. Its 60,000 acres are now home to about 6,000 members of the Eastern Band of the Cherokee.

Bradleys View →

Unusually fine views east into the deep-cut gorge of Bradley Fork and over the mountains in North Carolina.

False Gap →

"False" in contrast to nearby Porters Gap, with which it was often confused.

Porters Gap →

Between Porters Gap and Dry Sluice Gap is a narrow, jagged ridge of exposed rock known as the Sawteeth.

Dry Sluice Gap Trail →

Leads 8.5 miles to NPS Smokemont Campground. *Via* this trail and Grassy Branch Trail, it is 3.8 miles to Kephart Shelter: accommodates 14; creek water.

Dry Sluice Gap →

The gap probably got its name from the logging operations here.

N-S   TRAIL DESCRIPTION

21.1 Cross Hughes Ridge.   **10.2**

22.2 Reach **Bradleys View**.   **9.1**

23.5 Cross Woolly Tops Lead.   **7.8**

23.8 Pass around side of Laurel Top (elev. 5,865 feet).   **7.5**

24.8 Reach **False Gap** (elev. 5,400 feet), below Porters Moun-   **6.5**
          tain.

25.5 Reach **Porters Gap** (elev. 5,500 feet) on state line, near   **5.8**
          junction of Porters Mountain and state-line ridge.

26.9 Between here and mile 27.7/3.6 below, hikers have spec-   **4.4**
          tacular views in a Sawteeth section that was swept by fire
          in 1925 after the mountains were logged, before establish-
          ment of the park.

27.1 Pass **Dry Sluice Gap Trail**, formerly Richland Mountain   **4.2**
          Trail, which enters on east from Smokemont Camp-
          ground.

27.2 Reach **Dry Sluice Gap** (elev. 5,375 feet).   **4.1**

S-N

SECTION HIGHLIGHTS

Charlies Bunion →

So named by author Horace Kephart, who thought it stuck out like the bunion of Charlie Conner, an early hiker in the area accompanying him on a hike to Mt. LeConte. Views are extraordinary. To compass-west are the Jump-Off and Mt. Kephart; to compass-northwest is Mt. LeConte; to compass-north are gorges on the headwaters of Porters Creek and, beyond, the Great Valley of Tennessee and the Cumberland Plateau; slightly to compass-northeast is Greenbrier Pinnacle; to compass-east is the jagged knife-like section of the state line known as the Sawteeth Range. The spectacular formation of bare slate on an otherwise densely forested ridge crest was created when an avalanche swept the rock clean. This happened when a 1929 cloudburst washed away a slope, following a fire on the North Carolina slope (this, in turn, following timbering operations). See page 46, Hell Ridge. Several other areas of the park have bare rock slopes where heavy rainfall has caused avalanches of all vegetation and dirt (including the A.T.) down the slopes. The precipitous western (lower) peak of the Bunion is sometimes called Fodder Stack; the higher peak is Charlies Bunion.

Virgin forest →

Overstory canopy trees in most spruce-fir forests have died, allowing sunlight to reach the understory, resulting in massive blackberry growth, at times nearly blocking the Trail. The forests are in a period of decline because of attack by the balsam woolly adelgid, a killer of mature fir trees. The Smokies' hemlocks are also threatened by the hemlock woolly adelgid. Biologists estimate that about 125,000 acres of old-growth forest, or 90 percent of the total remaining in the eastern United States, are protected as part of the Great Smoky Mountains National Park.

Icewater Spring Shelter →

Accommodates 12, with spring and privy nearby. Unfenced, with bear cables. Next shelter: south, 8.0 miles (Mt. Collins Shelter); north, 7.8 miles (Pecks Corner Shelter).

	TRAIL DESCRIPTION	

27.4	Pass east around **Charlies Bunion**. A loop trail south of here leads around the west side of Fodder Stack and its famous views and profile, which are not visible from the A.T.	**3.9**
27.7	Pass southern end of fire-scarred area with **virgin forest** to south. See mile 26.9/4.4. The old-growth spruce-fir forest in this high-elevation section was never logged.	**3.6**
28.2	Pass spring to west.	**3.1**
28.3	Pass **Icewater Spring Shelter** to east.	**3.0**

Icewater Spring Shelter

SECTION HIGHLIGHTS

Boulevard Trail →

Leads west 5.3 miles to Mt. LeConte and LeConte Lodge and Shelter. "Boulevard" was applied ironically to the very rugged ridgeline before the trail was constructed. About 100 yards from the A.T., a spur trail off Boulevard Trail leads 0.8 mile to Mt. Kephart (elev. 6,150 feet) and the scenic Jump-Off (elev. 6,100 feet). Mt. Kephart was named for Horace Kephart, an early A.T. planner, distinguished authority on the region, and author of *Our Southern Highlanders*. Accommodations are available at LeConte Lodge from late March to early November; fee; reservations required and are very difficult to get, (865) 429-5704 or <www.leconte-lodge.com>; a shelter there accommodates 12.

Viewpoint →

Views to southwest include Clingmans Dome (elev. 6,643 feet), highest point in park; to south, of Thomas Ridge and Oconaluftee River gorge. *Oconaluftee* means "by the river" in Cherokee.

Sweat Heifer Trail →

Leads south 5.8 miles to U.S. 441 *via* Sweat Heifer Creek and Kephart Prong, through an area where disastrous fire occurred in 1995. Good views of Oconaluftee River Valley. Kephart Shelter is beside this trail, 3.7 miles from A.T.; accommodates 14; creek water.

Southern end of the section →

Newfound Gap is on U.S. 441/Tenn. 71, the highway that crosses the park. From the Trail crossing, it is 16 miles west (compass-north) to Gatlinburg, Tenn., *via* U.S. 441 and Tenn. 71, and 55 miles to Knoxville. Park headquarters is located 2 miles west of Gatlinburg; (865) 436-1200. To the east (compass-south), it is 20 miles *via* U.S. 441 to Cherokee, N.C., and the Cherokee Indian reservation. Both towns have a full range of accommodations for hikers. Public restrooms are located at Newfound Gap. Park shuttle bus between Gatlinburg and Cherokee stops here May to December; $12 round-trip, $7 one-way; (828) 497-5296.

N-S

	TRAIL DESCRIPTION	

28.6 Reach junction to west with **Boulevard Trail**.   2.7

28.9 High point (elev. 6,000 feet) above Newfound Gap.   2.4
■ SOUTHBOUND hikers begin 955-foot descent over 2.4
miles. ■ NORTHBOUND hikers follow ridge through
woods.

29.4 Reach **viewpoint**.   1.9

29.6 **Sweat Heifer Trail** leads east into North Carolina, down   1.7
Kephart Prong.

31.3 **Southern end of section** at U.S. 441/Tenn. 71 in New-   0.0
found Gap parking area (elev. 5,045 feet). ■ SOUTHBOUND
hikers cross the transmountain highway, U.S. 441, and
pass between guardrails to reach Trail. ■ NORTHBOUND
hikers take wide trail uphill past the rock overlook, marked
with a large plaque, and the Rockefeller Monument,
named for the mother of John D. Rockefeller, Jr., who
donated more than $5 million for land acquisition for the
park. President Franklin D. Roosevelt dedicated the park
here on September 2, 1940.

S-N

Newfound Gap
(Tenn. 71/U.S. 441)
to Little Tennessee River
at Fontana Dam

40.3 MILES

This section, also identified as Tennessee–North Carolina Section Eighteen, includes the longest roadless stretch of the Appalachian Trail outside Maine, and it leads up and over the highest point on the entire Trail, atop Clingmans Dome (elev. 6,643 feet). For most of its length, the Trail generally follows the state line on the crest of the ridge that marks the border. North to south, prominent summits include Mt. Collins, Mt. Love, Clingmans Dome, Silers Bald, Thunderhead and Rocky Top, Cold Spring Knob, Devils Tater Patch, Doe Knob, and Shuckstack Mountain. Between Doe Knob and Fontana Dam, the Trail follows a spur of the main ridge. The Trail along the ridge was cleared as a fire trail by the Park Service in 1931. Hikers share parts of the southern and middle thirds of the route with equestrians. The route is easier to hike north to south because of the difference in elevation between the two ends of the section. The climb north to south is about 5,200 feet; south to north, about 6,800 feet. The section's many deep gaps and high peaks involve considerably more climbing than a casual inspection of the route on a map would indicate. Allow for extra time and exertion. See the introductory section on the Great Smoky Mountains National Park (page 30). Please note that the actual compass orientation of the Trail through the Smokies is along a generally northeast-southwest axis, described as north-south in this guide; see page 14 for information on how compass directions are used in the A.T. guides.

Spence Field

Road Access—Both the northern (U.S. 441/Tenn. 71) and southern (Fontana Dam off N.C. 28) ends of the section are accessible by vehicle. A road from Newfound Gap to Clingmans Dome parallels the Trail and is accessible at several points, with parking below Clingmans Dome.

Maps—Refer to National Geographic Maps Great Smoky Mountains National Park map, accompanying this guide, for route navigation. For additional area detail, refer to USGS Clingmans Dome, Silers Bald, Thunderhead, Cades Cove, and Fontana Dam quadrangles.

Shelters, Campsites, and Water—This section has seven shelters (two on side trails) and one designated campsite: Mt. Collins (mile 4.5/35.8), Double Spring Gap (mile 10.8/29.5), Silers Bald (mile 12.5/27.8), Derrick Knob (mile 18.0/22.3), Spence Field (mile 24.3/16.0), Russell Field (mile 27.2/13.1), Mollies Ridge (mile 30.0/10.3), and Birch Spring Campsite (mile 35.1/5.2). Fontana Dam Shelter is just south of the southern end of the section. The entire section is within the Great Smoky Mountains National Park. Overnight use along the A.T. is by permit only. Tent camping is not allowed, except by thru-hikers and then only when the shelter is full. Campfires are allowed only in campfire rings or shelter fireplaces. Campfires should be attended at all times and completely extinguished when you leave a shelter. Be sure to pack out all food and trash.

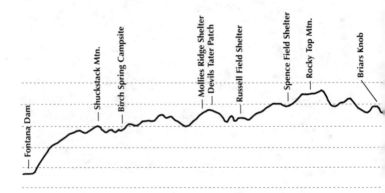

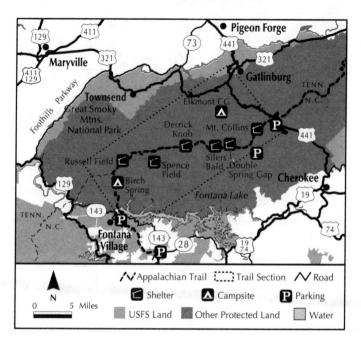

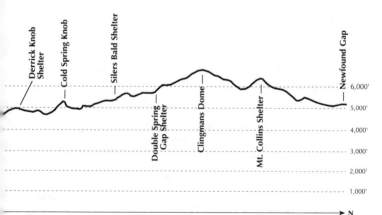

40.3 MILES

SECTION HIGHLIGHTS

Northern end of the section →

At Newfound Gap on the Tennessee–North Carolina state line, on U.S. 441/Tenn. 71, the highway that crosses the Great Smoky Mountains National Park. From the Trail crossing, it is 16 miles west (compass-north) to Gatlinburg, Tenn., and 55 miles to Knoxville. To the east (compass-south), it is 20 miles to Cherokee, N.C., and the Cherokee Indian Reservation. Both towns have a full range of accommodations for hikers. Public restrooms are located on the north side of U.S. 441. Park shuttle bus between Gatlinburg and Cherokee stops here May to December; $12 round-trip, $7 one-way; (828) 497-5296. The park headquarters is located two miles west of Gatlinburg; (865) 436-1200.

Newfound Gap →

Indian Gap (mile 1.7/38.6), site of an old Cherokee path across the ridge, was long thought to be the lowest pass across the Smokies. But, in the 1850s, the present route (elev. 5,045 feet) was discovered, and a road built.

Indian Gap →

Clingmans Dome Road from Newfound Gap to the parking area below Clingmans Dome is east, with a fine view of the North Carolina side. An old road (now a footpath) crosses the Trail here, at the point where the traditional Cherokee path crossed the ridge.

Road Prong Trail →

On the Tennessee side, the old road is known as Road Prong Trail, coming up from Chimney Tops along the stream named Road Prong. It is 3.3 miles west to Newfound Gap Road at Chimneys parking area, *via* the Road Prong Trail and Chimney Tops Trail. On the North Carolina side, it was the Oconaluftee Turnpike, the original trans-mountain road first built in 1839, then improved by Confederate Col. William Thomas during the Civil War, with the help of troops recruited from among the Cherokee.

N-S

TRAIL DESCRIPTION

Newfound Gap

0.0 **Northern end of section** is on U.S. 441/Tenn. 71 at parking lot. ■ SOUTHBOUND hikers cross U.S. 441 and pass through opening in highway guardrail from parking lot at **Newfound Gap**. Trail is graded and on Tennessee side (west) of the ridge, beginning 7.9-mile, 1,598-foot ascent to Clingmans Dome. ■ NORTHBOUND hikers ascend graded trail beside stone overlook with plaque (see Section One). **40.3**

0.9 Reach ridge crest and view of Mt. LeConte through balsam trees to west. **39.4**

1.2 Reach crest of Mt. Mingus Lead. The Trail leads across a barrier set up to exclude feral hogs from areas with fragile plant life, to provide a natural control for studying areas disturbed by the hogs. **39.1**

1.7 Reach **Indian Gap** (elev. 5,317 feet), intersection of **Road Prong Trail,** and cross grassy open slope on Tennessee side, with parking for the Clingmans Dome Road. **38.6**

S-N

Fork Ridge Trail →
Leaves A.T. 0.9 mile north of Mt. Collins; leads south 14.7 miles to public road at NPS Deep Creek Campground *via* Fork Ridge and Deep Creek to Bryson Place, 8.6 miles from A.T. through virgin hardwoods in last stretch.

Mountains-to-the-Sea Trail →
A 900-plus-mile trail consisting of footpaths, roads, and state bike routes, begun in 1973 when the North Carolina General Assembly passed the North Carolina Trails System Act and still being pieced together. It is mostly complete in the western mountains. From here, it follows the Fork Ridge Trail east toward the Blue Ridge Parkway.

Sugarland Mountain Trail →
Leaves A.T. 0.5 mile north of Mt. Collins; leads north 12.1 miles to Little River Road at Fighting Creek Gap. Excellent views of Mt. LeConte and Sugarland and Little River valleys.

Mt. Collins Shelter →
Built-in bunks accommodate 12; spring is nearby. Bear fence, bear cables, privy. Next shelter: south, 6.8 miles (Double Spring Gap); north, 8.0 miles (Icewater Spring).

Clingmans Dome →
The highest point on the Appalachian Trail. It was known as Smoky Dome until renamed for Thomas Lanier Clingman, U.S. senator, mining prospector, and Civil War general who explored these mountains during the 1850s and extolled their virtues. Rare mountain cranberry is abundant here. Many fir trees have been killed by woolly adelgid insects. From a summit tower, a paved path leads downhill 0.5 mile to Forney Ridge parking area at end of the Clingmans Dome Road, 7.6 miles from Newfound Gap; restrooms are at the parking area. South of Clingmans Dome, the Trail passes through northern hardwood forests, in marked contrast to the coniferous forests of the eastern Great Smokies. Some of the Trail is along a grassy ridge dotted with mature timber, affording delightful travel.

N-S

| | TRAIL DESCRIPTION | |

4.1 Pass side trail, which leads east 35 yards to road and **Fork Ridge Trail.** From here to Clingmans Dome (mile 7.9/32.4 below), the A.T. route hosts the **Mountains-to-the-Sea Trail.**   **36.2**

4.5 Pass **Sugarland Mountain Trail**, which leads west 0.5 mile to **Mt. Collins Shelter.**   **35.8**

5.0 Reach summit of Mt. Collins (elev. 6,188 feet).   **35.3**

5.6 Reach Collins Gap (elev. 5,886 feet).   **34.7**

6.7 Summit of Mt. Love (elev. 6,446 feet). ■ SOUTHBOUND hikers descend toward a minor gap (elev. 6,366 feet) between Mt. Love and Clingmans Dome summit. ■ NORTHBOUND hikers descend toward Collins Gap.   **33.6**

7.9 Reach highest point of A.T. just west of summit of **Clingmans Dome** (elev. 6,643 feet). A side trail to east leads 50 yards to a wheelchair-accessible observation tower on the summit, providing a splendid view above red-spruce and scattered fir trees. ■ SOUTHBOUND hikers descend slightly along narrow ridgecrest to a gap at the northern base of Mt. Buckley, beginning 7.3-mile, 1,826-foot descent to Buckeye Gap. ■ NORTHBOUND hikers descend steeply to a minor gap (elev. 6,366 feet) between Clingmans Dome summit and Mt. Love, beginning 7.9-mile, 1,598-foot descent to Newfound Gap.   **32.4**

S-N

SECTION HIGHLIGHTS

Clingmans Dome Bypass Trail →

Leads 1.0 mile to Forney Ridge Trail, on which it is 1.5 miles to Andrews Bald and 11.5 miles to Fontana Lake. It also leads to Forney Ridge parking area. Andrews Bald is one of two balds in the park being preserved as grassy, open areas. Since the establishment of the park and the suspension of grazing, most balds have become overgrown, and their open features, which were their outstanding attraction, are disappearing rapidly. Gregory and Andrews balds are being kept open by cutting woody growth, however. A portion of the original A.T. route has been officially designated as Gregory Bald Trail (mile 32.8/7.5) and continued as a side trail.

Goshen Prong Trail →

Leads east (compass-north) 10.0 miles along the stream of Goshen Prong to public road one mile south of NPS Elkmont Campground. The first 0.2 mile is through spruce; 1.2 miles is through rhododendron and hemlock; balance is through hardwoods. The last 2.3 miles are on the Little River Trail.

Double Spring Gap Shelter →

Built-in bunks for 12. Fenced, with bear cables, and a privy nearby. Gap is named for two unreliable springs, one on each slope. The better spring is 15 yards from crest on North Carolina (east) slope; the other, 35 yards on Tennessee (west) side. Next shelter: south, 1.7 miles (Silers Bald); north, 6.8 miles (Mt. Collins).

Welch Ridge Trail →

Leads east (compass-south) 7.5 miles on crest of Welch Ridge to High Rocks. Traverses second-growth hardwoods and offers views of adjacent valleys. From High Rocks, it is 10.1 miles farther to Fontana Lake at Hazel Creek *via* Cold Spring Gap Trail.

N-S

TRAIL DESCRIPTION

8.3	Reach **Clingmans Dome Bypass Trail** to east.	32.0
8.4	Reach summit of Mt. Buckley (elev. 6,582 feet).	31.9
8.8	Reach narrow ridgecrest.	31.5
10.2	Pass junction of **Goshen Prong Trail** to west.	30.1
10.8	Reach Double Spring Gap (elev. 5,507 feet) and **Double Spring Gap Shelter.** ■ SOUTHBOUND hikers ascend through beech woods. ■ NORTHBOUND hikers ascend steeply.	29.5
11.3	Reach Jenkins Knob. Magnificent view west of Silers Bald, with Welch Ridge and High Rocks to compass-south, Miry Ridge to compass-northwest, and Thunderhead to compass-southwest. South of this knob, few high-elevation spruce, hemlock, fir, and balsam trees survive.	29.0
12.1	**Welch Ridge Trail** intersects to east.	28.2

Ascending Mt. Buckley

S-N

Silers Bald →

Silers Bald is named for the Siler family, which pastured cattle on it in summer.

Silers Bald Shelter →

Built-in bunks accommodate 12; no fence, no privy; bear cables. Water can be found 100 yards down a trail that leaves the A.T. on the west side, just north of the shelter and at the edge of the woods. Next shelter: south, 5.5 miles (Derrick Knob); north, 1.7 miles (Double Spring Gap).

Buckeye Gap →

Faint trails lead away on both sides; water can be found 200 yards down the North Carolina (east) slope.

Miry Ridge Trail →

Leads 8.2 miles west (compass-north) to public road at developed NPS Elkmont Campground. Follows Miry Ridge and Dripping Springs Mountain to Jakes Gap and then down Jakes Creek Trail.

Greenbrier Ridge Trail →

Leads west 4.2 miles to Indian Flats Falls (a series of four falls cascading 60 feet) and 8.3 miles *via* the Middle Prong Trail to a public road above the Great Smoky Mountains Institute, a park educational center at Tremont, along the Middle Prong of Little River. A good spring is 100 yards down and to left on Greenbrier Ridge Trail.

Derrick Knob Shelter →

Built-in bunks accommodate 12; spring nearby; no fence; bear cables; no privy. Shelter is located where a herder's cabin once stood. Water is 50 yards to west on Tennessee slope. Next shelter: south, 6.5 miles (Spence Field); north, 5.5 miles (Silers Bald).

N-S

TRAIL DESCRIPTION

12.3 Reach partially wooded crest of **Silers Bald** (elev. 5,607   **28.0**
feet) with panoramic view. Between here and Buckeye
Gap (mile 15.2/25.1), hikers share the Trail with horseback
riders. ■ SOUTHBOUND hikers descend along open slope.
■ NORTHBOUND hikers descend on switchbacks.

12.5 Reach **Silers Bald Shelter** on west side of Trail.   **27.8**

15.2 Reach **Buckeye Gap** (elev. 4,817 feet). ■ SOUTHBOUND   **25.1**
hikers ascend toward Cold Spring Knob. Between here
and Devil's Tater Patch (mile 29.4/10.9), the Trail is a
"roller-coaster," with frequent ascents and descents, but
little over-all gain or loss of elevation. ■ NORTHBOUND hikers begin 7.3-mile, 1,826-foot ascent to Clingmans Dome.
Between here and Silers Bald (mile 12.3/28.0), hikers share
the Trail with horseback riders.

15.4 Graded **Miry Ridge Trail** intersects to west.   **24.9**

16.0 Reach Cold Spring Knob (elev. 5,240 feet).   **23.4**

17.5 Skirt North Carolina slope of Mt. Davis, formerly known   **22.8**
as Greenbrier Knob.

17.8 Reach Sams Gap (elev. 4,840 feet) and junction with   **22.5**
graded **Greenbrier Ridge Trail** entering from west.

17.9 Reach spur of knob at north end of open field.   **22.4**

18.0 Reach **Derrick Knob Shelter** on west side of Trail.   **22.3**

18.3 Reach Chestnut Bald.   **22.0**

S-N

SECTION HIGHLIGHTS

Thunderhead →

Heavy rhododendron growth has all but obscured the once-outstanding views from here; glimpses may be possible from rock piles. Ridgecrest is mostly open and grassy between Thunderhead and Spence Field, but those open areas are rapidly being reclaimed by the surrounding forests.

Rocky Top →

Some of the graffiti on the rocks here dates back 150 years or more.

Jenkins Ridge Trail →

Leads east 8.9 miles to the Hazel Creek Trail (Pinnacle Creek Trail at Pickens Gap is now closed).

Bote Mountain Trail →

Leaves A.T. near center of Spence Field and leads west (compass-north) 6.5 miles to Laurel Creek Road. First 0.5 mile is rocky through yellow birch; next 0.5 mile, through rhododendron with trail down to bedrock; next mile, laurel slick; balance, on old road through pine and hardwoods. It is the old Anderson Road, named for the founder of Maryville College, Issac Anderson, who promoted its construction from Tuckaleechee Cove up to the state line. The majority of the Cherokee labor force building the road voted to follow this ridge. Having no "v" sound in their language, they pronounced "vote" as "bote." The trail provides an excellent connection between Cades Cove and the A.T.—1.7 miles to Anthony Creek Trail and 3.5 miles farther on that to the cove.

Eagle Creek Trail →

Leads east 8.0 miles to Lakeshore Trail at Fontana Lake, along Spence Cabin Branch of Gunna Creek, a tributary of Eagle Creek.

Spence Field Shelter →

Built-in bunks accommodate 12. No fence. Bear cables, privy. Spring nearby. Next shelter: south, 3.1 miles (Russell Field); north, 6.5 miles (Derrick Knob).

N-S

TRAIL DESCRIPTION

19.1	Reach Sugar Tree Gap (elev. 4,435 feet), with sugar maple trees.	**21.2**
19.9	Reach Starkey Gap (elev. 4,500 feet).	**20.4**
20.7	Traverse east (North Carolina) slope of wooded Brier Knob (elev. 5,215 feet).	**19.6**
20.8	Pass ledge, with view east into North Carolina.	**19.5**
21.5	Reach Mineral Gap (elev. 5,030 feet).	**18.8**
22.2	Reach Beechnut Gap. Water is 75 yards down Tennessee (west) slope.	**18.1**
22.5	Reach eastern summit of **Thunderhead** (elev. 5,527 feet).	**17.8**
23.1	Reach **Rocky Top** (elev. 5,441 feet), which has views of Fontana Lake and southwest along the ridge toward Spence Field. Pass between jutting boulders. Watch for a turn, particularly in foggy or rainy weather.	**17.2**
23.9	Pass trail junction with **Jenkins Ridge Trail** in grassy sag at north end of Spence Field. From here to Sassafras Gap (mile 34.9/4.3), hikers share the Trail with equestrians.	**16.4**
24.3	**Bote Mountain Trail** intersects to west; a spring is 0.2 mile down this trail below A.T. And, 200 yards south, **Eagle Creek Trail** intersects to east. **Spence Field Shelter** is 250 yards down Eagle Creek Trail.	**16.0**
24.4	South end of Spence Field.	**15.9**

S-N

Russell Field Shelter →

Located at intersection; built-in bunks accommodate 14; spring is 150 yards down trail toward Cades Cove. Bear fence. Bear cables. No privy. Next shelter: south, 2.5 miles (Mollies Ridge); north, 3.1 miles (Spence Field).

Russell Field Trail →

Graded footpath leads west 5.1 miles to Cades Cove Picnic Area *via* Anthony Creek Trail. The grassy, open area at Russell Field is gradually being reclaimed by forest 0.25 mile west along this trail.

Gant Lot →

Appalachian dialect term, reported by Horace Kephart, for a pen in which livestock normally allowed to graze on the mountain balds were collected "gaunt" (without grass to graze on).

Mollies Ridge Shelter →

Built-in bunks accommodate 12; spring nearby. No privy. No bear fence. Bear cables nearby. Next shelter: south, 11.3 miles (Fontana Dam); north, 2.5 miles (Russell Field).

Ekaneetlee Gap →

On an early Cherokee route from valley towns to over-hill towns. Water is found 100 yards down the western slope. *Ekaneetlee* is an alternate spelling of *Oconaluftee*, which means "by the river."

Gregory Bald Trail →

Leads 3.1 miles along the main ridge of the Smokies to Gregory Bald, passing Rich Gap and intersection with Gregory Ridge Trail at 2.0 miles. Between here and Fontana Dam, the A.T. follows a side ridge oriented north–south. Gregory Bald Trail follows the original A.T. route, which continued west over Gregory and Parson balds and along the state line to Deals Gap. Russell Gregory was the first person to settle in the area. Gregory Bald is renowned for its spectacular view into Cades Cove and its population of rare varieties of flame azaleas. The Park Service is preserving the bald.

N-S	TRAIL DESCRIPTION	

26.5	Reach McCampbell Gap (elev. 4,328 feet), just north of a section that skirts the North Carolina side of wooded McCampbell Knob.	**13.8**
27.2	Reach Russell Field, with **Russell Field Shelter** and trail junction with **Russell Field Trail** to west.	**13.1**
27.6	Reach Big Abrams Gap (elev. 4,080 feet).	**12.7**
28.0	Reach Little Abrams Gap (elev. 4,120 feet). ■ SOUTHBOUND hikers ascend toward Locust Knob. ■ NORTHBOUND hikers traverse east slope of knob.	**12.3**
29.4	Reach Devil's Tater Patch (elev. 4,775 feet). ■ SOUTHBOUND hikers will descend 3,035 feet over next 10.9 miles to Fontana Dam (with a significant climb out of Ekaneetlee Gap, below). ■ For NORTHBOUND hikers, between here and Buckeye Gap (mile 15.2/25.1 above), the Trail is a "roller-coaster," with frequent steep ascents and descents, but little over-all gain or loss of elevation.	**10.9**
30.0	Reach **Gant Lot** (Rich Gap) and **Mollies Ridge Shelter.**	**10.3**
31.4	Reach **Ekaneetlee Gap** (elev. 3,842 feet).	**8.9**
32.3	Skirt North Carolina (east) side of Powell Knob (elev. 4,439 feet).	**8.0**
32.4	Reach Mud Gap (elev. 4,260 feet).	**7.9**
32.8	Reach summit of Doe Knob (elev. 4,520 feet) and, to south, intersection with **Gregory Bald Trail** to west.	**7.5**
33.3	Pass viewpoint.	**7.0**

Birch Spring Gap →

Birch Spring Shelter was removed in 2000, and a complex of tent pads installed, with bear cables. Campsite is 100 yards to west down slope. Camping along the A.T. is not permitted. Next shelter: south, 5.9 miles (Fontana Dam Shelter); north, 5.1 miles (Mollies Ridge).

Lost Cove Trail →

Leads east 3.5 miles to Eagle Creek and the Lakeshore Trail. The Benton MacKaye Trail intersects the A.T. here.

Twentymile Trail →

Leads west, 4.5 miles, to Twentymile Creek and ranger station at N.C. 28, 3.7 miles from Deals Gap and U.S. 129.

Shuckstack Mountain →

The fire tower here, on the high side of a north-south spur, makes accessible one of the most extraordinary panoramic views of the southern Appalachians. The crestline of the Great Smokies, running southwest–northeast from Thunderhead to Clingmans Dome, is prominent. Hangover Mountain and other peaks in the Joyce Kilmer-Slickrock Creek Wilderness to southeast and mountains to south in Nantahala National Forest are particularly impressive.

Fontana Lake →

This 11,685-acre lake in the valley of the Little Tennessee River has a shoreline of 240 miles. It was formed when the Tennessee Valley Authority built Fontana Dam in 1942–45. Its 480-foot-tall, 2,365-foot-long dam is the highest east of the Rockies and took 2.8 million cubic yards of concrete to build. Three generating units in its hydro-electric plant produce 250,000 kilowatts of electricity.

N-S

TRAIL DESCRIPTION

33.9 Skirt west side of Greer Knob. **6.4**

34.3 Reach gap where water is located 100 yards down slope **6.0**
to west.

35.1 Reach **Birch Spring Gap** (elev. 3,834 feet) and campsite. **5.2**

35.4 Reach Red Ridge Gap. **4.9**

36.0 Reach Sassafras Gap (elev. 3,653 feet) and intersection of **4.3**
Lost Cove Trail on east side and **Twentymile Trail** on west
side. Between here and Jenkins Ridge Trail (mile
23.9/16.4), hikers share the Trail with equestrians.
■ SOUTHBOUND hikers follow old road up Shuckstack.

36.3 Old road on east side of A.T. leads 0.1 mile steeply uphill **4.0**
to firewarden's cabin and firetower on crest of **Shuckstack
Mountain** (elev. 4,020 feet). ■ SOUTHBOUND hikers begin
2,200-foot descent to Fontana Dam. ■ NORTHBOUND hikers follow old road, descending toward Sassafras Gap.

36.5 Pass a viewpoint above **Fontana Lake**. **3.8**

View of Fontana Lake

S-N

<table>
<tr><td>SECTION HIGHLIGHTS</td></tr>
</table>

Lakeshore Trail →

Leads east 33.6 miles, past numerous campsites, along the shore of Fontana Lake to Lakeview Drive, the paved "road to nowhere" constructed between 1948 and 1970.

Fontana Dam bypass trail →

An alternate, blue-blazed route along roads and trails that crosses the Little Tennessee River on a highway bridge below the dam and rejoins the A.T. south of the dam.

Southern end of section →

At Fontana Dam on the Little Tennessee River. The Tennessee Valley Authority (TVA) Fontana Visitors Center at the dam is open seven days a week, May–November, 9 a.m.–7 p.m. The phone number is (828) 498-2234. It is closed when the homeland-security alert level is high (orange or higher). Fontana Village Resort at Fontana Village, N.C., is two miles from the southern end of this section *via* S.R. 1245 and N.C. 28, with stores, cafeteria, a post office, and accommodations available. Bryson City, N.C., is 34 miles east *via* N.C. 28 and U.S. 74. The dam may also be reached from Tennessee by taking U.S. 129 to Deals Gap on the Tennessee–North Carolina state line and then N.C. 28 east for nine miles. No bus service is available. North of the dam, a hard-surfaced road leads downstream 0.2 mile to a parking overlook, which has a spectacular view of dam and powerhouse. On the southern end of the dam is the visitors center (showers and toilets); Fontana Dam Shelter is to east, at top of hill.

N-S

TRAIL DESCRIPTION

37.1 Reach gap between Shuckstack Mountain and Little   **3.2**
Shuckstack.

37.4 Pass an unreliable water source a few yards to east, at   **2.9**
bend in the Trail.

39.4 Pass unreliable spring, ten yards to west.   **0.9**

39.7 Reach hard-surfaced road. The **Lakeshore Trail** leads east   **0.6**
along the road from its intersection with the A.T. ■ SOUTH-
BOUND hikers follow paved road to right toward Fontana
Dam. ■ NORTHBOUND hikers leave road, going left at bul-
letin board, and begin 2,200-foot ascent of Shuckstack
Mountain.

40.1 Blue-blazed **Fontana Dam bypass trail** intersects to   **0.2**
west.

40.3 **Southern end of section** and end of hard-surfaced road   **0.0**
at Fontana Dam (elev. 1,740 feet). Road to viewpoint to
west. *Note: During times of heightened national security
and terrorism alerts, the route across the dam may be
closed, and an alternate blue-blazed route (mile 40.1/0.2
above) along roads and trails will take hikers across the
Little Tennessee River on a highway bridge below the dam.*
■ SOUTHBOUND hikers continue across dam (see Section
Three). ■ NORTHBOUND hikers follow paved road to right
along shore of Fontana Lake. Between here and Devil's
Tater Patch (mile 29.4/10.9), northbound hikers will ascend 3,035 feet in 10.9 miles.

S-N

Nantahala National Forest

In the rugged Nantahala National Forest, the largest of four national forests in North Carolina, most of the A.T. passes through mature hardwood forest. Rhododendron, mountain laurel, flame azalea, mountain ash, fern, galax, wildflowers, streams, springs, and the fall coloring all contribute to the A.T. in the South being a distinctive experience. A.T. pioneer A. Rufus Morgan (page 17), described it this way:

> "A trip in October will give opportunity of seeing grouse, wild turkeys, squirrels, deer, and occasionally other wildlife. The coloring, also, makes a fall trip a beautiful experience.... A spring trip, perhaps in late April, will show the white-flowering trees, such as dogwood, bellwood, service, and black locust.... During June and July..., a wealth of flame azalea and rhododendron, especially the purple rhododendron on Standing Indian Mountain."

The Cherokee and their predecessors flourished in this region for thousands of years. Although Hernando de Soto explored the area

View from Cheoah Bald

in 1539, European settlers did not arrive until the eighteenth century. Most Cherokee were forced out onto the "Trail of Tears" to Oklahoma in 1838, but a few hid in the hills and finally–in 1973–secured a reservation to call home. The national forest was established in 1920.

North to south, the first part of the A.T. here parallels the Little Tennessee River. It heads east from near the southern end of the Great Smokies to the northern end of the Nantahala range. Particularly impressive are the panoramic views of the Great Smokies on one side and the Nantahala, Cowee, and Snowbird mountains on the other. Cheoah Bald affords one of the outstanding views of the southern Appalachians. Those views of endless, misty ridges are true signatures of the Appalachian Trail experience.

South of the Nantahala River, the A.T. climbs out of Nantahala Gorge and proceeds over a series of 5,000-foot summits (heath balds characteristic of the southern Appalachians) and 4,000-foot gaps. It flanks the headwaters of the Nantahala, Little Tennessee, and Tallulah rivers. At Ridgepole Mountain, the southern end of the Nantahala Range, it turns to the eastern arm of the Blue Ridge for the remainder of its journey to Georgia.

Little Tennessee River (Fontana Dam) to Yellow Creek Gap (S.R. 1242)

8.2 MILES

This section climbs out of (or descends into) the valley of the Little Tennessee River near the boundary between the Great Smoky Mountains National Park and the Nantahala National Forest. At the northern end is the Tennessee Valley Authority (TVA) Fontana Dam and its visitors-center complex at the southern entrance of the Smokies, two miles from the resort community of Fontana Village. At the southern end is Yellow Creek Gap, where the Trail swings south, away from the river valley. In between is a ridgewalk along 3,720-foot Yellow Creek Mountain. The A.T. originally extended the length of the Great Smokies and used the only available crossing of the river, at Tapoco, North Carolina. After 1946, Fontana Dam made a new crossing of the river feasible. Hard-surfaced N.C. 28 leads from U.S. 129 to Fontana Dam (9.5 miles from Tapoco) and continues to a junction with U.S. 19 about nine miles south of Bryson City.

Road Approaches—Both the northern (S.R. 1245) and southern ends (S.R. 1242) of the section are accessible by road. The Trail crosses N.C. 28 near the northern end of the section.

Maps—See ATC's Nantahala National Forest map with this guide and the TVA Fontana Dam quadrangle.

Shelters and Campsites—Fontana Dam Shelter is located in the TVA complex south of Fontana Dam. Cable Gap Shelter is 7.3 miles from the northern end of the section. Both shelters have reliable water sources. The Trail corridor in this section lies mostly within the Nantahala National Forest, and camping is permitted except where noted otherwise. Campfires should be attended at all times and completely extinguished when you leave a campsite.

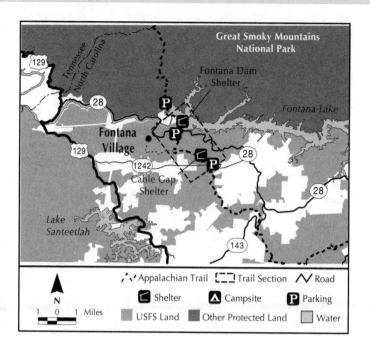

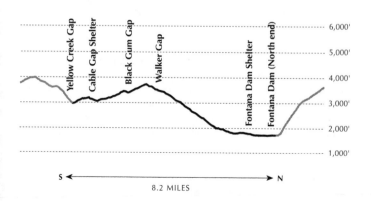

8.2 MILES

Northern end of section →

Fontana Village Resort at Fontana Village, N.C., is two miles from the southern end of this section *via* S.R. 1245 and N.C. 28, with stores, outfitter, cafeteria, a post office (ZIP code 28733), and accommodations available. Bryson City, N.C., is 34 miles east *via* N.C. 28 and U.S. 19. The dam may also be reached from Tennessee by taking U.S. 129 to Deals Gap at the Tennessee–North Carolina state line and then N.C. 28 east for nine miles. No bus service is available. North of the dam, a hard-surfaced road leads downstream 0.2 mile to a parking overlook, which has a spectacular view of the dam and powerhouse.

Fontana Dam →

TVA constructed this dam on the Little Tennessee River during and after World War II to furnish hydroelectric power. It is 480 feet high, the highest dam east of the Rockies. The dam impounded the Little Tennessee River for 29 miles to create Fontana Lake, making the southern boundary of the Great Smoky Mountains National Park a water boundary. The TVA Fontana Visitors Center at the dam is open seven days a week, May–November, 9 a.m.–7 p.m. The visitors center telephone number is (828) 498-2234. It will be closed when the homeland-security-alert level is orange or higher.

Fontana Dam bypass trail →

An alternate, blue-blazed route along roads and trails that crosses the Little Tennessee River on a highway bridge below the dam and rejoins the A.T. north of the dam.

Fontana Dam Shelter →

A concrete-floored shelter near the picnic area, constructed by the Tennessee Valley Authority and fondly known to hikers as the "Fontana Hilton." Accommodates 24. Running water and restrooms are nearby, and showers are available at the visitors center. Next shelter: south, 6.6 miles (Cable Gap); north, 11.3 miles (Mollies Ridge).

N-S

TRAIL DESCRIPTION

0.0 The **northern end of section** is the northern bank of the   **8.2**
Little Tennessee River, on the north side of Fontana Dam
(elev. 1,740 feet). ■ SOUTHBOUND hikers follow the road-
way across the dam. *Note: During times of heightened
national-security and terrorism alerts, the route across the
dam may be closed; an alternate, blue-blazed route along
roads and trails takes hikers across the Little Tennessee
River on a highway bridge below the dam.* ■ NORTHBOUND
hikers follow paved road along northern shore of Fontana
Lake (see Section Two).

0.4 Southern end of **Fontana Dam**. At the southern abutment   **7.8**
of the dam are a visitors center with exhibits, a refreshment
stand, restrooms, and public showers. ■ SOUTHBOUND
hikers ascend on hard-surfaced road. ■ NORTHBOUND hikers cross dam (see note at mile 0.0/8.2).

0.5 Blue-blazed **Fontana Dam bypass trail** intersects at west,   **7.7**
next to TVA police station.

0.7 At ridgecrest, pass parking overlook on hard-surfaced   **7.5**
road, with good views of Fontana Lake, its dam and
powerhouse, and the Great Smokies and a picnic area
with water fountains and restrooms (closed in winter).
Fontana Dam Shelter is 100 yards east on paved sidewalk.
■ SOUTHBOUND hikers follow hard-surfaced road. ■ NORTH-
BOUND hikers descend along road to the dam. Hikers
planning to camp in Great Smoky Mountains National
Park must register (see page 20); a self-registration station
for thru-hikers only is located near the shelter.

S-N

SECTION HIGHLIGHTS

Fontana Lake Marina →

A shuttle (small fee) to Fontana Village will stop here; dial 265 from boat dock. Parking is available near the bulletin board.

N.C. 28 →

Leads west 1.8 miles to Fontana Village, N.C., with stores, outfitter, cafeteria, a post office (ZIP code 28733), and accommodations available. Bryson City, N.C., is 34 miles east *via* N.C. 28 and U.S. 19.

Nantahala Mountains →

A transverse ridge of the Blue Ridge mountains, extending along a north-south axis between the Great Smoky Mountains and the eastern face of the Blue Ridge. Between here and Ridgepole Mountain (see Section Nine), the Trail is generally considered to be in the Nantahalas. See pages 78–79.

Bee Cove Lead →

In 1971, the U.S. Forest Service relocated the A.T. from the boat dock parking area at N.C. 28 to ascend to Walker Gap on Yellow Creek Mountain *via* Bee Cove Lead. Water sources are infrequent, and even well-recognized sources may fail in dry seasons. Make ample provisions for water.

TRAIL DESCRIPTION

1.0 Trail intersects with hard-surfaced road. ■ SOUTHBOUND hikers follow footpath east into woods, continuing along curving ridgecrest, with gentle ascents and descents. ■ NORTHBOUND hikers follow road to right. **7.2**

1.7 Cross S.R. 1245 near swimming pool, south of **Fontana Lake Marina** (elev. 1,710 feet). ■ SOUTHBOUND hikers ascend toward **N.C. 28**, beginning 2,310-foot ascent to crest of Yellow Creek Mountain. ■ NORTHBOUND hikers ascend gently through wooded area. **6.5**

1.8 Cross **N.C. 28**. ■ SOUTHBOUND hikers ascend stone steps, then ascend along narrow ridgecrest toward switchbacks up Bee Cove Lead, into the **Nantahala Mountains**. ■ NORTHBOUND hikers descend stone steps and turn right down grassy slope to **Fontana Lake Marina**. Pass a concrete comfort station on the right and boat docks in the valley of the Little Tennessee River. **6.4**

2.5 Pass water source to west, immediately below Trail. **5.7**

3.0 Pass through gap. ■ SOUTHBOUND hikers switch back sharply right and ascend along right side of ridgecrest of **Bee Cove Lead.** ■ NORTHBOUND hikers switch back sharply left, leaving Bee Cove Lead. **5.2**

3.5 Pass rock cliffs to west. **4.7**

4.0 Crest of **Bee Cove Lead**. ■ SOUTHBOUND hikers bear right. ■ NORTHBOUND hikers descend steeply along crest of Bee Cove Lead toward switchbacks. **4.2**

4.1 Trail crosses stream. **4.1**

4.2 Trail crosses small stream. **4.0**

SECTION HIGHLIGHTS

Yellow Creek Mountain Trail →

Former A.T. route leads 9.3 miles west along Yellow Creek Mountain to U.S. 129. Blazed blue. A short cut to Fontana Village is possible by following the trail 1.6 miles to its intersection with Lookout Rock Trail, which leads 1.1 miles down to the resort. This short-cut to the resort is difficult and not well-marked.

Fontana Village →

In May 1946, Fontana Village was constructed at Welch Cove to house as many as 5,000 Tennessee Valley Authority construction workers building the nearby dam. For years after the dam was built, it was operated by the government as a public recreation development. It was turned over to private interests in the 1980s. The village is two miles from the dam at an elevation of 1,800 feet, immediately at the base of the Yellow Creek Mountains. Today, Fontana Village Resort offers rentals and timeshares, as well as extensive facilities, including a lodge, restaurants, drugstore, grocery store, post office, and laundry. About 300 houses, which were used in the original construction, are now available for guests. The resort, on the Internet at <www.fontanavillage.com>, has an extensive recreation program that features hiking, fishing, and horseback riding.

Cable Gap Shelter →

Built in 1939 by the Civilian Conservation Corps under the direction of the Nantahala National Forest; refurbished in 1988 by the Smoky Mountains Hiking Club. Accommodates 6. A privy is close by, and a spring is adjacent to the shelter. Next shelter: south, 6.1 miles (Brown Fork Gap); north, 6.6 miles (Fontana Dam).

Southern end of section →

At intersection of hard-surfaced S.R. 1242. To east, it is 4.0 miles to N.C. 28, where several motels are near the intersection. Fontana Village is nine miles farther to left on N.C. 28 (a total of 13 miles from Yellow Creek Gap). U.S. 129 is about ten miles west. No services or amenities are available at road crossing. A gravel parking lot here accommodates a few cars.

N-S

TRAIL DESCRIPTION

4.5   Reach Walker Gap (elev. 3,450 feet) on the crest of Yellow   **3.7**
Creek Mountain. **Yellow Creek Mountain Trail** to **Fontana Village** intersects to west. ▪ SOUTHBOUND hikers ascend along ridge of Yellow Creek Mountain. ▪ NORTHBOUND hikers begin 1,740-foot descent to Fontana Lake.

5.1   Cross high point (elev. 3,720 feet) on ridge of Yellow   **3.1**
Creek Mountain, with rocks on summit. ▪ SOUTHBOUND hikers follow ridge. ▪ NORTHBOUND hikers begin 2,010-foot descent to Walker Gap and Fontana Lake.

5.2   Cross high point on ridgecrest. ▪ SOUTHBOUND hikers   **3.0**
descend and continue along a ridgecrest that ascends and descends. ▪ NORTHBOUND hikers follow ridgecrest.

5.9   Reach Black Gum Gap (elev. 3,400 feet).   **2.3**

6.2   Skirt High Top (highest point on Yellow Creek Mountain,   **2.0**
elev. 3,786 feet) on west side. ▪ SOUTHBOUND hikers leave ridgecrest. ▪ NORTHBOUND hikers continue along ridgecrest, with Fontana Lake visible to east.

6.5   Trail switches back below High Top. ▪ SOUTHBOUND hikers   **1.7**
descend, with views to the south. ▪ NORTHBOUND hikers follow spur.

7.1   Trail turns sharply.   **1.1**

7.3   Trail turns sharply to the east of **Cable Gap Shelter.**   **0.9**

8.2   S.R. 1242 intersects at Yellow Creek Gap (elev. 2,980   **0.0**
feet) at **southern end of section**. ▪ SOUTHBOUND hikers continue directly opposite, up steps into woods (see Section Four). ▪ NORTHBOUND hikers proceed along west side of ridge, ascending gradually.

S-N

Yellow Creek Gap (S.R. 1242) to Stecoah Gap (N.C. 143)

7.6 MILES

Between Yellow Creek Gap (2,980 feet) and Stecoah Gap (elev. 3,165 feet), the Trail follows an up-and-down path over the Cheoah Mountains, with a slight elevation gain for southbound hikers. The section offers some excellent views of Cheoah Bald and a side trail to Wauchecha Bald. The Trail formerly went to the lookout tower at the summit of Wauchecha (elev. 4,385 feet), but that route is now part of a side-trail loop of less than one mile.

Road Approaches—Both the northern (S.R. 1242) and southern (N.C. 143) ends of the section are accessible by car.

Maps—See ATC's Nantahala National Forest map with this guide and the TVA Fontana Dam and Hewitt quadrangles.

Shelters and Campsites—Brown Fork Gap Shelter is near the southern end of the section (mile 5.2/2.4). The Trail corridor in this section lies within the Nantahala National Forest, and camping is permitted except where noted otherwise. Campfires should be attended at all times and completely extinguished when you leave a campsite.

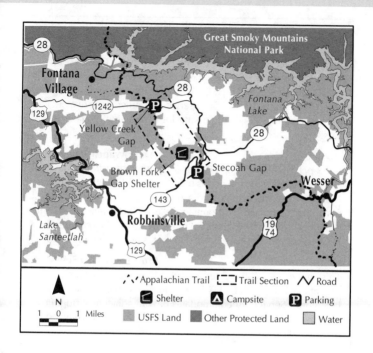

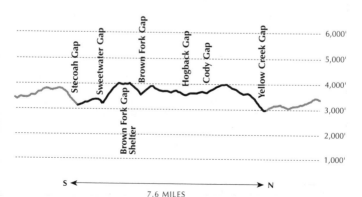

S ← → N

7.6 MILES

Northern end of section →

In Yellow Creek Gap, the A.T. crosses the Yellow Creek Mountain Road (hard-surfaced S.R. 1242). Four miles east of this crossing is N.C. 28, where several motels are near the intersection. To the west, U.S. 129 is about 10 miles. No services or amenities are available at road crossing. A gravel parking lot here accommodates a few cars.

Wauchecha Bald →

A steep, blue-blazed loop (former A.T. route) leads from Cody and Hogback gaps to the top of this bald (elev. 4,385 feet), where there is a fire tower (no access) and a partially obstructed view. Forest roads there are used by mountain bikers. USFS Trail No. 47, the Wauchecha Bald Trail, leads 7.3 miles west to a USFS campground at Cheoah Point, on Lake Santeelah, but is not well-maintained.

Brown Fork Gap Shelter →

This shelter was constructed in 1997 by volunteers from Smoky Mountains Hiking Club, ATC's Konnarock volunteer crew, and the U.S. Forest Service. Accommodates 8, with adjacent spring. Privy is below shelter. Next shelter: south, 9.1 miles (Sassafras Gap); north, 6.1 miles (Cable Gap).

N-S

TRAIL DESCRIPTION

0.0 S.R. 1242 intersects at Yellow Creek Gap (elev. 2,980   **7.6**
feet) at **northern end of section**. ■ SOUTHBOUND hikers
continue directly opposite, up stone steps into woods,
beginning 1,000-foot ascent to ridgecrest. ■ NORTHBOUND
hikers proceed along west side of ridge, ascending
gradually (see Section Three).

0.4 Cross stream at foot of small cascade above Yellow Creek   **7.2**
Gap.

1.4 Trail turns sharply. ■ SOUTHBOUND hikers bear right, fol-   **6.2**
lowing ridgecrest. ■ NORTHBOUND hikers bear left, leaving
ridgecrest and descending.

1.6 Cross knob (elev. 4,000 feet), with view of Cheoah Bald   **6.0**
to east.

2.4 Reach Cody Gap (elev. 3,600 feet) along ridgecrest; water   **5.2**
usually available at nearby spring, except during dry
seasons. ■ SOUTHBOUND hikers bear left, with little elevation change, around side of **Wauchecha Bald**. ■ NORTH-
BOUND hikers bear right along ridgecrest.

3.2 Pass through Hogback Gap (elev. 3,500 feet). ■ SOUTH-   **4.4**
BOUND hikers ascend toward knob at 3,912 feet. ■ NORTH-
BOUND hikers bear east on Trail and continue, with little
elevation change, around side of **Wauchecha Bald**.

5.0 Pass through Brown Fork Gap (elev. 3,580 feet). Water   **2.6**
usually can be found just south of the gap, 35 yards to
the east of the A.T.

5.2 Trail intersects to east, leading about 70 yards to **Brown**   **2.4**
Fork Gap Shelter.

S-N

SECTION HIGHLIGHTS

Nantahala National Forest →

The forest covers 1.3 million acres in western North Carolina and was established in 1920. The land was purchased under the authority of the Weeks Act of 1911, which Congress passed in response to devastating eastern floods blamed on unchecked timber harvesting in the Appalachians. At the time, most national forests were in western states, but the act allowed the purchase of eastern lands that were "forested, cut-over or denuded...within the watersheds of navigable streams," and most early land purchases were of land that was inaccessible or had been stripped of timber. *Nantahala* is a Cherokee word that has been translated by the Forest Service as meaning "land of the noonday sun."

Southern end of section →

In Stecoah Gap, where the Trail crosses N.C. 143 (Sweetwater Creek Road); parking available. No public transportation. N.C. 28 is about three miles to the east, and Robbinsville is 10.0 miles to the west, with public accommodations and services, including grocery stores, restaurant, and post office.

N-S

TRAIL DESCRIPTION

5.6   Reach narrow ridgecrest, which Trail follows, descending **2.0**
      in southerly course.

5.8   Pass cliffs, 15 yards to west, with excellent views of **1.8**
      Snowbird Mountains and the surrounding **Nantahala**
      National Forest. ■ SOUTHBOUND hikers descend steeply.

6.6   Pass through Sweetwater Gap (elev. 3,220 feet). ■ NORTH- **1.0**
      BOUND hikers ascend steeply toward cliffs.

6.8   Reach ridgecrest above Stecoah Gap. **0.8**

7.6   N.C. 143 intersects at Stecoah Gap (elev. 3,165 feet), at **0.0**
      southern end of section. ■ SOUTHBOUND hikers cross
      highway and follow Trail up steps to left of ridgecrest,
      gradually ascending (see Section Five). ■ NORTHBOUND
      hikers enter woods and begin 800-foot ascent to cliffs
      above Sweetwater Gap.

S-N

Stecoah Gap (N.C. 143) to the Nantahala River (U.S. 19/74)

13.6 MILES

This section involves long ascents and descents in both directions but is especially tough for northbound hikers, who must gain 3,339 feet over the eight miles from the Nantahala River to the summit of Cheoah Bald (elev. 5,062 feet), one of the toughest hauls on the Appalachian Trail south of New England. Southbound hikers must deal with switchbacks and small knobs while climbing out of Stecoah Gap, a gain of 1,897 feet before the long, knee-testing descent to the gorge. At the summit of Cheoah Bald, a short side trail leads to a lookout point, with views that are among the best in the southern Appalachians; another long-distance trail, the Bartram Trail, terminates here. Also worth noting are the rock formations of Nantahala slate that form a knife edge south of the Cheoah summit. Farther south, the route offers good views of the Nantahala Gorge and passes through a beautiful hardwood cove on the Trail into (or out of) the gorge.

Road Approaches—Both ends of this section are accessible by car, but there are no road crossings in between.

Maps— See ATC's Nantahala National Forest map with this guide and the TVA Hewitt and Wesser quadrangles.

Shelters and Campsites—The Sassafras Gap Shelter is located almost midway along this section (mile 6.7/6.9), about 120 yards off the A.T. The A. Rufus Morgan Shelter is 0.8 mile south of the southern end of the section, in Section Six. The Trail corridor in this section lies within the Nantahala National Forest, and camping is permitted except where noted otherwise. Campfires should be attended at all times and completely extinguished when you leave a campsite.

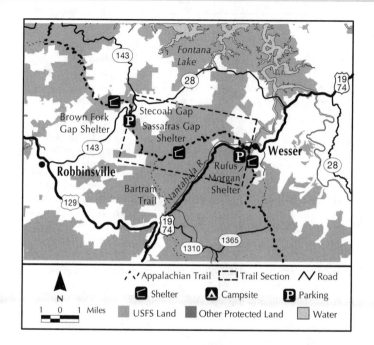

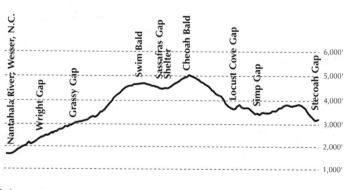

SECTION HIGHLIGHTS

Northern end of section →

In Stecoah Gap, where the Trail crosses N.C. 143 (Sweetwater Creek Road); parking available. No public transportation. N.C. 28 is about three miles to the east, and Robbinsville is 10.0 miles to the west on hard-surfaced N.C. 143, with public accommodations and services, including grocery stores, lodging, restaurant, and post office.

Ridgecrest →

In 1819, a line separating Cherokee lands from those of North Carolina settlers was drawn along the crest of the Nantahalas.

Bartram Trail →

This 78-mile national recreation trail, blazed yellow, leads compass-south along Ledbetter Creek 6.6 miles down to the Nantahala River. It traces the route that pioneer naturalist William Bartram took through the high country of North Carolina and Georgia in the eighteenth century. From its terminus at Cheoah Bald, it extends through western North Carolina and Georgia and is maintained by volunteers from trail associations in both states. It intersects the A.T. at Cheoah Bald and Wayah Bald, making a 57-mile loop possible along the two trails (see page 222). For more information and maps, contact N.C. Bartram Trail Society, P. O. Box 144, Scaly Mountain, NC 28775; e-mail, <info@ncbartramtrail.org>.

Sassafras Gap Shelter →

Accommodates 14. Built in 2002. Spring is in front of the shelter. Privy. Next shelter: south, 7.7 miles (Rufus Morgan); north, 9.1 miles (Brown Fork Gap).

N-S

| | TRAIL DESCRIPTION | |

0.0   N.C. 143 intersects at **northern end of section.** ■ SOUTH- **13.6**
BOUND hikers follow Trail up steps to left of ridgecrest,
gradually ascending along a series of switchbacks. ■
NORTHBOUND hikers cross highway, enter woods, and
begin 800-foot ascent to cliffs above Sweetwater Gap (see
Section Four).

0.7   Reach high point of ridge. A good spring is about 0.1 mile **12.9**
to the west on a logging road. ■ SOUTHBOUND hikers pass
over a series of small knobs along crest. ■ NORTHBOUND
hikers turn sharply to the left and follow Trail on gradual
descent through a series of switchbacks to Stecoah Gap.

2.1   Pass through Simp Gap. **11.5**

3.1   Reach Locust Cove Gap. Water is located 150 yards to **10.5**
the west (spring is variable). ■ SOUTHBOUND hikers ascend
gradually toward ridgecrest, beginning two-mile ascent
to Cheoah Bald.

3.4   Trail turns sharply at **ridgecrest.** **10.2**

5.1   Yellow-blazed **Bartram Trail** intersects with A.T. from **8.5**
west.

5.5   Reach the summit of Cheoah Bald (elev. 5,062 feet), **8.1**
terminus of the **Bartram Trail.** A side trail leads east to a
view of the Great Smokies, one of the most splendid
panoramas in the southern Appalachians. ■ SOUTHBOUND
hikers begin 8.1-mile, 3,339-foot descent into Nantahala
Gorge along a knife edge of blue Nantahala slate.
■ NORTHBOUND hikers begin 1,897-foot descent to Stecoah Gap along A.T. and, for a short distance, the Bartram
Trail.

6.7   Reach Sassafras Gap. Side trail leads east 120 yards to **6.9**
Sassafras Gap Shelter.

S-N

SECTION HIGHLIGHTS

Nantahala Gorge →

One of the premier whitewater rivers in the southern Appalachians runs through here. A.T. geologist V. Collins Chew explains that the gorge was formed where the Nantahala River cuts along a ten-mile belt of marble and mica that erodes more easily than surrounding rocks. "The marble was originally limestone, laid down in a sea by chemical precipitation or by animals building their shells, 400 to 570 million years ago.... Erosion appears to have formed a long valley through the mountains here, but, rather than being one stream valley, it includes several streams that cross or follow the lowland belt. They twist, turn, and branch over rocks beside the belt but flow in much straighter channels where they follow the traces of the marble. The Nantahala River flows north in a curvy path. When it reaches marble, it turns sharply northeast, cutting a long, straight gorge to the Little Tennessee River, where the gorge and the marble belt end. The A.T. crosses the gorge near its northeastern end."

The Jump-up →

This spot originally got its name from a short and very steep scramble here. A graded switchback now takes the Trail around the steep part, but a good view is available. Another "Jump-up," also known as the "Jump-off," with a view, is in Section Six.

N-S

TRAIL DESCRIPTION

7.0 Cross gap. ■ SOUTHBOUND hikers ascend toward summit   **6.6**
of Swim Bald. ■ NORTHBOUND hikers proceed along right
side of knob.

7.6 Reach summit of Swim Bald (elev. 4,720 feet). An unreli-   **6.0**
able spring is approximately 50 yards east of the summit
of Swim Bald. ■ SOUTHBOUND hikers follow main ridge.
(**Note:** Another ridge extends compass-north from Swim
Bald and is often confused with the one running almost
directly compass-east, which the Trail follows.) Along the
ridge that the A.T. follows are good views of the **Nantahala Gorge**. This knife-edge ridge becomes exceed-
ingly sharp, especially on the western slope. ■ NORTH-
BOUND hikers bear slightly to the right and descend. On
the opposite side is a splendid view of the Smokies.

8.3 Trail switches back sharply at **the Jump-up.** ■ SOUTHBOUND   **5.3**
hikers descend into a beautiful hardwood cove, passing
a reliable spring. ■ NORTHBOUND hikers ascend to knife
edge of rock.

8.8 Trail switches back sharply, passing a reliable spring.   **4.8**

9.3 Reach a gap.   **4.3**

10.1 Reach crest of Grassy Top.   **3.5**

10.5 Reach Grassy Gap (elev. 3,050 feet). ■ SOUTHBOUND hik-   **3.1**
ers bear right along heavily used trail around side of Tyre
Knob. ■ NORTHBOUND hikers ascend and skirt eastern side
of ridge.

10.9 Pass through sag. Trail to west leads about 100 yards to   **2.7**
spring and campsite.

11.3 Skirt southeast side of Tyre Knob (elev. 3,760 feet).   **2.3**

S-N

SECTION HIGHLIGHTS

Railroad tracks →

Formerly the tracks of the **Southern Railway**, running between Asheville and Murphy, N.C. The line mainly transported logs from the mountains, beginning in the late nineteenth century. Logging operations wound down in the 1940s, and passenger service was discontinued in 1948. Freight service was discontinued by Norfolk Southern in 1988, and the right-of-way was sold to the state of North Carolina. It was leased by the Great Smoky Mountains Railroad, Inc., a group of shippers and investors, which today operates dinner trains and steam excursions up the gorge. In recent years, it has been used as a set for such movies as "The Fugitive," starring Harrison Ford and Tommy Lee Jones, and "Forces of Nature," with Sandra Bullock and Ben Affleck.

Southern end of section →

The former whistle-stop town of Wesser is now the site of the Nantahala Outdoor Center. Lodging, restaurants, a coin laundry, and an outdoor-recreation store are located at NOC, with limited groceries available. Supermarkets and a full selection of hiker amenities are available at Bryson City, N.C., 15 miles compass-northeast *via* U.S. 19/74; Murphy, N.C., is 38 miles compass-south. Long-distance hikers can pick up supply packages mailed to Nantahala Outdoor Center, 13077 Highway 19 W, Bryson City, NC 28713. No public transportation is available. South of the river, the Trail is maintained by the Nantahala Hiking Club. North of the river, it is maintained by the Smoky Mountains Hiking Club.

N-S	TRAIL DESCRIPTION	

12.0	Reach dirt road at Wright Gap. ▪ SOUTHBOUND hikers cross road and ascend to ridgecrest. ▪ NORTHBOUND hikers begin steep ascent of ridge.	**1.6**
12.3	Cross under powerline below Flint Ridge.	**1.3**
12.9	Reach crest of ridge spur.	**0.7**
13.5	Reach **railroad tracks**. ▪ SOUTHBOUND hikers cross tracks and continue straight through parking lot of Nantahala Outdoor Center to footbridge across the Nantahala River. ▪ NORTHBOUND hikers leave railroad tracks and take Trail to left, gradually ascending to ridge spur.	**0.1**
13.6	The **southern end of section** is in the Nantahala Gorge, on the southern bank of the Nantahala River in the center of Nantahala Outdoor Center facilities in Wesser, N.C. (elev. 1,723 feet). ▪ SOUTHBOUND hikers continue on A.T., cross U.S. 19/74, cross a small paved road, and ascend graded Trail into woods (see Section Six). ▪ NORTHBOUND hikers cross footbridge and continue straight across parking lot to railroad tracks, beginning 3,339-foot, 8.1-mile ascent of Cheoah Bald.	**0.0**

S-N

Nantahala River (U.S. 19/74) to Tellico Gap (S.R. 1365)

7.9 MILES

This section presents southbound hikers leaving from Wesser with a long climb out of Nantahala Gorge (elev. 1,723 feet) over Wesser Bald (elev. 4,627 feet) and northbound hikers with a long descent into it. Near the middle of the section is the "Jump-up," with extensive views of Cheoah Bald to the west, the Smokies to the north, and the Balsam Mountains to the east. Wesser Bald, now tree-covered, still offers a superb view from a lookout tower, from which hikers can see mountain ranges in all directions. Water is scarce in this section. There is no water in Tellico Gap (elev. 3,850 feet).

Road Approaches—Both ends of the section are accessible by car. On the northern end, Wesser is on U.S. 19. Tellico Gap, at the southern end of the section, can be reached from the west by gravel N.C. 1365 (Otter Creek Road).

Maps—See ATC's Nantahala National Forest map (with this guide) and the TVA Wesser quadrangle. See also the U.S. Forest Service Nantahala National Forest map.

Shelters and Campsites—This section includes two shelters: The A. Rufus Morgan Shelter, mile 0.8/7.1, and the Wesser Bald Shelter, mile 5.7/2.2. The Trail corridor in this section lies within the Nantahala National Forest, and camping is permitted except where noted otherwise. Campfires should be attended at all times and completely extinguished when you leave a campsite.

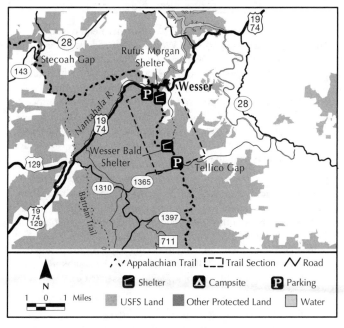

Appalachian Trail ┌┈┈┐ **Trail Section** ⋀ **Road**

🏠 **Shelter**   ▲ **Campsite**   🅿 **Parking**

1 0 1 Miles

USFS Land   Other Protected Land   Water

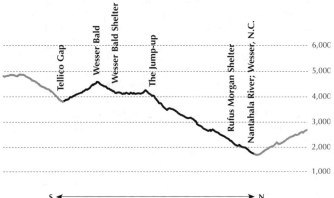

S ◄─────────────────► N

7.9 MILES

SECTION HIGHLIGHTS

Northern end of section →

The former whistle-stop town of Wesser is now the site of the Nantahala Outdoor Center (NOC). Lodging, restaurants, a coin laundry, and an outdoor-recreation store are located at NOC, with limited groceries available. Supermarkets and a full selection of hiker amenities are available at Bryson City, N.C., 15 miles compass-northeast *via* U.S. 19/74; Murphy, N.C., is 38 miles compass-south. Long-distance hikers can pick up packages mailed to Nantahala Outdoor Center, 13077 Highway 19 W, Bryson City, NC 28713. No public transportation is available.

A. Rufus Morgan Shelter →

Built after a relocation took the Trail away from Wesser Creek in the 1980s. It was rebuilt after a falling tree smashed it in 1993. Accommodates 6. No privy. Rev. Morgan (1885–1983), an Episcopal priest who founded the Nantahala Hiking Club, was an A.T. pioneer who singlehandedly maintained the Trail between Wesser and the Georgia state line in the 1940s and early 1950s. Next shelter: south, 4.9 miles (Wesser Bald); north, 7.7 miles (Sassafras Gap).

Wesser Creek Trail →

This blue-blazed former route of the A.T. leads east (compass-north) from the A.T. to Wesser Creek Road. It can be used for an 11.9-mile loop hike from Wesser, using the A.T. to return to starting point. Southbound from Wesser (mile 0.0/7.9), roadwalk along U.S. 19 east 0.9 mile. This roadwalk can be dangerous, so it's better to get a ride. Turn right onto Wesser Creek Road (trail not blazed along road), and follow road to footpath junction at mile 2.6. Begin graded footpath, reaching Wesser Creek at mile 3.0. At mile 4.3, the path leaves the creek and climbs toward Wesser Bald along switchbacks. Reach junction with present A.T. at mile 6.2 on ridge. To complete loop, follow A.T. north and generally downhill for 5.7 miles (see page 223).

N-S	TRAIL DESCRIPTION	

0.0	The **northern end of section** is on the southern bank of the Nantahala River, just north of U.S. 19/74 in Wesser (elev. 1,723 feet), near the Nantahala Outdoor Center office. ■ Southbound hikers cross highway, cross small paved road, and ascend graded Trail into woods, beginning 2,904-foot, 6.5-mile ascent of Wesser Bald. ■ Northbound hikers cross footbridge over river and continue straight across parking lot to railroad tracks, beginning 3,339-foot, 8.1-mile ascent to Cheoah Bald (see Section Five).	7.9
0.8	Enter clearing. **A. Rufus Morgan Shelter** is 200 feet to east; a stream is to west.	7.1
1.1	Old road intersects at gap. ■ Southbound hikers follow road to right for 600 feet, then turn left into woods. ■ Northbound hikers turn left on sidehill trail.	6.8
3.9	Pass small cave to west. Trail leads over rock-and-wood steps.	4.1
4.1	Reach the "Jump-up" (also called the "Jump-off"), a rocky outcrop boasting outstanding views. Do not confuse it with the "Jump-up" in Section Five. ■ Southbound hikers follow ridge with many short ups and downs. ■ Northbound hikers descend steeply.	3.8

Wesser Bald Shelter →

Built by the Nantahala Hiking Club in 1994. Accommodates 8. Privy nearby. A campsite is located near the shelter, and water for both is available from the spring 0.1 mile south on the Trail. Next shelter: south, 5.8 miles (Cold Spring); north, 4.9 miles (Rufus Morgan).

Wesser Bald →

There are many theories about how southern mountain balds were formed, but those that the U.S. Forest Service doesn't keep open by burning, mowing, or livestock-grazing soon end up like Wesser Bald, with the view obscured by new trees. Fortunately for hikers, the open platform of a former fire lookout here provides magnificent views of the Nantahalas and the Smokies.

Southern end of section →

Gravel S.R. 1365 leads 4 miles west (Otter Creek Road) to S.R. 1310 and 8 miles east (Tellico Road) to N.C. 28, 12 miles north of Franklin, N.C. Parking available at graded area. The road to the east of the northbound Trail leads to the Wesser Bald fire tower and may be used for a three-mile loop hike. No services available.

N-S

TRAIL DESCRIPTION

5.7 Blue-blazed **Wesser Creek Trail** (former A.T. route) inter- **2.2**
sects to east. To west, on side trail, is **Wesser Bald Shelter**.
■ SOUTHBOUND hikers ascend toward Wesser Bald.
■ NORTHBOUND hikers follow ridge, with many short ups
and downs for next two miles.

5.8 Trail turns sharply. Blue-blazed trail leads 125 feet east to **2.1**
excellent spring.

6.5 Reach high point near **Wesser Bald** summit (elev. 4,627 **1.4**
feet). An observation tower is 100 yards south on a side
trail. ■ SOUTHBOUND hikers bear right and descend.
■ NORTHBOUND hikers bear left and begin 2,904-foot, 6.5-
mile descent into Nantahala Gorge.

7.9 Reach gravel S.R. 1365 and **southern end of section** at **0.0**
Tellico Gap (elev. 3,850). ■ SOUTHBOUND hikers cross road
and ascend under powerline (see Section Seven). ■ NORTH-
BOUND hikers begin 777-foot ascent of Wesser Bald on
graded trail to left of gravel road.

Observation tower on Wesser Bald

S-N

Tellico Gap (S.R. 1365) to
Wayah Gap (S.R. 1310)

13.5 MILES

This high, remote section of the A.T. follows the main ridge of the Nantahala range, going near the tops of seven balds above 5,000 feet in elevation. Both ends are at gaps, with challenging climbs or descents of more than 1,000 feet of elevation leading into or out of them and additional climbs/descents in between. The Trail is graded throughout, with a few steep places, and avoids the summits of peaks without views and of Wine Spring Bald, which has multiple radio and television tower installations. The observation tower on the summit of Wayah Bald (elev. 5,342 feet) has extensive views of the surrounding mountains. The long-distance Bartram Trail coincides with the A.T. for part of this section.

Road Approaches—Both the northern (S.R. 1365) and southern (S.R. 1310) ends of the section are accessible by gravel secondary roads. Another gravel road (S.R. 1397), reached from S.R. 1310 at a sign for Burningtown Gap, provides access to the A.T. at Burningtown Gap near the middle of the section. The A.T. at the summit of Wayah Bald can be reached from Wayah Gap by USFS 69.

Maps—ATC Nantahala National Forest map (with this guide), USFS map of the Nantahala National Forest, and the TVA Wayah Bald and Wesser quadrangles.

Shelters and Campsites—Cold Spring Shelter (mile 3.6/9.9) is small, but there is good camping nearby. Wayah Shelter (mile 8.4/5.1) also has five campsites. The developed picnic area around the observation tower on Wayah Bald (no water) is off-limits to camping. The Trail corridor in this section lies within the Nantahala National Forest, and camping is generally permitted.

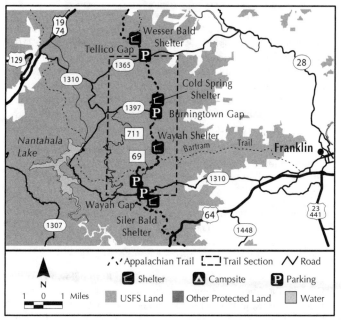

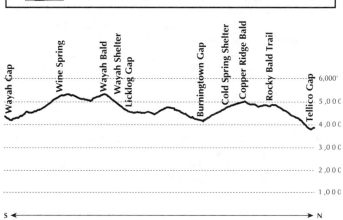

S ← → N

13.5 MILES

Northern end of section →

Gravel S.R. 1365 leads 4 miles west (Otter Creek Road) to S.R. 1310 and 8 miles east (Tellico Road) to N.C. 28, 12 miles north of Franklin, N.C. S.R. 1310 links U.S. 19 south of Wesser and U.S. 64 west of Franklin and also crosses the A.T. at Wayah Gap (southern end of section). Parking available at graded area. The rough road to the east of the northbound Trail leads to Wesser Bald fire tower and may be used for a three-mile loop. No services available.

Copper Ridge Bald →

Summit (elev. 5,256 feet) to east of A.T. is now wooded, but nice views can be had from A.T. of Little Tennessee River Valley.

Cold Spring Shelter →

A campsite is located on the ridge just above the shelter and is reached by a side trail just north of the shelter, which accommodates 6. Privy, bear cables; water 5 yards in front of shelter. Next shelter: south, 4.8 miles (Wayah); north, 5.8 miles (Wesser Bald).

Burningtown Gap →

In 1776, the Cherokee town of Tikaleyasuni on present-day Burningtown Creek, in the valley east of here, was put to the torch by troops of Col. Andrew Williamson, on his way to join Gen. Griffith Rutherford's punitive expedition against the Indians. The militia marched through this part of North Carolina, burning Cherokee crops and settlements as it went, trying to intimidate and keep the Cherokee from siding with the British in the Revolutionary War. The lower, middle, and overhill settlements (classifications based on location and dialect) were highly developed farming communities, usually run by women while the men hunted, fought, and roamed the mountains. Cherokee families fled to high ridges such as this one, above the burning settlements, but soon were forced to sign treaties in exchange for peace. Most of the towns never recovered their earlier prosperity, and many were later burned again in 1838, when the U.S. Army forced the Cherokee out of the lands granted by the earlier treaties.

N-S

	TRAIL DESCRIPTION	

0.0 **Northern end of section** is at Tellico Gap (elev. 3,850   **13.5**
feet) and gravel S.R. 1365. ■ SOUTHBOUND hikers ascend
under powerline, beginning 1,230-foot ascent of Copper
Ridge Bald. ■ NORTHBOUND hikers cross road and begin
777-foot ascent of Wesser Bald on graded trail to left of
gravel road (see Section Six). Graded A.T. crosses Tellico
Gap (3,850 feet) under powerline.

1.4 Reach a good spring to west.   **12.1**

1.7 Blue-blazed side trail to east leads 0.2 mile to nice view-   **11.8**
point on summit of Rocky Bald. ■ For SOUTHBOUND hikers,
the grade on A.T. becomes moderate as Trail skirts Rocky,
Black, and Tellico balds and returns to ridge between
them. ■ NORTHBOUND hikers descend more steeply.

2.9 Reach vista just west of Trail (elev. 5,080 feet), near **Cop-**   **10.6**
per Ridge Bald. Trail descends in either direction.

3.6 Reach **Cold Spring Shelter** and spring below Burningtown   **9.9**
Bald. This very old shelter (1933), built by the Civilian
Conservation Corps, still has remnants of the fencing that
kept cattle and hogs out when they were allowed to forage through the woods here.

4.8 Reach **Burningtown Gap** (elev. 4,236 feet), a large clear-   **8.7**
ing with apple trees. Dirt S.R. 1397 leads west from the
gap to S.R. 1310 at Kyle, N.C. Burningtown Gap is not
accessible from the east. ■ SOUTHBOUND hikers enter
woods. ■ NORTHBOUND hikers cross field and ascend,
skirting Burningtown Bald to west on graded trail.

5.6 Reach small clearing where several grassed roads inter-   **7.9**
sect.

S-N

SECTION HIGHLIGHTS

Licklog Gap →

Got its name from salt licks put out to attract animals. A stream is west about half a mile downhill along the logging road.

Wayah Shelter →

Built in 2007 by the Nantahala Hiking Club with, in part, contributions from Appalachian Long Distance Hikers Association members in memory of Ann and Larry McDuff, A.T. thru-hikers who were killed in eerily similar bicycle accidents more than a year apart. Accommodates 8 with overhang for cooking shelves and seating; five tentsites with a fire-ring nearby. Privy. Water source is Little Laurel Creek, 600 feet west of the A.T. on a blue-blazed trail. Next shelter: south, 7.8 miles (Siler Bald); north, 4.8 miles (Cold Spring).

Bartram Trail →

Leads east 10.0 miles to Wallace Branch. The Bartram Trail runs east–west from South Carolina to Cheoah Bald. This section begins at Wallace Branch, on S.R. 1315, 1.7 miles from its junction with "Old 64" on the outskirts of Franklin, near the USFS Nantahala District offices. Walking west from there, hikers reach junction at mile 1.3 with old Trimont Trail from Franklin to Wayah Bald. Bartram Trail turns left. At mile 10.0, hikers reach junction with A.T. 0.5 mile north of Wayah Bald (mile 8.8/4.7). The section between Wallace Branch and Wayah Bald ascends more than one mile, over numerous knobs. At mile 12.4 (A.T. mile 9.4/2.3), Bartram Trail turns, descending west on McDonald Ridge. At mile 14.1, hikers reach paved USFS 711 at Sawmill Gap. Bartram jogs left across road, then continues to S.R. 1310 along the shore of Nantahala Lake.

Wayah Bald →

Wayah is Cherokee for "wolf." The stone tower here offers superb views of the Smoky Mountains to the west and northwest. It was built in 1937 by the CCC as a fire tower. Two water-damaged floors were removed in the late 1940s. A roof of hemlock beams and cedar shakes was added in 1983, when it was renovated as a memo-

N-S

TRAIL DESCRIPTION

Privy at Wayah Shelter

7.1	Reach **Licklog Gap**. A logging road and wildlife clearing are a short distance to the west.	6.4
8.4	Reach **Wayah Shelter,** built in 2007, with tentsites.	5.1
8.8	Yellow-blazed **Bartram Trail** intersects here to east (route coincides with A.T. for 2.4 miles between here and mile 11.2/2.3 below).	4.7
8.9	Pass spring to west of Trail.	4.6
9.1	Cross dirt road.	4.4
9.3	Reach summit of **Wayah Bald** (elev. 5,342 feet) and stone observation tower. Macadam path leaving tower area goes to **USFS 69**. No camping on summit.	4.2
9.4	Pass latrines and parking area near edge of woods.	4.1

S-N

rial to John B. Byrne, former supervisor of the Nantahala National Forest, who first proposed the route of the Appalachian Trail in this area.

USFS 69 →

The A.T. at the summit of Wayah Bald can be reached from Wayah Gap by USFS 69, which roughly parallels the southern half of this section to the west.

Bartram Trail →

See mile 8.8/4.7. Leads west 1.7 miles to USFS 711 at Sawmill Gap and S.R. 1310.

Wilson Lick ranger station →

Built in 1913, it was the first such station in the Nantahala National Forest. Displays at the site tell its story. It is no longer used as a ranger station.

Wayah Gap →

See page 118.

Southern end of section →

From Wayah Gap, it is seven miles east to U.S. 64 and 12 miles east *via* S.R. 1310 and U.S. 64 to Franklin. The Wayah Crest picnic area is near the Trail crossing. Public accommodations are available in Franklin, but there are none at the Trail crossing.

N-S

TRAIL DESCRIPTION

9.6	Cross woods road near log steps.	**3.9**
11.0	Woods road intersects. ■ SOUTHBOUND hikers follow Trail along woods road. ■ NORTHBOUND hikers bear left into woods.	**2.5**
11.2	Below summit of Wine Spring Bald, reach Wine Spring (elev. 5,360 feet), to west of A.T. and 100 feet north of intersection with yellow-blazed **Bartram Trail** to west. ■ SOUTHBOUND hikers pass Bartram Trail and continue descending. ■ NORTHBOUND hikers continue to ascend along A.T. and Bartram Trail, which coincides with A.T. for the next 2.4 miles, between here and mile 8.8/4.7.	**2.3**
11.7	Cross gravel USFS 69, near log steps. A piped spring is located a few yards to east.	**1.8**
12.2	Reach blue-blazed side trail to historic **Wilson Lick ranger station** to west.	**1.3**
13.5	**Southern end of section** is one hundred feet east of crest of **Wayah Gap**, at paved S.R. 1310 (elev. 4,180 feet), 200 yards north of picnic area (latrines and trash cans). ■ SOUTHBOUND hikers cross road and climb log steps (see Section Eight). ■ NORTHBOUND hikers ascend into woods, paralleling USFS 69, beginning 1,180-foot ascent to Wine Spring.	**0.0**

S-N

Wayah Gap (S.R. 1310) to Wallace Gap ("Old 64")

9.0 MILES

This section includes three major road crossings of the Nantahala range—the oldest, at Wayah Gap (elev. 4,180 feet) at the northern end; the newest, at Winding Star Gap (elev. 3,850 feet) in the middle; and the "old" route that was used for most of the 20th century at Wallace Gap (elev. 3,738 feet) at the southern end. In between the gaps, the Trail climbs a shoulder of Siler Bald (elev. 5,216 feet) and crosses a series of knobs. The 0.2-mile side trail to the summit of Siler Bald is well worth the trip; views include the route of the A.T. from Tray Mountain in Georgia to the Great Smokies.

Road Approaches—Both the northern (S.R. 1310) and southern (S.R. 1448, "Old 64") ends of the section are accessible by car. U.S. 64, a major highway, crosses the Trail at Winding Stair Gap and is an access point for the Trail.

Maps—ATC Nantahala National Forest map (with this guide); TVA Wayah Bald and Rainbow Springs quadrangles.

Shelters and Campsites—One shelter, Siler Bald Shelter, is located along the section on a 1.1-mile blue-blazed loop trail at mile 1.7/7.3 and mile 2.2/6.8. The Trail corridor in this section lies within the Nantahala National Forest, and camping is permitted except where noted otherwise. Campfires should be attended at all times and completely extinguished when leaving a campsite.

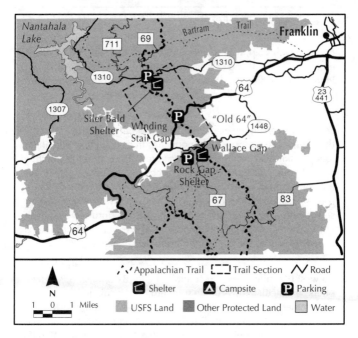

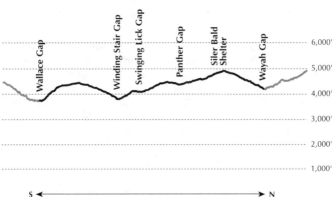

Northern end of section →

From Wayah Gap, it is seven miles east to U.S. 64 and 12 miles east, *via* S.R. 1310 and U.S. 64, to Franklin, N.C. The Wayah Crest Picnic Area is near the Trail crossing. Public accommodations are available in Franklin but not at the Trail crossing.

Wayah Gap →

For many years in the eighteenth and ninteenth centuries, this was the main route west over the mountains from Franklin. Militiamen fought a skirmish with the Cherokee here in 1776, during a punitive raid, although accounts differ as to whether the raiders were under the command of Gen. Griffith Rutherford or Col. Andrew Williamson. According to one account, the Cherokee, trying to defend their settlements, were waiting here to ambush Rutherford's force, which got lost and crossed the mountains elsewhere; Williamson's troops later walked into the ambush but routed the Cherokee.

Siler Bald →

To west 0.2 mile, the open summit of Siler Bald (elev. 5,216 feet) offers spectacular views of the southern Appalachians. The summit was named for William Siler, whose great-grandson, the Rev. A. Rufus Morgan, helped establish the A.T. in North Carolina. This bald is maintained as a grassy summit by the North Carolina Wildlife Resources Commission. Do not confuse it with Siler*s* Bald in the Smokies, page 68.

Siler Bald Shelter →

Built in 1959 and renovated in 1997. Reached by a loop trail along old logging roads. Accommodates 8; campsites and privy nearby. A spring is located 300 feet south of the shelter on the loop trail. Bear cables have been installed to hang food. Do not confuse with Silers Bald Shelter in the Smokies, page 68. Next shelter: south, 8.0 miles (Rock Gap); north, 7.8 miles (Wayah).

N-S

TRAIL DESCRIPTION

0.0 **Northern end of section** is one hundred feet east of crest of **Wayah Gap**, at paved S.R. 1310 (elev. 4,180 feet). ■ SOUTHBOUND hikers ascend, skirting Wayah Crest picnic area, beginning 900-foot ascent to Snowbird Leap below **Siler Bald**. ■ NORTHBOUND hikers ascend into woods paralleling USFS 69, beginning 1,180-foot ascent to Wine Spring (see Section Seven). **9.0**

1.7 Reach grassy wildlife clearing (elev. 4,980 feet) and trail junction below **Siler Bald**. Blue-blazed **Siler Bald Shelter** loop trail intersects to east, descending 0.6 mile on logging roads to shelter and spring. Spur trail to Siler Bald summit is to west. ■ SOUTHBOUND hikers continue straight into woods. ■ NORTHBOUND hikers begin 900-foot descent to Wayah Gap. **7.3**

2.0 Cross old, overgrown road. **7.0**

2.1 Turn sharply at log steps. **6.9**

2.2 Southern end of blue-blazed **Siler Bald Shelter** loop trail, which leads 0.5 mile to shelter and spring. ■ SOUTHBOUND hikers bear right, downhill. ■ NORTHBOUND hikers bear left and continue on woods road, ascending. **6.8**

3.9 Reach Panther Gap, a level area with no water. **5.1**

4.8 Turn sharply at Swinging Lick Gap, descending to south, ascending to north. **4.2**

4.9 Cross stream. **4.1**

5.6 Cross stream by waterfall. **3.4**

S-N

SECTION HIGHLIGHTS

U.S. 64 →

Franklin, N.C., is 10.0 miles east along this major east-west highway, with motels, restaurants, post office, groceries, outdoor equipment, and a hospital. Parking is available at Trailhead. Trash cans are located at the parking area. Cross-continental U.S. 64 is North Carolina's longest road, stretching 549 miles from the Tennessee line to the Outer Banks. The highway's western terminus is Teec Nos Pos, Arizona, and it extends 2,326 miles from end to end.

"Old 64" →

S.R. 1448, also known as Old Murphy Road. Originally N.C. 28, it became a U.S. highway in the late 1920s as part of a fledgling federal highway system. Development of the system during the late 1920s over existing primary roads was partly responsible for prompting A.T. founder and regional planner Benton MacKaye to dream up the idea of a "townless highway" that would allow traffic to flow across the country while avoiding local congestion. That concept later led to development of the modern interstate highway system. U.S. 64 was rerouted farther north in the 1970s and now crosses the Trail at Winding Stair Gap.

Southern end of section →

Wallace Gap is on "Old 64." Franklin, N.C., is 10.0 miles east, with motels, restaurants, post office, groceries, outdoor equipment, and a hospital. Rock Gap, with parking (see Section Nine), is a better Trailhead. USFS Standing Indian Campground has a public telephone and is located 1.5 miles south of Wallace Gap on paved USFS 67.

N-S

	TRAIL DESCRIPTION	

5.9 Reach Winding Stair Gap (elev. 3,850 feet) and **U.S. 64**. **3.1**
■ SOUTHBOUND hikers turn right after crossing highway, go
500 feet, then ascend steps just beyond parking area. A
piped spring is beside the steps. ■ NORTHBOUND hikers
turn right, go 500 feet, then descend bank after crossing
highway, beginning 1,130-foot ascent of Siler Bald.

6.6 Cross stream. **2.4**

7.6 Reach ridge at gap (elev. 4,400 feet) with eastern view, **1.4**
below Rocky Cove Knob.

8.4 Cross log steps near a small clearing. **0.6**

8.9 Cross stream. ■ SOUTHBOUND hikers bear right down long **0.1**
flight of log steps. ■ NORTHBOUND hikers ascend into
woods, beginning 660-foot ascent of Rocky Cove Knob.

9.0 **Southern end of section** is at Wallace Gap (elev. 3,738 **0.0**
feet). ■ SOUTHBOUND hikers cross **"Old 64"** and continue
along Trail to the left of USFS 67 (see Section Nine).
■ NORTHBOUND hikers ascend narrow path up road
bank.

S-N

Wallace Gap ("Old 64") to Deep Gap (USFS 71)

21.3 MILES

The Trail here completes (or begins, for northbound hikers) its traverse of the Nantahala Range, where the range joins the Blue Ridge. It makes a long hook to the south and east, around the headwaters of the Nantahala River and Standing Indian Campground. With the notable exception of steep Albert Mountain, changes in elevation are gradual and afford pleasant hiking. Standing Indian Mountain (elev. 5,498 feet) is the highest point on the Trail south of the Great Smokies. For 11.8 miles, the Trail is within the congressionally designated Southern Nantahala Wilderness.

Road Approaches—Both the northern and southern ends are accessible by car. Road access on a Forest Service road is also possible below Albert Mountain, mile 6.6/14.7, and at Mooney Gap, mile 8.2/13.1.

Maps—ATC Nantahala National Forest map (with this guide); USFS map of the Southern Nantahala Wilderness Area; TVA Rainbow Springs and Prentiss quadrangles.

Shelters and Campsites—This section has four shelters, all located near water: Rock Gap Shelter (mile 0.7/20.6), Big Spring Shelter (mile 6.0/15.3), Carter Gap Shelter (mile 12.5/8.8), and Standing Indian Shelter (mile 20.4/0.9).

Trail Orientation—Note that, for a lengthy stretch of Trail in this section, a northbound hiker will actually be hiking compass-south; a southbound hiker, *vice versa*. Please see the note on page 14 on how compass directions are used in this guidebook.

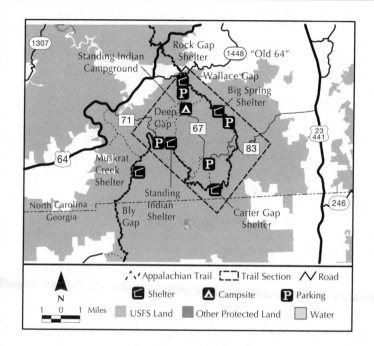

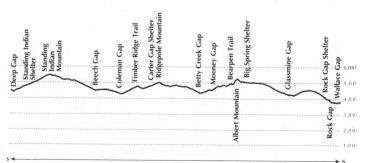

SECTION HIGHLIGHTS

Northern end of section →

At S.R. 1448, "Old 64," 10.0 miles west of Franklin, N.C., which has motels, restaurants, post office, groceries, outdoor equipment, and a hospital. Rock Gap, with parking (mile 0.6/20.7), is a better Trailhead. USFS Standing Indian Campground has a public telephone and is located 1.5 miles south of Wallace Gap on paved USFS 67. From Franklin, follow U.S. 64 12 miles west, then turn left at sign for "Appalachian Trail and Standing Indian Campground." Follow "Old 64" for about two miles to Wallace Gap. Hikers are advised to use the present U.S. 64 for access to Franklin (see Section Eight).

USFS 67 →

Starts at Wallace Gap and provides access to side trails at many points. It changes to gravel just past Standing Indian Campground and ends at a parking area 0.4 mile from the A.T. west of Albert Mountain.

Old 64 →

S.R. 1448, the "Old Murphy Road." See page 120.

Standing Indian Campground →

U.S. Forest Service campground, (828) 369-0442, open April 1– November 30, with restrooms, showers, and pay phone. It was originally a logging camp near the sawmill community of Rainbow Springs on the Nantahala River. Logs were shipped out on a narrow-gauge railroad along the river. The Forest Service took it over in 1920. It is a popular base of operations for loop hikes in the surrounding mountains.

Rock Gap Shelter →

Accommodates 8, and overhang offers additional cooking space sheltered from the rain. Privy nearby, bear cables. Spring may dry up during droughts. Next shelter: south, 5.3 miles (Big Spring Gap); north, 8.0 miles (Siler Bald).

N-S

TRAIL DESCRIPTION

0.0   **Northern end of section** is at Wallace Gap (elev. 3,738   **21.3**
feet). ■ SOUTHBOUND hikers leave pavement on trail to the
left of **USFS 67**, beginning 1,512-foot ascent of Albert
Mountain over next 6.6 miles. ■ NORTHBOUND hikers cross
"Old 64" and ascend narrow path up road bank (see
Section Eight).

0.6   Reach Rock Gap. Blue-blazed trail descends 0.7 mile east   **20.7**
to the enormous, 126-foot, now dead John Wasilik Memo-
rial Poplar, second-largest poplar in the East. To west is
trash can, parking area on USFS 67, and road to **Standing
Indian Campground**.

0.7   Blue-blazed trail intersects to west; leads 300 feet to **Rock**   **20.6**
Gap Shelter.

1.1   Pass a seasonal spring 25 feet below Trail. Several sea-   **19.1**
sonal water sources are near the Trail for a mile in either
direction.

View from Albert Mountain

S-N

Long Branch Trail →

Leads west, downhill, 2.0 miles to USFS 67 near Standing Indian Campground. The trailhead is across the road from the backcountry information center on USFS 67 near the campground. It intersects an orange-blazed horse trail and crosses Long Branch Creek before descending through a hardwood forest.

Big Spring Shelter →

Built in 1959, accommodates 8, with an overhang offering additional cooking space. Privy nearby. Bear cables. Water is 75 feet below shelter at a spring that may go dry during droughts. Next shelter: south, 6.8 miles (Carter Gap); north, 5.3 miles (Rock Gap).

Bypass trail →

Leads 0.8 mile to A.T. at mile 6.9/14.4. A parking area is at end of USFS 67, midway through the detour.

Albert Mountain →

The summit features one of the few remaining fire towers along the southern Trail and offers superb views of the Blue Ridge to the east and the Little Tennessee River Valley below. The Trail here follows the western boundary of Coweeta Hydrologic Laboratory Area, one of the longest continuous environmental studies in North America. Its focus is on the relationship between trees and water in the landscape and is sponsored by the National Science Foundation, University of Georgia, and the USDA Forest Service.

Blue-blazed trails →

Bearpen Trail crosses the gravel road and descends 2.5 miles to USFS 67, 3.2 miles south of Standing Indian Campground; the lower 0.4 mile follows a grassed logging road, and hikers ascending from the road should watch for easy-to-miss turn into woods from the road. The rest of the trail traverses several different kinds of woodland while climbing to meet the A.T. The Albert Mountain bypass trail follows road uphill to left (see mile 6.4/14.9).

N-S

TRAIL DESCRIPTION

3.2 Reach Glassmine Gap in small clearing. Blue-blazed **Long Branch Trail** intersects to west.   **18.1**

4.0 Cross stream in wet area.   **17.3**

6.0 Reach Big Spring Gap. Blue-blazed trail leads west 280 feet to **Big Spring Shelter**.   **15.3**

6.4 Reach clearing. Blue-blazed trail to west (old road) is Albert Mountain **bypass trail**, a bad-weather alternative to the exposed summit and steep south face of Albert Mountain.   **14.9**

6.6 Reach summit of **Albert Mountain** (elev. 5,250 feet). Summit has a firetower and a magnificent view. ■ SOUTH-BOUND hikers begin steep, scrambling descent of southern slope of Albert Mountain. ■ NORTHBOUND hikers descend gradually from summit.   **14.7**

6.9 Two **blue-blazed trails** intersect beneath south face of Albert Mountain. Gravel USFS 67 is a few feet to the west. ■ SOUTHBOUND hikers follow ridge. ■ NORTHBOUND hikers scramble up the steep, rocky, and memorable southern side of Albert Mountain for 0.3 mile.   **14.4**

7.3 Pass near gravel USFS 67 in Bearpen Gap. ■ SOUTHBOUND hikers skirt Big Butt Mountain with occasional views into Coweeta area. ■ NORTHBOUND hikers follow level Trail toward Albert Mountain.   **14.0**

7.9 Log steps. ■ SOUTHBOUND hikers descend, turn right onto old road, and cross culvert that conducts water from spring above. ■ NORTHBOUND hikers cross above cliff along very steep eastern face of Big Butt Mountain, with some views east into Coweeta valley.   **13.4**

S-N

USFS 83 →

Comes up gravel road to east from U.S. 441; continues west to join USFS 67 in 1.2 miles.

Southern Nantahala Wilderness →

Designated by Congress in 1984. The area includes a total of 23,473 acres, split evenly between Georgia and North Carolina, mostly on the eastern side of the Blue Ridge. According to the 1964 Wilderness Act, wilderness is "where the Earth and its community of life are untrammeled by man, where man himself is a visitor who does not remain." The act requires that wilderness retain "its primeval character and influence" and that it be protected and managed in such a way that it "appears to have been affected primarily by the force of nature." For A.T. hikers, this means few access roads, minimal blazing, and fewer Trailside structures. For volunteer Trail maintainers, it means building and clearing the path without benefit of motorized equipment, such as chain saws and Weed-eaters.

Betty Creek Trail →

Leads 0.2 mile west to stream and USFS 67, 6.3 miles south of Standing Indian Campground area.

Blue Ridge Mountains →

The eastern escarpment of the Appalachians, extending southwestward 615 miles from north of Carlisle, Pa., to Mt. Oglethorpe, Ga. For most of its length, the range is a narrow ridge, but, in Georgia and North Carolina, it broadens to about 65 miles wide. In practice, people referring to the "Blue Ridge" generally mean the eastern side of the range and don't think of it as including the Nantahalas or the highlands on the Tennessee–North Carolina border that the Trail follows. The A.T. follows the eastern Blue Ridge through Georgia and most of Virginia, Maryland, and part of Pennsylvania. See page 33.

N-S

| TRAIL DESCRIPTION |

8.2   Cross **USFS 83** at Mooney Gap, an important watershed   **13.1**
      boundary. North of here, water flowing east from the ridge
      drains into the Mississippi River basin and the Gulf of
      Mexico. South of here, water flowing east from the ridge
      flows into the Savannah River basin and the Atlantic
      Ocean. West of here, water flowing west from the ridge
      also flows into the Mississippi River basin and the Gulf
      of Mexico. ▪ SOUTHBOUND hikers enter **Southern Nan-
      tahala Wilderness Area** 200 feet farther.

9.1   Reach clearing in Betty Creek Gap. A small spring is lo-   **12.2**
      cated to east, just north of the clearing. Blue-blazed
      Betty Creek Trail intersects to west. ▪ SOUTHBOUND hikers
      ascend gradually to Little Ridgepole Mountain. ▪ NORTH-
      BOUND hikers cross clearing and enter rhododendron
      tunnel.

11.1 Unmarked trail leads 25 feet east to excellent vista.   **10.2**

11.4 Trail turns sharply on the north (compass-east) side of   **9.9**
      Ridgepole Mountain. Between here and Springer Moun-
      tain (see Section Seventeen), the Trail mostly follows the
      eastern **Blue Ridge Mountains**. Between here and Fontana
      Lake (see Section Three), it follows the Nantahala Moun-
      tains. ▪ SOUTHBOUND hikers continue south along the **Blue
      Ridge Mountains**, ascending to shoulder of Ridgepole.
      ▪ NORTHBOUND hikers leave the eastern arm of the Blue
      Ridge to head along Little Ridgepole Mountain, following
      the **Nantahala Mountains** toward the Smokies.

S-N

Carter Gap Shelters →

Two shelters, old (1959, on west side of the gap, accommodates 6) and new (1998, on east side of the gap, accommodates 8). Bear cables. Privy nearby. Spring is 200 feet on blue-blazed trail to west and has been reliable during dry spells. Next shelter: south, 7.6 miles (Standing Indian); north, 6.8 miles (Big Spring).

Timber Ridge Trail →

Leads west (compass-north) 2.3 miles to parking area at USFS 67, 4.4 miles south of the backcountry information center at Standing Indian Campground. To reach the A.T. from the parking area, cross a log bridge over a large brook, turn left, and climb through rhododendron. About halfway, cross Big Laurel Branch on a new log bridge, climb to Timber Ridge, and proceed through open, fern-covered woods to the A.T., 0.4 mile south of Carter Gap.

Beech Gap Trail →

Blue-blazed, leads 2.8 miles west (compass-north) to parking area at USFS 67. To reach A.T., start at Beech Gap parking area on USFS 67, four miles south of backcountry information center at Standing Indian Campground. At 0.5 mile, Big Indian Horse Trail (orange blazes) intersects to right. At 2.0 miles, reach Big Indian Road (where horse trail leaves), and turn left. After pleasant, almost-level roadwalk, reach A.T. at Beech Gap.

Lower Trail Ridge Trail →

Blue-blazed, 4.2 miles. This trail is the most direct, but a strenuous way to reach Standing Indian Mountain from Standing Indian Campground. It originates from the backcountry information center, crosses the Nantahala River on the main campground road, skirts the campground area, then climbs rather steeply up Lower Trail Ridge directly to the mountain. It crosses the A.T. near the top of the mountain and continues 0.1 mile to end at the summit clearing.

N-S

TRAIL DESCRIPTION

12.8   Reach Carter Gap, a level area. Blue-blazed trail leads east to **Carter Gap Shelter**. ■ SOUTHBOUND hikers continue straight through gap. ■ NORTHBOUND hikers skirt Ridgepole Mountain.   **8.5**

13.2   Blue-blazed **Timber Ridge Trail** intersects to west.   **8.1**

14.2   Cross Coleman Gap (elev. 4,220 feet) in dense rhododendron thicket. ■ SOUTHBOUND hikers cross several small streams on gently rising Trail in next mile, beginning 4.7-mile, 1,278-foot ascent of Standing Indian Mountain.   **7.1**

16.0   Side trails and logging roads intersect at Beech Gap. Unreliable spring is 100 feet east of Trail. Blue-blazed trail on west is **Beech Gap Trail.** ■ SOUTHBOUND hikers continue steady climb up Standing Indian Mountain. ■ NORTHBOUND hikers cross several small streams on gently falling Trail in next mile.   **5.3**

18.9   Blue-blazed **Lower Trail Ridge Trail** intersects, leading 600 feet east to summit of **Standing Indian Mountain** (elev. 5,498 feet) and 4.2 miles west to Standing Indian Campground. One hundred feet south of the junction, an unmarked trail goes west 0.2 mile to a spring. ■ SOUTHBOUND hikers begin 2.4-mile, 1,157-foot descent to Deep Gap (see Section Ten). ■ NORTHBOUND hikers begin 4.7-mile, 1,278-foot descent to Coleman Gap.   **2.4**

S-N

SECTION HIGHLIGHTS

Standing Indian Mountain →

The summit area of Standing Indian Mountain offers a superb view of the Georgia Blue Ridge that southbound hikers will follow and northbound hikers have completed. Cherokee legend holds that a bolt of lightning struck there, killing a brood of monstrous creatures that had plagued the people and leaving the mountaintop bald. A warrior standing lookout nearby was turned to stone.

Standing Indian Shelter →

Built in 1996, accommodates 8. Privy. Water is available from reliable stream reached by side trail to west of A.T. just beyond shelter trail. Next shelter: south, 4.9 miles (Muskrat Creek); north, 7.6 miles (Carter Gap).

Southern Nantahala Wilderness →
See mile 8.2/13.1.

Kimsey Creek Trail →

Blue-blazed, 3.7 miles. This popular trail follows the course of Kimsey Creek from the campground to Deep Gap. It begins at the backcountry information center, crosses the river on the campground road, then turns right, and skirts the campground on the northern side. At 0.3 mile, it turns left and leaves the trails that follow the river. At 0.9 mile, it enters a clearing, where it turns right along a gated road following Kimsey Creek. At 2.1 miles, it crosses a log bridge over a side creek. The trail enters Deep Gap through an old picnic and camping area.

Standing Indian Campground →
See mile 0.6/20.7.

Southern end of section →

At parking area on USFS 71, a one-lane, gravel, six-mile-long road leaving U.S. 64 near the Clay–Macon county line, about 5.0 miles west of Wallace Gap (see northern end of section) and Winding Stair Gap (see Section Eight). Trash cans available. No public accommodations or facilities are nearby.

N-S

TRAIL DESCRIPTION

20.4   Blue-blazed side trail 250 feet east to **Standing Indian Shelter**. ■ NORTHBOUND hikers ascend steadily on grassy road.   **0.9**

21.3   Reach parking area at Deep Gap (4,341 feet) and **southern end of section** at boundary of **Southern Nantahala Wilderness**. USFS 71 intersects to west, leading 6.0 miles to U.S. 64. Seasonal water is available 150 feet west down the blue-blazed trail at the edge of an old camping area. Blue-blazed **Kimsey Creek Trail** to west descends on a gentle grade for 3.7 miles to **Standing Indian Campground**. ■ SOUTHBOUND hikers go straight across parking area and begin graded ascent of Yellow Mountain (see Section Ten). ■ NORTHBOUND hikers ascend on a graded trail between two logging roads, east of parking areas, beginning 2.4-mile, 1,157-foot ascent of Standing Indian Mountain.   **0.0**

Deep Gap

S-N

Deep Gap (USFS 71) to Bly Gap

6.8 MILES

Bly Gap, at the southern end of this section, marks a division between club maintaining responsibilities and a division in the terrain of the Trail. From here on, northbound hikers will generally find themselves at elevations of 4,500 feet or higher all the way north through the Smokies (see Sections One and Two). South of Bly Gap, the Trail averages about 3,500 feet in elevation. Between Deep Gap (elev. 4,341 feet) and Bly Gap (elev. 3,840 feet), the Trail follows the crest of the Blue Ridge, with views to the west of Shooting Creek Valley and Lake Chatuge. The northern part completes a long curve around the headwaters of the Tallulah River; the southern part climbs steeply north out of Georgia. This route skirts the Southern Nantahala Wilderness Area. Bly Gap offers an open view northwest to the Tusquitee Range, and a half-mile side trail near Muskrat Creek Shelter to Ravenrock Ridge affords an outstanding view to the north and west.

Road Approaches—The northern end at Deep Gap can be reached by following a long, gravel Forest Service road (USFS 71). There is no road approach to Bly Gap at the southern end.

Maps—ATC Nantahala National Forest map (with this guide); USFS map of Southern Nantahala Wilderness Area and Standing Indian Basin; TVA Rainbow Springs and Hightower Bald quadrangles.

Shelters and Campsites—The only shelter in this section is the Muskrat Creek Shelter (mile 4.0/2.8).

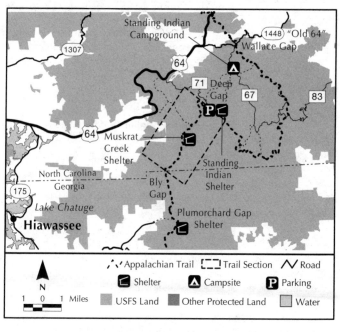

Standing Indian
Campground

1448 "Old 64"
Wallace Gap

1307

64

71 Deep
Gap

67

83

Muskrat
Creek
Shelter

P

Standing
Indian
Shelter

North Carolina
Georgia

Bly
Gap

Plumorchard Gap
Shelter

175

Lake Chatuge

Hiawassee

N

1 0 1 Miles

Appalachian Trail Trail Section Road
Shelter Campsite Parking
USFS Land Other Protected Land Water

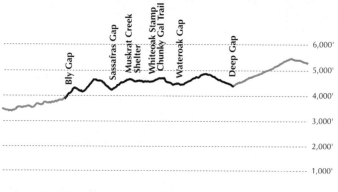

6,000'

5,000'

4,000'

3,000'

2,000'

1,000'

Bly Gap

Sassafras Gap

Muskrat Creek
Shelter

Whiteoak Stamp
Chunky Gal Trail

Wateroak Gap

Deep Gap

S N

6.8 MILES

SECTION HIGHLIGHTS

Northern end of section →

At parking area on USFS 71, a one-lane, gravel, six-mile-long road leaving U.S. 64 near the Clay-Macon county line, about 5.0 miles west of Wallace Gap (see northern end of Section Nine) and Winding Stair Gap (see Section Eight). Trash cans available. No public accommodations or facilities are nearby.

Southern Nantahala Wilderness Area →
See Section Nine.

Kimsey Creek Trail →
See Section Nine.

Standing Indian Campground →
See Section Nine.

Chunky Gal Trail →

Blue-blazed, leads 5.5 miles west to U.S. 64. This little-used trail (scenic when the trees are without leaves) follows the ridge of Chunky Gal Mountain. Trailhead is on U.S. 64 in Glade Gap, at the top of the long grade out of Shooting Creek Valley. The trailhead there is marked with a small sign and blazes but is not easy to locate. The name has brought a smile to many a hiker's face, but no one is quite sure where it comes from. One possibility is a legend about a portly native-American maiden, who left her family to pursue a lover. A more likely possibility is that it's simply a corruption of a Cherokee word. One old map from 1863 labels it "Chuckey Girl"; -*chucky* is a common element in Cherokee place names.

Whiteoak Stamp →

A fair spring is located about 400 feet southeast of Whiteoak Stamp on an unmarked trail.

N-S

TRAIL DESCRIPTION

0.0 Parking area at Deep Gap (elev. 4,341 feet) is the **north-**   **6.8**
ern end of section at boundary of **Southern Nantahala**
Wilderness Area. USFS 71 intersects to west, leading 6.0
miles to U.S. 64. Blue-blazed **Kimsey Creek Trail** to west
descends at a gentle grade for 3.7 miles to **Standing In-**
dian Campground. Seasonal water is available 150 feet
down the blue-blazed trail at the edge of an old camping
area. ■ SOUTHBOUND hikers go straight across parking area
and begin graded ascent. ■ NORTHBOUND hikers ascend
on a graded trail between two logging roads, east of parking areas, beginning 2.4-mile, 1,157-foot ascent of Standing Indian Mountain (see Section Nine).

0.7 Cross rock outcropping on switchbacks.   **6.1**

1.1 Reach view to compass-north and highest point in section   **5.7**
(elev. 4,840 feet).

2.1 Reach Wateroak Gap (elev. 4,460) in small clearing.   **4.7**

3.0 Blue-blazed **Chunky Gal Trail** intersects to west. ■ SOUTH-   **3.8**
BOUND hikers bear left. ■ NORTHBOUND hikers bear right.

3.2 Cross edge of clearing at **Whiteoak Stamp**.   **3.6**

S-N

Muskrat Creek Shelter →

Built in 1996, accommodates 8, with a latrine uphill from the shelter. Water is located at a spring behind the shelter. Next shelter: south, 7.4 miles (Plumorchard Gap); north, 4.9 miles (Standing Indian).

Blue-blazed trail →

Leads west about 0.5 mile to cliff view on Ravenrock Ridge.

Southern end of section →

Not accessible by road. North of here, the Trail is maintained by the Nantahala Hiking Club. South of here, it is maintained by the Georgia A.T. Club. USFS 72, sometimes impassable, is the nearest road that crosses the A.T., at Blue Ridge Gap (see Section Eleven), 3.2 miles south. USFS 71, 6.8 miles north on the A.T. at Deep Gap, at the northern end of this section, leads six miles to U.S. 64. Bly Gap has two springs, one on each side of the Trail, about 100 feet away. Several trails converge here, so take care to follow the A.T. To the west, a five-mile route down Eagle Fork of Shooting Creek begins as a worn woods road. Another trail, indicated on the TVA Hightower Bald quadrangle, leads to Tate City on the Tallulah River Fall Branch.

Side Trails in the Nantahalas—Side trails are an outstanding feature of this part of the Appalachian Trail. In conjunction with the A.T., a wide variety of loop hikes of one day or several days can be made. Hikers contemplating loop hikes are urged to acquire the USFS map entitled "Southern Nantahala Wilderness and Standing Indian Basin," which covers the A.T. from Wallace Gap south into Georgia and most of the side trails described in this book. Most north of Bly Gap are maintained cooperatively by the USFS and the Nantahala Hiking Club. See pages 220–225 for more information on loop hikes.

N-S

TRAIL DESCRIPTION

4.0   Blue-blazed trail leads east 100 feet to **Muskrat Creek Shelter**. ■ SOUTHBOUND hikers cross stream and pass **blue-blazed trail** leading west. ■ NORTHBOUND hikers follow mostly gentle terrain.   **2.8**

4.1   Pass viewpoint to west.   **2.7**

4.3   Cross logs over stream.   **2.5**

4.9   Sassafras Gap. ■ SOUTHBOUND hikers begin steep ascent of Courthouse Bald. ■ NORTHBOUND hikers follow gently rising Trail.   **1.9**

5.4   Skirt top of Courthouse Bald (elev. 4,690 feet). ■ SOUTHBOUND hikers begin steep descent to end of section and 4.5-mile, 1,580-foot descent to Blue Ridge Gap (see Section Eleven). ■ NORTHBOUND hikers descend steeply.   **1.4**

5.7   Pass fine view into Shooting Creek Valley to west of Trail.   **1.1**

6.0   Skirt Sharp Top (elev. 4,338 feet). ■ SOUTHBOUND hikers descend steeply. ■ NORTHBOUND hikers ascend through two small gaps.   **0.7**

6.8   Reach **southern end of section** at Bly Gap (elev. 3,840 feet), north of the Georgia line, on an open ridge below Sharp Top with fine views to west. ■ SOUTHBOUND hikers descend and turn sharply left, descend another 100 yards, then turn right (see Section Eleven). ■ NORTHBOUND hikers continue along crest straight ahead, beginning steep, 1,000-foot ascent of Sharp Top and Courthouse Bald in North Carolina.   **0.0**

S-N

Georgia

Seen from above, or on a relief map, the mountain ridges of northern Georgia might resemble an enormous V, open to the north. Both the eastern and western arms are part of a major geologic division of the Appalachian mountain system known as the Blue Ridge province. At the point of the V, where they join, is Springer Mountain (elev. 3,782 feet), the southern terminus of the fourteen-state Appalachian Trail. (The Blue Ridge extends from there south to the A.T.'s former terminus at Mt. Oglethorpe.)

In the early years of the Appalachian Trail Conservancy (called the Conference until 2005), volunteers from North Carolina and Tennessee argued that the northbound Trail should follow the western arm of this V, toward Cohutta Mountain and the Tennessee Valley (a route now followed by the Benton MacKaye Trail, which

connects at the West Fork of the Jacks River northwest of Springer with the Pinhoti Trail, into northern Alabama). The eastern arm led toward Standing Indian Mountain and the Nantahala range in western North Carolina. The eastern route was first walked and partially blazed in 1929 by volunteer Roy Ozmer, who at the time sought to thru-hike the entire Trail, even though most of it didn't exist yet. Everett B. Stone, assistant state forester of Georgia, took up the torch and developed Ozmer's route, successfully lobbying ATC's Arthur Perkins, Myron Avery, and other volunteer leaders to route the Trail along the U.S. Forest Service trails he had laid out.

When blazing of the A.T. began, most of north Georgia was woodlands. Timbering and farming had gone on for years, but, after establishment of eastern national forests in 1920, the woodlands began to revegetate and resemble the wilderness of Georgia's colonial days. Only one paved road crossed the eastern ridge, at Neels

Sunset from Wildcat Mountain

Gap, and the existing dirt roads were hazardous at best. Even after Prohibition was repealed in 1933, moonshining remained a fairly popular pursuit (and a necessary source of income for many mountain people). Cattle, sheep, and hogs roamed free over the hills. In 1930, major unpaved roads crossed the crest of the mountains at Dicks Creek Gap, Unicoi Gap, Woody Gap, Grassy Gap, Cooper Gap, and just south of Amicalola Falls.

When the Trail was established in Georgia, it was routed in part over a previously existing Forest Service trail along the Blue Ridge crest. Completion in the spring of 1931 of a twenty-mile link north of Tray Mountain allowed the first continuous route from Mt. Oglethorpe to the Great Smokies. Except for some minor relocations, almost all of the Georgia Trail north of Gooch Gap remains in its original location. Between Gooch Gap and Springer Mountain, however, after a forest road was built along the route of the A.T in the area, most of the original Trail was moved to return it to more pleasant areas within the forest.

The A.T. in Georgia is a "roller-coaster" of climbs from gaps to knobs, with little net change in elevation between Bly Gap and Springer Mountain.

During hunting season, particularly October through December, hikers should wear blaze orange and be on the alert for hunters.

Bears are common along the Trail in Georgia. Hang all food on the bear cables provided at the shelters.

Natural Setting of the Eastern Blue Ridge Mountains

The Trail in Georgia is entirely within the Chattahoochee National Forest, along the crest of the Blue Ridge Mountains. Although rising at times to elevations of more than 4,400 feet, the Trail mostly follows ridges of between 3,500 and 3,000 feet. It offers a hiking adventure of exceptional challenge and variety. Steep ascents and descents reward hikers with vistas from rocky outcrops and open summits. More than half of the Georgia Trail lies within congressionally designated wilderness areas, away from roads, the use of motorized equipment, and developed camping areas.

The ancient mountains of Georgia are made up generally of metamorphic rock, mostly gneiss. A good place to observe the characteristics of the Blue Ridge Mountains in Georgia is Woody Gap. The coarse-grained boulders around the parking area are gneiss, as are rocks in the abandoned quarry next to the Trail. The bare, smooth surface of the summit of Blood Mountain is made up of gneiss. Mica can be found at places along the Trail, particularly on Tray Mountain.

A normally high annual rainfall ensures lush vegetation in the Georgia mountains. Many hillsides are covered with ferns, galax, ground cedar, may apple, and false hellebore. Along the Trail, wildflowers, flowering trees and shrubs, and towering shade trees at times give the hiker the feeling of being in a vast park. Predominant trees are oak, hickory, and poplar.

Some of the flowers that can be found all along the Trail in early spring include bloodroot, trillium, violets, trailing arbutus, chickweed, dwarf iris, foamflower, bluets, wild geranium, jack-in-the-pulpit, Solomon's seal, Solomon's plume, lady's-slipper, bellwort, showy orchis, and many others. In early summer, look for rattlesnake weed, pipsissewa, beardtongue, scullcap, spiderwort, fire pink, ragwort, milkweed; in midsummer, Turk's-cap lily, saxifrage, jewelweed, wood sorrel, coreopsis, asters, phlox, mountain mint, and white snakeroot. Late-summer and fall flowers include black-eyed susan, harebell, cranefly orchid, goldenrod, golden aster, cardinal flower, false foxglove, and gentian. But, wildflower lovers, beware: Poison ivy abounds as well.

Common flowering shrubs include rhododendron, mountain laurel, azalea, and wild hydrangea. Common flowering trees include serviceberry, silverbell, dogwood, redbud, and sourwood.

Deer and wild turkeys are often seen, as well as bears. From many of the open summits, hawks and vultures can be seen sailing on the wind currents. A few of the other common birds along the Trail in Georgia are barred owl, ruffled grouse, woodpeckers, wood thrush, scarlet tanager, warblers, and red-eyed vireo.

Bly Gap to Dicks Creek Gap (U.S. 76)

9.0 MILES

The highlight of the section is Bly Gap, at the northern end, with its views of the western North Carolina mountains. The section also features views of the imposing Standing Indian Mountain (elev. 5,498 feet), as well as the Nantahala mountains in North Carolina. The isolated peak of Hightower Bald (elev. 4,568 feet) is conspicuous to the northwest. The southern end of this section, Dicks Creek Gap, is the lowest gap crossed by a paved road on the Trail in Georgia. In between there and Bly Gap, the Trail generally follows the crest of the Blue Ridge, ascending and descending through a series of gaps in the ridge. Between Bly Gap and Blue Ridge Gap, the Trail is within the Southern Nantahala Wilderness. High points between Bly Gap and Dicks Creek Gap include As Knob, Buzzard Knob, and Little Bald Knob. Low points include Blue Ridge Gap, Plumorchard Gap, and Cowart Gap.

Road Approaches—Only the southern end of this section at Dicks Creek Gap is accessible by car. Four-wheel-drive vehicles may be able to reach Blue Ridge Gap.

Maps—ATC Chattahoochee National Forest map (with this guide); USGS Hightower Bald quadrangle map.

Shelters and Campsites—The only shelter in this section is in the middle: Plumorchard Gap Shelter (mile 4.5/4.5). Campsites can be found at mile 7.9/1.1 and mile 2.2/6.8. The Trail corridor in this section lies within the Chattahoochee National Forest, and camping is permitted except where noted otherwise. Campfires should be attended at all times and completely extinguished when you leave a campsite. Verify current campfire bans with the local Forest Service office, or watch for postings at Trailheads.

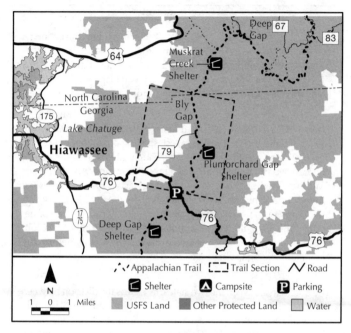

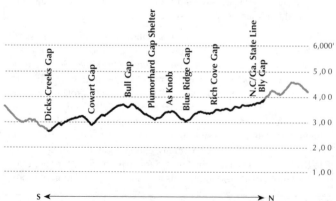

Northern end of section →

Not accessible by car. USFS 72, sometimes impassable, is the nearest road, at Blue Ridge Gap (mile 3.2/5.8) by way of the A.T. USFS 71, 6.8 miles north by way of the A.T. at Deep Gap, North Carolina, leads six miles to U.S. 64 (see North Carolina Section Ten).

Bly Gap →

Known years ago as Rich Gap, it offers good views to the west. The road in the distance to the northwest, snaking out of mountains and descending to a valley, is U.S. 64 through Glade Gap. Beyond it, you can see the ridge of the Tusquitee Mountains. An old woods road, obscured on the west and leading east to the Tallulah River Valley, crosses the gap. A log shelter, built by the Civilian Conservation Corps in the early 1930s, once was located near the spring. South of Bly Gap, the Trail is maintained by the Georgia A.T. Club. North of the gap to the Nantahala River, it is maintained by the Nantahala Hiking Club.

Boundary →

The boundary between the two states, as well as the division between the Chattahoochee National Forest (Georgia) and the Nantahala National Forest (North Carolina), has traditionally been referred to as Bly Gap. However, Bly Gap itself is in North Carolina, and the political boundary is south of Bly Gap.

Chattahoochee National Forest →

Includes 749,690 acres in northern Georgia and is administered jointly with the Oconee National Forest. The Forest Service first purchased 31,000 acres in four North Georgia counties in 1911 for $7 per acre, dividing it between Nantahala and Cherokee national forests. In 1936, the Chattahoochee was proclaimed a separate national forest, and the Forest Service began restoring lands that had been devastated by logging, farming, and mining. Deer and trout populations that had been virtually eliminated were brought back to healthy levels. Today, the Forest Service estimates a deer population of more than 30,000 animals and a turkey population of more

N-S

TRAIL DESCRIPTION

0.0 The **northern end of section** is at **Bly Gap** (elev. 3,840 feet), just north of the state line, on an open ridge below Sharp Top. A spring is east of the Trail about 250 feet south of the gap. ■ SOUTHBOUND hikers descend and turn sharply left, descend another 100 yards, then turn right. ■ NORTHBOUND hikers continue along crest straight ahead, beginning steep, 1,000-foot ascent of Sharp Top and Courthouse Bald (see North Carolina Section Ten). **9.0**

0.1 Cross Georgia–North Carolina state line **boundary** (unmarked) on eastern side of Rich Knob (elev. 4,132 feet). ■ SOUTHBOUND hikers enter **Chattahoochee National Forest**. ■ NORTHBOUND hikers enter **Nantahala National Forest**. **8.9**

Bly Gap

S-N

SECTION HIGHLIGHTS

than 6,000 birds. In 1970, the bear population totaled 106 bears. After 20 years of managing bear habitat, the forest boasts a healthy (and hungry) population of more than 650 bears; take precautions with your food when camping along the A.T.

Nantahala National Forest →

The forest covers 1.3 million acres in western North Carolina. See page 78.

Hightower Bald →

The fourth-highest mountain in Georgia (elev. 4,568 feet), it is visible to the west. Farther to the east is Dick's Knob (elev. 4,620 feet), the third-highest. (The highest in the state is Brasstown Bald, at 4,786 feet; second-highest is Rabun Bald, at 4,696 feet.) An obscure and overgrown trail once led from this level section to the west down into the valley of Hightower Creek.

Blue Ridge Gap →

The old road through Blue Ridge Gap (USFS 72) is often impassable by two-wheel-drive vehicles. To the east, the road leads approximately 1.5 miles down to Charlie's Creek and 3.0 miles to the Tallulah River, but it is not open to traffic. To the west, the road leads approximately 3.0 miles to the small community of Titus (no supplies) on Hightower Creek and 7.5 miles to U.S. 76, 2.8 miles west of Dicks Creek Gap. Space for vehicle parking in the gap is very limited.

Plumorchard Gap →

Water may be found at the shelter site to the east or to the west of Plumorchard Gap at a spring about 600 feet from the Trail. An old trail to the west leads about 2.0 miles down Big John Creek to Pleasant Hill School at a road on Hightower Creek.

N-S

TRAIL DESCRIPTION

0.4	Trail leads along narrow ridgecrest.	**8.6**
0.6	Near top of small knob is rock outcrop west of the Trail, with fine views.	**8.4**
0.9	Level section. Along here in fall and winter are views of **Hightower Bald** to west.	**8.1**
2.0	Cross Rich Cove Gap (elev. 3,400 feet) on ridgecrest between Rocky Knob and Wheeler Knob.	**7.0**
2.2	Swing around west side of Wheeler Knob (elev. 3,560 feet), passing a designated campsite.	**6.8**
3.2	**Blue Ridge Gap** (elev. 3,020 feet). Cross dirt road, USFS 72. ▪ SOUTHBOUND hikers ascend toward As Knob. ▪ NORTHBOUND hikers begin 4.5-mile, 1,580-foot ascent to Courthouse Bald (see North Carolina Section Ten).	**5.8**
3.8	The Trail crosses As Knob (elev. 3,440 feet), crossing high point below the summit.	**5.2**
4.5	Reach **Plumorchard Gap** (elev. 3,090 feet), midpoint of section. Blue-blazed trail leads 0.2 mile east to **Plumorchard Gap Shelter** and water.	**4.5**

S-N

Plumorchard Gap Shelter →

Built in 1993 in a cooperative effort by the Georgia A.T. Club, U.S. Forest Service, and Upper Loft Designs to replace a shelter built in 1959 by the USFS. Loft, privy; bear cables. Water may be found at creek that crosses trail to shelter. Accommodates 14. Below the shelter to the east, an old trail leads about 3.0 miles down Plumorchard Creek to a road at Plumorchard Church. Next shelter: south, 8.5 miles (Deep Gap); north, 7.4 miles (Muskrat Creek).

Cowart Gap →

Formerly called Tom Cowart Gap, possibly for a man who lived at the former homesite near the gap. Impassable old road crosses gap, leading to the east to Holden Branch and Plumorchard Church and to the west down Little Hightower Creek.

U.S. 76 →

Runs east-west 550 miles from Wrightsville Beach, North Carolina, through South Carolina and Georgia to Chattanooga, Tennessee.

Southern end of section →

In Dicks Creek Gap. Parking is available in the gap. U.S. 76 leads 11 miles west to Hiawassee, Georgia, with services for hikers, including outfitters, lodging, restaurants, groceries, and a hospital. Clayton is 18 miles east. An organic farm and hiker hostel is 3.5 miles to the west on the highway and offers many services for hikers, February 15–April 30. No public transportation is available at the Trailhead.

N-S	TRAIL DESCRIPTION	
5.0	Note green moss, laurel, and rhododendron covering rocky slopes above Trail along slope.	**4.0**
5.4	Cross over ridgecrest.	**3.6**
5.7	Reach Bull Gap (elev. 3,550 feet).	**3.3**
6.1	Fine views in winter from the slope of Buzzard Knob.	**2.9**
7.2	Reach **Cowart Gap** (elev. 2,920 feet) and a stand of tall pine trees.	**1.8**
7.9	Cross over spur (elev. 3,160 feet) of Little Bald Knob. A campsite is east of the Trail here. In wet seasons, water is available on Trail just north of spur and downhill about 600 feet.	**1.1**
9.0	Reach **southern end of section** at **U.S. 76**, in a picnic area at Dicks Creek Gap (elev. 2,675 feet). ■ SOUTHBOUND hikers cross highway and continue on Trail (see Section Twelve). ■ NORTHBOUND hikers follow Trail through picnic area and ascend along a small stream.	**0.0**

Dicks Creek Gap

Dicks Creek Gap (U.S. 76)
to Unicoi Gap (Ga. 75)

16.6 MILES

This section contains some of the longest climbs and highest peaks of the A.T. in Georgia. It rarely descends below 3,500 feet. Between its northern end at Dicks Creek Gap and its southern end at Unicoi Gap, the Trail crosses the summits of Powell Mountain, Kelly Knob, Tray Mountain (elev. 4,430 feet), and Rocky Mountain. It follows "The Swag of the Blue Ridge," a wide, low section, and descends to 3,113 feet at Indian Grave Gap. Between Addis Gap and Tray Gap, it leads through the Tray Mountain Wilderness. Highlights of the section include Tray Mountain, with a splendid viewpoint, and the Swag of the Blue Ridge, a long ridgewalk.

Road Approaches—Both the northern and southern ends of the section are accessible by car. Rough forest roads cross at Indian Grave Gap and Tray Gap (four-wheel-drive vehicles recommended).

Maps—ATC Chattahoochee National Forest map (with this guide); USGS Tray Mountain and Macedonia quadrangles.

Shelters and Campsites—Two shelters are found in this section: Deep Gap (mile 3.5/13.1) and Tray Mountain (mile 11.0/5.6). Designated campsites are located near Moreland Gap (mile 1.2/15.4), Addis Gap (mile 5.4/11.2), Sassafras Gap (mile 6.2/10.4), Steeltrap Gap (mile 9.1/7.5) and at the "Cheese Factory" (mile 13.0/3.6). The Trail in this section lies within the Chattahoochee National Forest, and camping is permitted except where noted otherwise. Campfires should be attended at all times and completely extinguished when you leave. Verify current campfire bans with the local Forest Service office, or watch for notices posted at Trailheads.

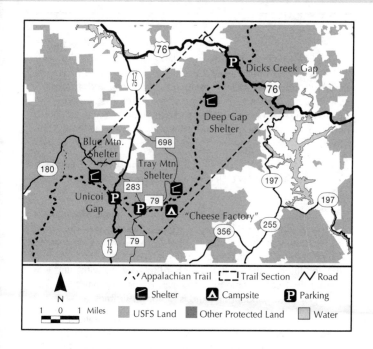

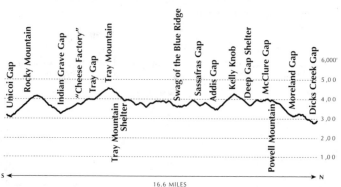

16.6 MILES

Northern end of section →

In Dicks Creek Gap. Parking is available in the gap. U.S. 76 leads 11 miles west to Hiawassee, Georgia, with services for hikers, including outfitters, lodging, restaurants, groceries, and a hospital. Clayton is 18 miles east. An organic farm and hiker hostel is 3.5 miles to the west on the highway and offers many services for hikers, Feb. 15–April 30. No public transportation is available at the Trailhead.

Hiawassee, Georgia →

The town was formerly called Hiwassee, as in the river of that name. It was changed, for unknown reasons, in 1870.

Snake Mountain →

At about mile 1.0/15.1, hikers pass a spring and the site of the former Snake Mountain Shelter, built in 1934 by the Civilian Conservation Corps at the urging of Georgia A.T. Club members. By the 1950s, the condition of the shelter was "hard to keep up with" and was "variously used as home by highway, logging, and other transient laborers." It was abandoned and is no longer visible.

Moreland Gap →

Known for many years as Hooper Gap or Jim Hooper Gap. The obscure trail to the west leads along Swallow Creek about 5.0 miles to Lower Hightower Church on U.S. 76.

Deep Gap Shelter →

Built in 1991 by the Georgia A.T. Club, Forest Service, and Upper Loft Designs. Accommodates 12. Loft, privy, bear cables. A spring is adjacent to the shelter. Next shelter: south, 8.0 miles (Tray Mountain); north, 8.5 miles (Plumorchard Gap).

N-S

TRAIL DESCRIPTION

0.0 Dicks Creek Gap (2,675 feet) on U.S. 76 is the **northern end of section**, east of **Hiawassee**, Georgia. ■ SOUTHBOUND hikers cross road from parking area and follow level Trail briefly, then bear to left uphill. ■ NORTHBOUND hikers follow Trail through picnic area and ascend along small stream (see Section Eleven).   **16.6**

0.6 Along east side of **Snake Mountain**, cross several small streams.   **16.0**

1.2 Reach **Moreland Gap** (elev. 3,050 feet). An obscure trail (old roadbed) leads west.   **15.4**

2.2 Reach top of Powell Mountain (elev. 3,850 feet).   **14.4**

2.4 Cross McClure Gap.   **14.2**

2.6 On ridgecrest, blue-blazed trail leads east several yards to small campsite and fine view.   **14.0**

3.5 Blue-blazed trail intersects to east at Deep Gap (elev. 3,550 feet), leading about 0.3 mile to **Deep Gap Shelter**.   **13.1**

4.2 Cross over ridge in shallow gap.   **12.4**

4.4 Reach high point along crest of Kelly Knob. The A.T. goes over the shoulder of Kelly Knob, but the summit of the mountain (elev. 4,276 feet) is about 0.2 mile west. This is the highest peak between the North Carolina line and Tray Mountain and one of the two peaks of Double Spring Knob.   **12.2**

SECTION HIGHLIGHTS

Addis Gap →

Good campsites and water may be found 0.5 mile down old road to the east. Until 1991, the Addis Gap Shelter, built in 1959 by the Forest Service, was located at the campsite. Be aware that, during turkey-hunting season, it is a popular "drive-in" camping spot locally. Addis Gap was named after the Addis family, who lived near the site of the former shelter until 1942 and perhaps at one time lived in the gap itself, where evidence of an old homesite has been found. Early members of the Georgia A.T. Club remember stopping by the Addis family home down the road and chatting with the impoverished family. One reported, "The last time we visited the Addises (mountain people), they ran inside and bolted their doors and windows. We left our surplus food on their doorstep." After the family abandoned the area, club members sometimes used the house or barn for a shelter. According to one, the barn had the best roof.

Swag of the Blue Ridge →

This area is called a "swag," or " low point," and is a long, broad ridgecrest with only moderate elevation change, extending for more than three miles—among the most remote areas of the Trail in Georgia.

Young Lick Knob →

An important watershed boundary. North of here, water flowing east from the ridge flows into the Savannah River basin and the Atlantic Ocean. South of here, water flowing east from the ridge flows into the Apalachicola River basin and the Gulf of Mexico. West of here, water flowing west from the ridge flows into the Mississippi River basin and the Gulf of Mexico.

Tray Mountain Shelter →

Built in 1971 by the Forest Service and modified in 2006 by the GATC. Water can be found about 800 feet downhill to the right of the shelter. Privy is to the left down a short trail. Bear cables. Accommodates 7. Next shelter: south, 8.0 miles (Blue Mountain); north, 8.0 miles (Deep Gap).

N-S

	TRAIL DESCRIPTION

5.4 Cross **Addis Gap** (3,304 feet). At the northern boundary   **11.2**
of the Tray Mountain Wilderness, an old fire road leads
east. The road continues east for about 8.0 miles to Ga.
197, near Lake Burton and Moccasin Creek State Park,
and also crosses Moccasin Creek, a beautiful rushing
stream, about 1.0 mile from the A.T. To the west from the
gap, the old road, generally impassable, leads about 5.0
miles out to Ga. 75.

6.2 Sassafras Gap (elev. 3,500 feet). A spring is about 150   **10.4**
yards downhill to east.

6.8 Continue around eastern side of Round Top, which is the   **9.8**
eastern peak of Dismal Mountain.

7.4 Cross **Swag of the Blue Ridge** (elev. 3,400 feet), and   **9.2**
continue along or near ridgecrest.

8.6 Swing around western side of **Young Lick Knob** (elev.   **8.0**
3,800 feet).

9.1 Steeltrap Gap (elev. 3,500 feet). ■ Southbound hikers   **7.5**
begin 930-foot ascent of Tray Mountain.

9.7 Wolfpen Gap (elev. 3,550 feet).   **6.9**

10.5 Come to gap (elev. 3,760 feet) below Tray Mountain   **6.1**
summit.

11.0 On ridgecrest, reach junction of A.T. and blue-blazed   **5.6**
trail leading approximately 0.2 mile to **Tray Mountain
Shelter**. This is the third shelter on Tray Mountain. The
first was built by the CCC in 1934; the second, by the
Forest Service in 1960, down the hill beside the spring.
The present shelter was moved back to the top of the hill,
near the site of the original one. On the east side of the
blue-blazed trail are excellent views from the rocky
ledges.

S-N

Tray Mountain →

Directly south is Yonah Mountain. The isolated peak to the southeast is Currahee Mountain, near Toccoa. Farther north on the Trail are views of the Blue Ridge. Brasstown Bald, the highest peak in Georgia, is the prominent peak to the northwest. Rabun Bald, the state's second-highest peak, is to the northeast. Rhododendron and mountain laurel are abundant on the summit area. Also look for witch hazel and sprouts of American chestnut. Tray Mountain is probably the southernmost breeding area in the United States for the Canada warbler. It was originally called Trail Mountain, which one source says was "so named by the Cherokee from the fact that they once had a number of trails leading to the summit, to which point they were in the habit of ascending for the purpose of discovering the campfires of their enemies during the existence of hostilities."

Tray Mountain Road →

To the east, it leads down the mountain to eventually join Ga. 197. To the west, USFS 698 leads about 12 miles to Ga. 75 at Mountain Scene, Georgia, 7.0 miles south of Hiawassee. USFS 79 leads south and west, crossing the Trail again at mile 12.2/4.4 near Indian Grave Gap. This road was an old circuit road connecting the towns of Helen and Clarkesville. It is usually passable by cars. Until 1970, the A.T. followed the road for about a mile and then for another half mile followed USFS 283 toward Indian Grave Gap. No services.

Cheese Factory →

The "factory" was actually a remote mountain dairy operated by a transplanted New Englander in the early nineteenth century. In *Letters from the Alleghany Mountains*, by Charles Lanman, "Letter VII" describes a trip to Trail (Tray) Mountain in May 1848 on muleback and in the company of Major Edward Williams, "principal proprietor of Nacoochee Valley." According to Lanman, a dairy was established at the site about 1848 by Williams, a New Englander, who had come to live in the valley twenty years earlier. Williams had hired as a dairyman by another New Englander who "knew how to make but-

N-S

TRAIL DESCRIPTION

Tray Mountain

11.4 Reach small, rocky summit of **Tray Mountain** (elev. 4,430 feet), with excellent views in all directions of the Georgia mountains. ■ Northbound hikers will encounter rough, rocky, steep Trail beginning 930-foot descent from summit toward Steeltrap Gap. ■ Southbound hikers begin 2.5-mile, 1,317-foot descent to Indian Grave Gap. **5.2**

12.2 At the southern boundary of the Tray Mountain Wilderness, reach Tray Gap (elev. 3,847 feet). **Tray Mountain Road** (USFS 698/USFS 79) intersects. ■ Southbound hikers cross road and enter woods on path to left of parking area. ■ Northbound hikers cross road and begin ascent of Tray Mountain. **4.4**

12.4 Rocky cliff with small overlook on east side of Trail. **4.2**

S-N

ter and cheese" and had given Williams the idea of establishing the dairy, which was said to be the only one in the entire state of Georgia. Lanman marveled that this dairy was "on top of a mountain, distant from the first farmhouse some fifteen miles, and inaccessible by any conveyance but that of a mule or well-trained horse," where the cattle fed on "the luxuriant weed of the wilderness."

Tray Mountain Road →

To the east, it leads down the mountain 8.0 miles to eventually join Ga. 75 at Robertstown, Georgia. To the west, it parallels the A.T. See mile 12.2/4.4.

Indian Grave Gap →

The Trail crosses USFS 283, which leads east about 0.5 mile to connect with Tray Mountain Road (USFS 79) and 7.5 miles farther to Robertstown. It leads west about 4 miles to Ga. 75, north of Unicoi Gap. The blue-blazed Rocky Mountain Trail intersects 0.6 mile west of the A.T. and leads 1.0 mile to rejoin the A.T. at mile 15.7/0.9. To the east, an old, possibly obscured trail leads about 1.5 miles down Andrews Cove to Ga. 75. It is said that the name of the gap derives from a rock cairn monument about 2 feet high, down a side trail, which supposedly marked the grave of a lone Indian.

Unicoi Gap →

The road through Unicoi Gap was built in 1813–1816 and was the first road across the Georgia Blue Ridge. Called Unicoi Turnpike, it was a major thoroughfare from South Carolina through North Georgia into North Carolina and Tennessee during early settlement days. *Unicoi* is said to be the Cherokee word for "white man's (or new) way." The route was actually cleared in 1812 by a group of coastal merchants seeking an inland trade route into the area. A former Indian trail, it became a wagon road from the upper limit of navigation on the Tugaloo River, near Toccoa, north of Clarkesville, and through the Nacoochee Valley. It turned north through Helen, crossing the Blue Ridge at Unicoi Gap, paralleling the Hiwassee River into Tennessee. The road was paved in the late 1940s.

N-S

TRAIL DESCRIPTION

13.0 Reach gap. Just to west of the Trail is the site of the old **Cheese Factory**, a popular campsite. About 50 yards to west is Tray Mountain Road and a spring. **3.6**

13.3 Cross **Tray Mountain Road** (USFS 79). **3.3**

14.0 Cross USFS 283 at **Indian Grave Gap** (elev. 3,113 feet). **2.6**
■ SOUTHBOUND hikers bear slightly west and begin 1.2-mile, 904-foot ascent of Rocky Mountain. ■ NORTHBOUND hikers bear slightly to east and ascend through laurel, rhododendron, and beds of galax, beginning 2.5-mile, 1,317-foot ascent of Tray Mountain.

Trillium on Rocky Mountain

S-N

SECTION HIGHLIGHTS

Southern end of section →
Parking is available in the gap on Ga. 75, which leads 8.0 miles east to Robertstown, one mile farther to Helen, or 14.0 miles west to Hiawassee (supplies and services available in all three towns). No public transportation or services at the gap. Near the Trail is a classic plaque depicting a hiker with pack climbing a mountain, one of three created by early GATC members and embedded in the rock here in 1934; club president Warner Hall modeled for sculptor G.H. Noble. Similar bronze plaques are located at Neels Gap and at Springer Mountain, the Trail's southern terminus. A spring, located on the northeast side of Unicoi Gap about 400 yards down an old road bed, is the headwaters of the Hiwassee River. Just north on the Trail out of the gap, look for maidenhair fern, Canada violet, Dutchman's pipe, and clintonia. Farther up the Trail can be found New York fern and southern lady fern.

N-S

TRAIL DESCRIPTION

15.1 Excellent views to south from rocky ledges.   **1.5**

15.3 Summit of Rocky Mountain (elev. 4,017 feet). ■ SOUTH-   **1.3**
BOUND hikers begin 1.3-mile, 1,068-foot descent to **Unicoi
Gap**. ■ NORTHBOUND hikers begin 1.2-mile, 904-foot
descent to Indian Grave Gap.

15.7 Junction with blue-blazed Rocky Mountain Trail (leads   **0.9**
1.0 mile west to USFS 283).

16.0 Cross stream.   **0.6**

16.6 Reach Unicoi Gap (elev. 2,949 feet) and **southern end of** **0.0**
section at Ga. 75. ■ SOUTHBOUND hikers go right (compass-
west) to end of parking area and cross road (see Section
Thirteen). ■ NORTHBOUND hikers go right (compass-east)
to end of parking area and climb steps, beginning 1.3-
mile, 1,068-foot ascent to Rocky Mountain.

S-N

Unicoi Gap (Ga. 75) to Tesnatee Gap (Ga. 348)

14.7 MILES

This section skirts the headwaters of Georgia's Chattahoochee River, the water source for Atlanta as well as many other municipalities all the way to Florida and the Gulf of Mexico. From north to south, the Blue Ridge in this section turns northwest, then southwest to form the upper rim of a huge bowl, enclosing the Chattahoochee's headwaters. Between Unicoi Gap and Tesnatee Gap, the Trail ascends Blue Mountain, Sheep Rock Top, Poor Mountain, and Wildcat Mountain. It drops into Chattahoochee Gap, Low Gap (the lowest point on the section), and Hogpen Gap. For about 3.5 miles south of Unicoi Gap, the Trail passes over several rock slides and through rocky areas—north-facing rocky slopes that are home to a variety of interesting and unique plant life. The Trail between Unicoi Gap and Hog Pen Gap is in the Mark Trail Wilderness.

Road Approaches—Both ends of the section, as well as Hogpen Gap, at mile 13.8/0.9, are accessible by vehicle.

Maps—ATC Chattahoochee National Forest map (with this guide); USGS Cowrock, Jacks Gap, and Tray Mountain quadrangles.

Shelters and Campsites—This section has three shelters. Blue Mountain Shelter is at mile 2.2/12.5; Low Gap Shelter, at mile 9.4/5.3; Whitley Gap Shelter, 1.2 miles from the A.T. at mile 14.0/0.7. Popular campsites are Rocky Knob (mile 2.7/12.0), a site at mile 3.1/11.6, Chattahoochee Gap (mile 4.4/10.3), and Poplar Stamp Gap (mile 8.0/6.7). The Trail corridor in this section lies within the Chattahoochee National Forest, and camping is generally permitted.

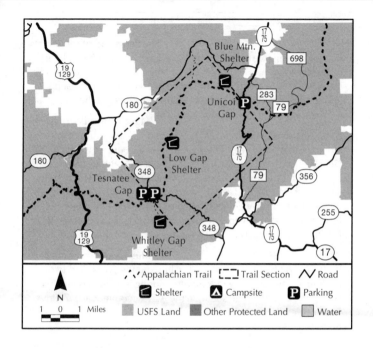

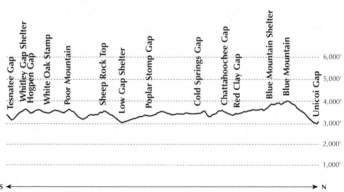

Northern end of section →

Parking is available in the gap on Ga. 75, which leads 8.0 miles east to Robertstown and 9.0 miles on to Helen (supplies and services available at both towns) and 14.0 miles west to Hiawassee (supplies and services). No public transportation or services at the gap.

Mark Trail Wilderness →

A 16,400-acre area managed by the Forest Service, it is the only federal wilderness area to be named after a comic-strip character. Georgian Ed Dodd created the character of the naturalist Mark Trail after World War II, and the daily adventure strip was widely syndicated in the 1950s and 1960s, with Sunday strips featuring educational panels about wildlife. Dodd died in 1991, the year the wilderness area was designated. The strip, written by Jack Elrod since 1978, is still carried in nearly 175 newspapers.

Blue Mountain Shelter →

Built in 1988 by the Georgia A.T. Club and the Forest Service. Affords fine views in the winter months. Spring is located on the west side of the Trail 0.1 mile south on the A.T. Accommodates 7. Privy. Bear cables. Next shelter: south, 7.2 miles (Low Gap); north, 8.0 miles (Tray Mountain).

Henson Gap →

Named for a man who is said to have been ambushed and killed here. Perhaps a moonshiner or a "revenuer"?

Rocky Knob →

The large, flat area here was the site of two shelters. The first, actually a cabin, was built in 1933 by the Civilian Conservation Corps and was called the "pride of the GATC." When it deteriorated to "better than nothing," a second shelter was built by the Forest Service in 1960; that was removed in the late 1980s and replaced by the Blue Mountain Shelter above. In the cove south of this area are large stands of umbrella leaf and waterleaf.

N-S

TRAIL DESCRIPTION

0.0 Unicoi Gap (elev. 2,949 feet) at Ga. 75, at the northern   **14.7**
boundary of the **Mark Trail Wilderness,** is the **northern
end of the section**. ■ SOUTHBOUND hikers go right (compass-west) to western end of parking area and cross road,
beginning 1.4-mile, 1,076-foot ascent of Blue Mountain.
■ NORTHBOUND hikers go right (compass-east) to end of
parking area and climb steps (see Section Twelve).

1.2 Reach ridgecrest. ■ SOUTHBOUND hikers ascend, following   **13.5**
narrow ridge. ■ NORTHBOUND hikers bear left off ridge and
descend.

1.4 Top of Blue Mountain (elev. 4,025 feet). ■ SOUTHBOUND   **13.3**
hikers descend gradually on narrow ridge. ■ NORTHBOUND
hikers begin 1.4-mile, 1,076-foot descent to Unicoi Gap
along ridge.

2.2 Blue-blazed side trail leads west about 50 yards to **Blue**   **12.5**
Mountain Shelter.

2.3 Pass spring on west side of Trail.   **12.4**

2.6 Reach **Henson Gap** (elev. 3,550 feet).   **12.1**

2.7 Reach flat area known as **Rocky Knob**. Water is ap-   **12.0**
proximately 150 yards down slope on west side of
Trail.

S-N

Old roadbed →

The old road leads south from here all the way to Low Gap and has a story behind it. In 1934, the CCC, under instructions from the local Forest Service, began building a road from Low Gap to Indian Grave Gap (part of the same national initiative to construct ridgetop roads that produced Skyline Drive and the Blue Ridge Parkway in Virginia). When the Georgia A.T. Club got wind of the progress of this road and saw stakes leading right by their brand-new Rocky Knob Shelter, they went as a group to investigate. Upon finding the evidence, they were "all in an uproar." They appealed to higher authorities in the Forest Service, who were very cooperative and ended the road-building at that point "because of the conflict of the road with the Appalachian Trail." Unfortunately, it was too late for about five miles of the Trail that had been destroyed by the road.

Jacks Knob Trail →

Also called the Jacks Gap Trail, it was blazed by pioneering A.T. hiker Roy Ozmer in the early 1930s. The blue-blazed trail entering the gap from the west leads 2.4 miles down Hiwassee Ridge to Jacks Gap (elev. 2,950 feet), on Ga. 180, and from there climbs another 2.5 miles to the observation-tower summit of Brasstown Bald (elev. 4,788 feet), Georgia's highest mountain.

Cold Springs Gap →

Between here and Low Gap, the Trail follows an old road (see mile 3.8/10.9). For about twenty years, the Trail followed the ridgecrest over Horsetrough Mountain, as well as the ridge south of Poplar Stamp Gap. During the Second World War, however, maintenance of the Trail was at a low ebb, and the old CCC road was easier to follow than the Trail across the ridgeline. After the war, the club decided to leave the Trail on the road, in spite of some protests from club members. The road was closed to traffic.

N-S

TRAIL DESCRIPTION

2.9 Pass spring several yards to west of Trail down rocky   **11.8**
slope. ■ SOUTHBOUND hikers cross several rock slides along
western slopes of Rocky Knob.

3.1 Pass a designated campsite to west of Trail.   **11.6**

3.8 Cross Red Clay Gap (elev. 3,450 feet). ■ SOUTHBOUND   **10.9**
hikers proceed from gap on footpath that becomes an **old
roadbed**. ■ NORTHBOUND hikers cross several rock slides
along western slope of Rocky Knob.

4.4 Reach Chattahoochee Gap (elev. 3,500 feet). **Jacks Knob**   **10.3**
Trail intersects to the west. The blue-blazed trail to the
east leads about 200 yards steeply down to a spring, which
is considered the beginning of the Chattahoochee River.
The Trail along this area turns north (for northbound hikers) and then southeast to partly encircle the huge "bowl"
enclosing the headwaters of the river.

5.6 Descend to **Cold Springs Gap** (elev. 3,450 feet), where,   **9.1**
despite the name, you won't find a spring. ■ SOUTHBOUND
hikers bear to east of ridge and follow old road for the
next 3.8 miles to Low Gap. Several small streams cross
the road.

8.0 Descend to Poplar Stamp Gap (elev. 3,350 feet). A stream   **6.7**
is several hundred feet to east down an old roadbed.

S-N

Low Gap Shelter →

Built in 1972 by the Forest Service. Accommodates 7. Privy. Bear cables. Next shelter: south, 5.8 miles (Whitley Gap); north, 7.2 miles (Blue Mountain).

Choestoe →

A Cherokee word meaning "the place where rabbits dance" (see page 186).

Poor Mountain →

Look for Bowman's root (or Indian physic) along the Trail, particularly near here.

White Oak Stamp →

"Stamp" or "Stomp" is sometimes seen in Appalachian place names to indicate a place where livestock were kept. Today, it seems odd to think of the mountains as a place where people raised cattle, sheep, and hogs. But, until the early 20th century, isolated people here still were part of what historians call a "farm and forest economy" typical of many parts of the mountains. They lived in the hollows and would burn the forest floor on the ridges, then let livestock roam free to eat the mast and new growth. Seasonally, drovers would come through and take the livestock to market, providing a little cash to the local folk. Otherwise, the mountain families lived off what they could grow or hunt.

Hogpen Gap →

Parking is available in the gap. The Richard B. Russell Scenic Highway (Ga. 348) leads to the east about 10.0 miles to Ga. Alt. 75 near Robertstown and about 5.0 miles west to Ga. 180. North on the highway from the gap is a superb view of the mountains, including Brasstown Bald, as well as deep, steep, rugged Lordamercy Cove below the road. No services available at road crossing.

N-S

TRAIL DESCRIPTION

9.4 Descend to Low Gap (elev. 3,050 feet), low point of the **5.3**
section. A blue-blazed trail leads about 60 yards east to
Low Gap Shelter and stream. Water can be found at a
small stream near the shelter. Two old trails, no longer
visible, led from Low Gap into the valley to the west,
converging at Stink Creek (which is joined by Smell Creek)
and connecting with an old road leading out to **Choestoe**
on Ga. 180. ■ NORTHBOUND hikers bear to east of ridge
and follow old road for the next 3.8 miles to Cold Springs
Gap. Several small streams cross road.

10.2 Rocky summit of Sheep Rock Top (elev. 3,575 feet). **4.5**
■ SOUTHBOUND hikers descend steadily toward Wide Gap.
■ NORTHBOUND hikers descend steadily toward Low
Gap.

11.3 Wide Gap (elev. 3,150 feet). Continue along narrow **3.4**
ridge.

11.9 Reach summit of **Poor Mountain** (elev. 3,650 feet). **2.8**

12.6 Pass to east of Strawberry Top. **2.1**

12.9 Reach **White Oak Stamp** on ridgecrest. **1.8**

13.8 Descend to **Hogpen Gap** (elev. 3,450 feet) and Richard **0.9**
Russell Scenic Highway (Ga. 348), at the southern bound-
ary of the Mark Trail Wilderness. ■ SOUTHBOUND hikers
turn left in parking area, parallel highway for about 200
feet, cross highway, and begin ascent of Wildcat Mountain. ■ NORTHBOUND hikers cross highway, turn left, parallel highway for about 200 feet to western end of parking
area, and enters woods.

S-N

SECTION HIGHLIGHTS

Whitley Gap Shelter →

Accommodates 6. Reached by way of a 1.2-mile, blue-blazed trail along the ridgecrest. Built by the Forest Service in 1973. About 0.2 mile beyond the shelter is a spring. Privy. Bear cables. The trail to the remote shelter follows a ridgetop that offers wonderful views from grassy spots between stands of mountain laurel and rhododendron and many wildflowers. From the ridgetop, the blue-blazed trail drops steeply down into an isolated hollow where the shelter is located. Next shelter: south, 9.8 miles (Blood Mountain); north, 5.8 miles (Low Gap).

Southern end of section →

Parking is available in the gap. Ga. 348 (Richard Russell Scenic Highway) leads east about 10.5 miles to Ga. Alt. 75 near Robertstown and almost 5 miles to the west to Ga. 180. No services at the road crossing. To reach gap from the south, go north on Ga. 75 in Robertstown, turn left across the Chattahoochee River bridge onto Ga. Alt. 75, and, in 2.5 miles, turn right onto Ga. 348. From the north, go south on U.S. 129 from Blairsville about 8 miles to Ga. 180, turn left and go about 1 mile, and turn right onto Ga. 348 for about 5 miles.

N-S

| TRAIL DESCRIPTION |

14.0 Crest of Wildcat Mountain (elev. 3,600 feet). Blue-blazed **0.7**
trail to east leads 1.2 miles to **Whitley Gap Shelter**.
■ SOUTHBOUND hikers descend by way of switchbacks
toward Tesnatee Gap.

14.2 Rock cliff with views of Cowrock Mountain and 1,200- **0.5**
foot-deep gorge of Town Creek.

14.7 The **southern end of the section** is at Tesnatee Gap (elev.
3,138 feet) and Richard Russell Scenic Highway (Ga.
348). ■ SOUTHBOUND hikers cross parking area to continue on Trail and ascend (see Section Fourteen). ■ NORTH-
BOUND hikers ascend up switchbacks toward crest of
Wildcat Mountain.

Tesnatee Gap

S-N

Tesnatee Gap (Ga. 348)
to Neels Gap (U.S. 19/129)

5.5 MILES

The A.T. in this section follows broad, rocky ridgetops offering excellent viewpoints, including rock outcroppings on Cowrock Mountain, Wolf Laurel Top, and Levelland Mountain. Before Ga. 348 was built in 1966, this area was considered the most remote on the Georgia Trail, and Trail-builders called Tesnatee Gap "a delightful locality… deeply entrenched in a beautiful hardwood forest." The section of Trail between Unicoi Gap (see Section Thirteen) and Neels Gap was the longest section of the A.T. in Georgia not crossed by a paved highway. The Georgia A.T. Club and other interested parties fought the building of the "road to nowhere" to no avail. The road displaced the A.T. between Tesnatee and Hogpen gaps, and the Trail was rerouted to cross Wildcat Mountain. The longest climbs are on the north sides of Cowrock and Levelland mountains. The entire section is within the Raven Cliffs Wilderness.

Road Approaches—Both ends of the section are accessible by vehicle.

Maps—ATC Chattahoochee National Forest map (with this guide); USGS Neels Gap and Cowrock quadrangles.

Shelters and campsites—This section has no shelters. Popular campsites are at Baggs Creek Gap (mile 1.3/4.2) and at Bull Gap (mile 4.4/1.1). The Trail corridor in this section lies within the Chattahoochee National Forest, and camping is permitted except where noted otherwise. Campfires should be attended at all times and completely extinguished when you leave a campsite. Verify current campfire bans with the local Forest Service office, or watch for posted notices at Trailheads.

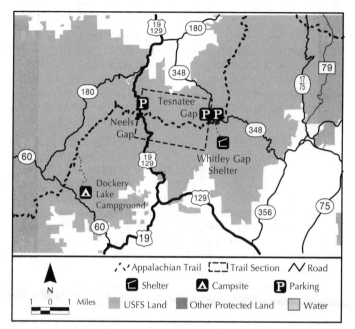

Appalachian Trail Trail Section Road
Shelter Campsite Parking
USFS Land Other Protected Land Water

N
1 0 1 Miles

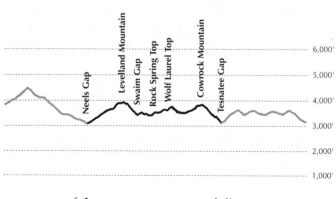

S ◄————————► N
5.5 MILES

SECTION HIGHLIGHTS

Northern end of section →

Parking is available in the gap. Ga. 348 leads east about 10.5 miles to Ga. Alt. 75 near Robertstown and almost 5 miles west to Ga. 180. To reach gap from the south, go north on Ga. 75 in Robertstown, turn left across the Chattahoochee onto Ga. Alt. 75, and, in 2.5 miles, turn right onto Ga. 348. From the north, go south on U.S. 129 from Blairsville about 8 miles to Ga. 180, turn left and go about 1 mile, then turn right onto Ga. 348 for about 5 miles.

Tesnatee Gap →

Tesnatee meant "wild turkey" in Cherokee. In 1938, a shelter was built just above the gap in a flat area that is now right along the Trail, but it was removed in 1975 when its proximity to the road left it exposed to vandalism and litter. On a winter hike to Tesnatee Gap in 1940, several GATC members described their first look at the new shelter: "We found a sturdy shelter of open Adirondack style, built of stout chestnut logs with a fireplace, table, log benches, and a surrounding rail fence (to keep out hogs)."

The Logan Turnpike—An abandoned road entering Tesnatee Gap from east of the Trail was called the Logan Turnpike—one of the first toll roads. It was originally an Indian trail leading up Town Creek Valley through the mountain pass. First called the Union Turnpike, the road was constructed in 1821 and provided a "lifeline for commerce and transportation" between Gainesville and Blairsville, Georgia. The discovery of gold in the area played an important role in the development of both the Union Turnpike and the Unicoi Turnpike, as gold was hauled across the mountains to a mint in North Carolina. After the Cherokee were expelled in the mid-1800s, Major Willis Logan purchased extensive lands on the south slope of the mountains, which included the turnpike. The name of the road was changed to Logan Turnpike, and the route extended from Loudsville over Tesnatee Gap to Choestoe, a length of 7.5 miles. A toll gate and stagecoach stop/hotel were established at the Logan

N-S

| TRAIL DESCRIPTION |

0.0 **Northern end of section** at **Tesnatee Gap** (elev. 3,138 feet) and Richard Russell Scenic Highway (Ga. 348), at northern boundary of Raven Cliffs Wilderness area. ■ SOUTHBOUND hikers cross parking area to continue on Trail and ascend. ■ NORTHBOUND hikers ascend up switchbacks toward crest of Wildcat Mountain (see Section Thirteen). **5.5**

0.4 Pass through small gap. **5.1**

S-N

homeplace. Toll charges varied according to the type of vehicle, the purpose of travel, and the number of livestock used to pull the vehicle. A stagecoach line, as well as wagon trains carrying merchandise back and forth, made regular trips across the gap. The road was used by mail carriers, "pleasure vehicles," cattle drovers, wagon trains, as well as individual covered wagons. In 1917, the first automobile—a "snappy gray roadster" with red wire wheels—was driven over it by a woman from Atlanta. The Logan Turnpike officially closed in 1925, when U.S. 129 was opened through Neels Gap, but four-wheel drive vehicles still traveled the road until 1981, when the Forest Service barricaded it. The Richard Russell Highway was built over a portion of the turnpike north of Tesnatee Gap. Today, the piles of rocks and boulders along the sides of the road are reminders of those who kept the road open and passable by constantly removing the obstructing stones.

SECTION HIGHLIGHTS

Cowrock Mountain →

The view from the rock overlook near the summit of Cowrock shows the valley of Town Creek gorge below, bound by the north–south ridges of Cowrock itself and Wildcat Mountain to the east. The view to the southeast includes the steep rock face of Yonah Mountain; to the north, Brasstown Bald, the state's highest mountain, with its lookout tower.

Neels Gap →

Although it is now referred to as Neels Gap, the gap was officially named Neel Gap, in honor of the engineer who built the highway, W.R. Neel. Before 1925, it was called Walasi-yi Gap or Frogtown Gap. The highway was completed in 1925, "a 20-foot graded road with a ten-foot paved strip," considered at the time to be an engineering marvel and the first paved road over the Georgia Blue Ridge. It was repaved and widened to two lanes in 1949.

U.S. 19/129 →

U.S. 19 leads 1,386 miles from Erie, Pennsylvania, to Memphis, Florida, generally following the Appalachians. The A.T. crosses it in Georgia, North Carolina, and Tennessee. U.S. 129 leads 582 miles between Knoxville, Tennessee, and Chiefland, Florida.

N-S   TRAIL DESCRIPTION

0.8	Cross open rock face just north of summit of **Cowrock Mountain**, with good views of valley below and Wildcat Ridge. ■ SOUTHBOUND hikers turn sharply to right and ascend briefly to summit (elev. 3,842 feet). ■ NORTHBOUND hikers turn sharply to left and descend.	**4.7**
1.3	Cross through Baggs Creek Gap (elev. 3,591 feet), not a distinctive gap. A spring is located down an overgrown road to west.	**4.2**
2.1	Trail crosses Wolf Laurel Top (elev. 3,766 feet). An open rock face east of the Trail offers excellent views.	**3.4**
2.7	Pass to west of Rock Spring Top (elev. 3,526 feet). Spring to west of Trail.	**2.8**
3.4	Descend to Swaim Gap (elev. 3,450 feet).	**2.1**
3.8	Cross open rocky area on crest of Levelland Mountain.	**1.7**
4.0	Cross wooded summit of Levelland Mountain (elev. 3,942 feet). ■ SOUTHBOUND hikers begin 1.5-mile, 817-foot descent to **Neels Gap** and **U.S. 19/129**. ■ NORTHBOUND hikers follow crest of mountain.	**1.5**
4.4	Reach Bull Gap (elev. 3,644 feet). Blue-blazed trail to west leads downhill about 200 yards to spring.	**1.1**

S-N

SECTION HIGHLIGHTS

Vogel State Park →
See Section Fifteen.

Walasi-Yi Center →

Arguably the only building on the A.T. that the Trail actually passes through. The smaller building, to the west of the covered walkway that the Trail goes through, was originally a wooden structure built by the Pfister-Vogel Land Company, which conducted logging and tanning operations there in the early 1900s. The house was used as a tea room and for lodging. During 1933–34, the Civilian Conservation Corps built the main building at Walasi-Yi and veneered the older building with rock. It also built two log cabins behind the structure, added a 10,000-gallon, spring-fed reservoir and sewage system, and "developed" Walasi-Yi, as it was called. The inn has been over the years a restaurant, an inn, a gift shop, and a hiker hostel. The state of Georgia owns the building and surrounding land (a gift to the state from the Vogel family in 1927) and leases it to concessionaires. For decades, under different managers, it has been operated by Mountain Crossings at Walasi-Yi as a hiking store and a hostel.

Southern end of section →

U.S. 19/129 through Neels Gap leads east (compass-south) 19.0 miles to Cleveland, Georgia (on U.S. 129), and 22.0 miles to Dahlonega, Georgia (on U.S. 19). Cabins and a store are 0.3 mile east from Neels Gap. To the west (compass-north), it is 14.0 miles to Blairsville and 3 miles to Vogel State Park, where cabins, tentsites, showers, laundry service, and a supply concession are located (fee charged). Cabins are located 0.5 mile beyond Vogel Park. Mountain Crossings at Walasi-Yi offers showers, rooms, laundry, and other hiker services and excellent hiker equipment and supplies. For more information, call (706) 745-6095. Hiker parking is available 0.3 mile west of Neels Gap on U.S. 129 at the Byron Reece Memorial. Hikers may either walk back to Neels Gap along the highway or reach the A.T. by way of a blue-blazed trail leading from the parking area to the Trail on Blood Mountain.

N-S

TRAIL DESCRIPTION

5.5 Reach **southern end of section** and of Raven Cliffs Wilderness at U.S. 19/129 at Neels Gap (elev. 3,125 feet) and the **Walasi-Yi Center**. **Vogel State Park** is 3.0 miles west (compass-north) by road. ■ SOUTHBOUND hikers cross highway and begin ascent of Blood Mountain (see Section Fifteen). ■ NORTHBOUND hikers pass through breezeway of Walasi-Yi building and enter woods, beginning 1.5-mile, 817-foot ascent of Levelland Mountain.

0.0

Walasi-Yi Center breezeway

S-N

Neels Gap (U.S. 19/129) to Woody Gap (Ga. 60)

10.6 MILES

Blood Mountain, the highlight of this section, is the highest point on the Georgia A.T. as well as its most-hiked section. Its open, rocky summit affords spectacular views. Between Blood Mountain, near the northern end of the section, and Big Cedar Mountain, near the southern end, the Trail crosses a number of knobs and gaps and reaches a low point below Miller Gap. Several side trails offer opportunities for loops. Another side trail leads down to the Dockery Lake Recreation Area. Most of the Trail between Neels Gap and Woody Gap is in, or borders, the Blood Mountain Wilderness.

Road Approaches—Both ends of this section are accessible by vehicle. Another access point is by way of Lake Winfield Scott Recreation Area on Ga. 180 and either of the side trails from it.

Maps—ATC Chattahoochee National Forest map (with this guide); USGS Neels Gap quadrangle.

Shelters and Campsites—Two shelters are located in this section. Blood Mountain Shelter is at mile 2.4/8.2 below, and a side trail leads to Woods Hole Shelter at mile 3.6/7.0. Good campsites are located on the south side of Blood Mountain at mile 3.2/7.4 and at Bird Gap at mile 3.6/7.0. Camping is also available at the Byron Reece Memorial, 0.3 mile west of Neels Gap on U.S. 19/129 or about one mile west of the A.T. at mile 1.0/9.6. The Trail corridor in this section lies within the Chattahoochee National Forest, and camping is permitted except where noted otherwise. *Campfires are not permitted in the northernmost 3.3 miles.*

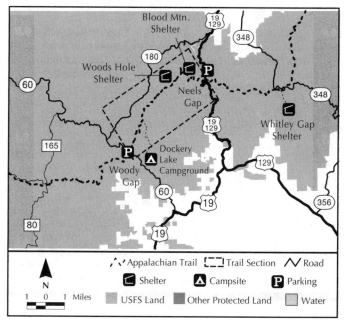

Appalachian Trail   Trail Section   Road

Shelter   Campsite   Parking

N

1 0 1 Miles

USFS Land   Other Protected Land   Water

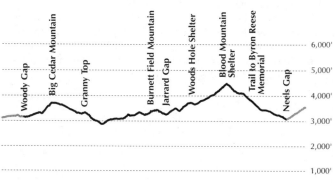

S ←————————————————→ N

10.6 MILES

SECTION HIGHLIGHTS

Northern end of section →

U.S. 19/129 through Neels Gap leads east (compass-south) 19.0 miles to Cleveland, Georgia (on U.S. 129), and 22.0 miles to Dahlonega, Georgia (on U.S. 19). Cabins and store are 0.3 mile east from Neels Gap. Cabins are also located 3.5 miles west, beyond Vogel State Park. It is 14.0 miles west to Blairsville, Georgia. Mountain Crossings at Walasi-Yi offers showers, rooms, laundry, other hiker services, and excellent hiker equipment and supplies. For more information, call (706) 745-6095. Hiker parking is available 0.3 mile west of Neels Gap on U.S. 129 at the Byron Reece Memorial. Hikers may either walk back to Neels Gap along the highway or reach the A.T. by way of a blue-blazed trail leading from the parking area to the Trail on Blood Mountain. No public transportation available.

Walasi-yi →

The word *Walasi-yi* means "frog place" or "giant frog" in Cherokee, reflecting a legend of a great mythical frog who was chieftain of the animal council and made his home high in the gap, frightening the Indians who came there. See Section Fourteen.

Vogel State Park →

To the west (compass-north), it is 3.0 miles to Vogel State Park, where cabins, tentsites, showers, laundry service, and a supply concession are located (fee charged). The park was built by the Civilian Conservation Corps. The main CCC camp was located down the road at Goose Creek; the large building there is the only remaining one built by the Corps at that location.

Plaque →
See page 164.

N-S

TRAIL DESCRIPTION

0.0 Reach **northern end of section** at U.S. 19/129 at Neels   **10.6**
Gap (elev. 3,125 feet) and the **Walasi-Yi Center**, at the
northern boundary of the Blood Mountain Wilderness.
Vogel State Park is 3.0 miles west (compass-north) by
road. ■ SOUTHBOUND hikers pass the **plaque** and begin
2.4-mile, 1,336-foot ascent of Blood Mountain.
Campfires are banned within 300 feet of the Trail between here and
Slaughter Creek (mile 3.3 below). ■ NORTHBOUND hikers
pass through breezeway of Walasi-Yi building on rock
walkway and enter woods (see Section Fourteen).

0.9 Pass balanced rock on east side of Trail.   **9.7**

Rock work on Blood Mountain

S-N

SECTION HIGHLIGHTS

Byron Reece Memorial →

Parking and picnic area along U.S. 129, named for a lyrical, melancholy Georgia poet, Byron Herbert Reece, who committed suicide at the age of 41. Reece lived on a farm in Choestoe, a few miles down the road. He wrote of Choestoe, "the place where rabbits dance":

> It's not that rabbits ever really danced here,
> Though sometimes, in the dusk, when nothing happens,
> We could believe they danced and wish them dancing;
> They came to sport forever in the name our country bears,
> One that the Indians gave it.

Freeman Trail →

This 1.8-mile trail was named for Larry Freeman, outstanding member of the GATC from the 1940s to the 1960s. Freeman, among other accomplishments, was instrumental in rejuvenating the club and the Trail after World War II. The trail offers a bad-weather bypass of the Blood Mountain climb. Just south of the trail junction, on the large flat area of rock, look for mountain saxifrage and St. John's wort.

Blood Mountain →

At 4,461 feet, it is the highest point on the Georgia A.T. The Trail leads across several large rock outcrops that afford fine views in all directions. In the spring and early summer, the mountainside is in bloom with rhododendron and mountain laurel, as well as flame, sweet white, and pink azalea. Most accounts attribute the names of Blood Mountain and nearby Slaughter Mountain to a fierce battle between the Cherokee and Creek Indians in the late 1600s, as pressure from Euroamerican settlers began pushing native Americans to the west; the mountains reportedly "ran red with blood." Other scholars believe the names, which are "white man's names," resulted from a last stand of the Cherokee against the colonists during the Revolutionary War. The Cherokee in the area, angered by settlers moving into their lands, slaughtered entire families and destroyed

N-S

TRAIL DESCRIPTION

1.0 Reach Flatrock Gap (elev. 3,420 feet); an unreliable water source is located here. Trail to west leads about one mile to **Byron Reece Memorial**. The **Freeman Trail** leads east 1.8 miles around southern slope of Blood Mountain and back to A.T. at Bird Gap, mile 3.6/7.0. ▪ SOUTHBOUND hikers continue ascent of Blood Mountain. ▪ NORTHBOUND hikers proceed across level area.   **9.6**

1.4 Series of rock steps leads through boulders. Be careful. Midway along steps, path jogs to left for several yards and continues on steps.   **9.2**

1.8 Rocky slope with fine views at sharp turn in Trail. ▪ NORTHBOUND hikers, watch for 90-degree turn off the rock slab into the woods.   **8.8**

2.3 Trail follows face of steep rock slope with excellent views.   **8.3**

2.4 Summit of **Blood Mountain** (elev. 4,461 feet). **Blood Mountain Shelter** is just to south of open rocky summit. Descent from summit is steep and rocky in both directions. ▪ SOUTHBOUND hikers begin 5.0-mile, 1,581-foot descent over knobs to near Miller Gap. ▪ NORTHBOUND hikers begin 2.4-mile, 1,336-foot descent to Neels Gap.   **8.2**

SECTION HIGHLIGHTS

farmlands of colonists; the colonists responded by sending troops of militiamen into Cherokee territory to retaliate (see page 110). Still others say that Blood Mountain might have derived its name from the reddish lichens that cover its rocky slopes (which doesn't explain the name of nearby Slaughter Gap).

Blood Mountain Shelter →

The two-room stone shelter at the summit of the mountain was built in 1934 by the Civilian Conservation Corps. It was refurbished in 1981 by the GATC and the USFS. Unfortunately for hikers, the top of Blood Mountain has no firewood or water, and campfires are banned on the mountain in an effort to allow overused areas to return to their natural state. Fires are prohibited in the shelter as well. Blood Mountain is the most-visited spot on the A.T. south of Clingmans Dome, and the impact of more than 40,000 visitors a year has taken its toll. The nearest water sources are near Flatrock Gap (mile 1.0/9.6) and sometimes at Slaughter Creek (mile 3.3/7.3; camping also available). A privy and bear cables are available near the shelter. Next shelter: south, 1.7 miles (Woods Hole); north, 9.8 miles (Whitley Gap).

Campsites →

Eight tent pads have been constructed here to relieve the often crowded conditions on top of Blood Mountain. Water is available about 200 yards down the Trail at Slaughter Creek. Fires are prohibited.

Slaughter Creek Trail →

Leads west 2.5 miles to Lake Winfield Scott Recreation Area. The recreation area can also be reached by the 1.0-mile Jarrard Gap Trail (mile 5.0/5.6). Some facilities may be closed in winter, but, in season, there are tentsites, swimming, a lake, restrooms, picnic areas, and water. Lake Winfield Scott is located on Ga. 180, about 22.0 miles north of Dahlonega by way of Ga. 60. From the entrance to the recreation area on Ga. 180, it is approximately 5.0 miles west to Ga. 60 and approximately 6.0 miles east to U.S. 129.

N-S

TRAIL DESCRIPTION

Blood Mountain Shelter

2.5	Reach a sharp turn in the Trail. ■ SOUTHBOUND hikers, avoid the old roadbed leading down the mountain. ■ NORTHBOUND hikers continue to ascend.	**8.1**
3.2	Reach **campsites**.	**7.4**
3.3	Reach source of Slaughter Creek, an unreliable water source. ■ SOUTHBOUND hikers continue descent toward Bird Gap. ■ For NORTHBOUND hikers, campfires are banned within 300 feet of the Trail between here and Neels Gap (mile 0.0/10.6). From this point, the blue-blazed **Slaughter Creek Trail** leads west to Ga. 180 and Lake Winfield Scott.	**7.3**

S-N

Freeman Trail →
See mile 1.0/9.6 above.

Woods Hole Shelter →

This shelter was built in 1998 by the Georgia A.T. Club. Accommodates 7. Water can be found at a small stream crossing the trail to the shelter about midway; unreliable in dry months. Privy is on a side trail leading from the front of the shelter. Bear cables are available. Woods Hole is named for, and dedicated to, the late Roy and Tillie Wood of Roswell, Georgia, known for providing food and shelter to hikers at their "Wood's Hole" hostel in Virginia. Funds to build the shelter were donated by Mr. and Mrs. Jerry Bowden. Along the Trail south of the shelter, look for large stands of Turk's-cap lily. Next shelter: south, 12.4 miles (Gooch Mountain); north, 1.7 miles (Blood Mountain).

Jarrard Gap Trail →

Blazed blue. A stream crosses this trail about 0.3 mile west of A.T. Leads 1.0 mile west to Lake Winfield Scott (see mile 3.3/7.3).

N-S

	TRAIL DESCRIPTION	

3.6 Bird Gap (elev. 3,650 feet). Two blue-blazed side trails intersect. In the middle of the gap, the **Freeman Trail** leads east around southern slope of Blood Mountain and rejoins A.T. above. At the southern end of the gap, a trail leads west about 0.5 mile to **Woods Hole Shelter**.   **7.0**

3.9 Skirt shoulder of Turkey Stamp Mountain.   **6.7**

4.6 Reach western shoulder of Gaddis Mountain.   **6.0**

5.0 Descend to Jarrard Gap (elev. 3,250 feet). An unpaved private road crosses Trail. To west, beginning on old road, blue-blazed **Jarrard Gap Trail** leads to Lake Winfield Scott Recreation Area.   **5.6**

5.1 Pass intermittent springs on east side of Trail. (Unreliable water source.)   **5.5**

5.5 Pass over flat area known as Burnett Field Mountain.   **5.1**

5.6 Trail turns sharply.   **5.0**

6.1 Come to wide, flat area. ■ SOUTHBOUND hikers skirt eastern side of ridge for next mile.   **4.5**

6.6 Trail passes to east of Henry Gap (elev. 3,100 feet).   **4.0**

7.1 Trail leads along side of wooded ridge. ■ SOUTHBOUND hikers descend, reaching old roadbed. ■ NORTHBOUND hikers skirt eastern side of ridge for next mile.   **3.5**

7.4 Reach Lance Creek (elev. 2,880 feet) below Miller Gap. ■ SOUTHBOUND hikers cross stream and bear left up slope, beginning 2.2-mile, 857-foot ascent of Big Cedar Mountain. ■ NORTHBOUND hikers follow old road briefly and ascend along southern side of Baker Mountain, beginning 5.0-mile, 1,581-foot ascent over knobs and gaps to Blood Mountain.   **3.2**

S-N

SECTION HIGHLIGHTS

Dockery Lake Trail →

This blue-blazed trail leads about 3.0 miles east to Dockery Lake Recreation Area (no facilities), about one mile from Ga. 60.

Big Cedar Mountain →

The rock outcrop just south of the summit, often called "Preaching Rock," affords fine views of the mountains to the east and south.

Woody Gap →

Arthur Woody was the state's first ranger. It is said that he saw his father kill the last deer in the forest, during a time of little respect for wildlife and deteriorating forests. Woody vowed that he would some day put back what the mountain men of his time had taken away. In time, he began to restock the forest with deer and the streams with fish. His outstanding achievements in forest-fire prevention, game restoration and preservation, land reclamation, and timber management paved the way for today's advanced methods used by the Forest Service. Woody was a large, rough mountain man. The story goes that he asked the federal government to build a road from Suches to Stone Pile Gap but was told the government did not build roads, it only improved them. So, Woody "scraped out a trail through the mountains" and then told the government, "I have my road. Now, you come and improve it." Ga. 60 is that road.

Southern end of section →

At Woody Gap, where Ga. 60 crosses the ridge. Ga. 60 leads 15.0 miles east to Dahlonega, with most services, and 2.0 miles west to Suches, where a grocery store and a post office can be found at the intersection of Ga. 60 and Ga. 180. A commercial campground is located near Suches. Parking is available in the gap. The gap has picnic tables and a restroom. In the spring, the roadside east of the Trail crossing is in bloom with a variety of wildflowers. The road was built around 1930 (see Section Sixteen) and paved in the mid-1940s. The old quarry site just to the east of the Trail on the north side of the gap provided rock in the building of the road.

N-S

| TRAIL DESCRIPTION |

7.7 At Miller Gap, cross **Dockery Lake Trail**. Spring approximately 100 yards east on Dockery Lake Trail. ■ SOUTHBOUND hikers ascend Granny Top Mountain and turn sharp left at top of ridge. ■ NORTHBOUND hikers continue descent. **2.9**

8.3 Reach Dan Gap. ■ SOUTHBOUND hikers ascend toward ridge of Big Cedar Mountain. ■ NORTHBOUND hikers ascend Granny Top Mountain and turn sharply right, descending from ridge. **2.3**

8.4 Cross small stream on eastern slope of ridge. **2.2**

8.7 Sharp turn in Trail, just below large boulder and steps. **1.9**

9.1 Small spring on west side of Trail at Augerhole Gap. **1.5**

9.6 Reach open, rocky face of **Big Cedar Mountain** just south of summit (elev. 3,737 feet). ■ SOUTHBOUND hikers begin 1.0-mile, 587-foot descent toward Woody Gap. ■ NORTHBOUND hikers begin 2.2-mile, 857-foot descent to near Miller Gap. **1.0**

9.9 Pass just to west of Lunsford Gap (elev. 3,300 feet). **0.7**

10.6 Reach **southern end of section** at Ga. 60 in **Woody Gap** (elev. 3,150 feet). The southern boundary of Blood Mountain Wilderness is just to the north. ■ SOUTHBOUND hikers cross highway and continue through small parking lot on east side of picnic area (see Section Sixteen). ■ NORTHBOUND hikers pass through large parking lot and begin 1.0-mile, 587-foot ascent to Big Cedar Mountain. **0.0**

S-N

Woody Gap (Ga. 60) to Hightower Gap (USFS 42)

11.8 MILES

This section is, on average, the lowest on the Georgia Trail. It consists of long ridges that break gently to the north (or west) and more steeply to the south (or east). Almost all of the section south of Gooch Gap has been relocated over the years to remove it from a forest road that was built on top of the Trail in the early 1930s. Part of the present route, completed more than twenty-five years ago, takes the Trail into a valley known as the "Devil's Kitchen" that once was the location of farms and communities. Part takes it to ridgetops that offer fine views. USFS 42, which parallels the A.T. for most of the section, affords access to the Trail at several points.

Road Approaches—Both ends of the section are accessible by vehicle, as are Gooch Gap, Cooper Gap, and Horse Gap. All except Woody Gap are reached by way of a sometimes rough forest road.

Maps—ATC Chattahoochee National Forest map (with this guide); USGS Suches and Noontootla quadrangles.

Shelters and Campsites—The one shelter on this section is Gooch Mountain Shelter at mile 5.0/6.8 south of Woody Gap. Camping is available at Gooch Gap at mile 3.6/8.2 south of Woody Gap and at Gooch Mountain Shelter, where there are tent pads. The Trail corridor in this section lies within the Chattahoochee National Forest, and camping is permitted except where noted otherwise. Campfires should be attended at all times and completely extinguished when you leave a campsite. Verify current campfire bans with the local Forest Service office, or watch for posted notices at Trailheads.

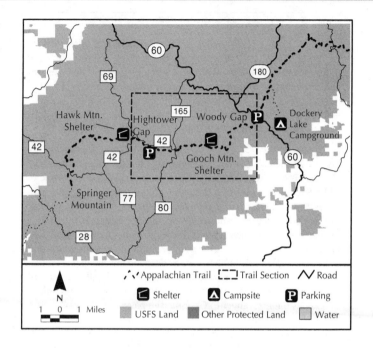

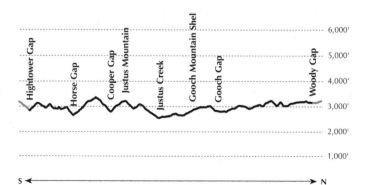

11.8 MILES

SECTION HIGHLIGHTS

Northern end of section →

At Woody Gap, where Ga. 60 crosses the ridge. Ga. 60 leads 15 miles east to Dahlonega, with most services, and 2 miles west to Suches, where a grocery store and post office can be found at the intersection with Ga. 180. A commercial campground is located near Suches. Parking is available in the gap. The gap, designated Woody Gap Recreation Area, has picnic tables and a restroom.

Suches →

The small town of Suches, Georgia, called "the valley above the clouds," is the highest town in Georgia. It is named for Cherokee Chief Suches, who lived in the valley in the early 1800s. For centuries, the area was inhabited by the Cherokees, but, after gold was discovered in nearby counties in the late 1820s and early 1830s, the Cherokee were forced out. Settlers subsequently developed flat land along Suches Creek. One of the earliest inhabitants was John, or Johnathan, Woody, who has many descendants living in the area today. When the U.S. Forest Service began to develop the surrounding land as a national forest in the early 1900s, they appointed Arthur Woody as the first ranger in Georgia (see page 194). A gravel road was built a few miles from the Suches settlement, and a ranger station was constructed on the road. Electricity and telephone lines were installed. Later, the Civilian Conservation Corps set up camp nearby to help construct buildings, create a lake, and improve the road. The residents of Suches gradually moved homes and businesses toward the developing area nearer the mountain crests.

N-S

TRAIL DESCRIPTION

Woody Gap

0.0 Woody Gap (3,150 feet) is the **northern end of the section**, 2.0 miles east of **Suches**. ■ SOUTHBOUND hikers leave small parking lot on south side of highway and continue around eastern slope of Black Mountain. ■ NORTHBOUND hikers leave large parking lot on north side of highway and begin 1.0-mile, 587-foot ascent to Big Cedar Mountain (see Section Fifteen).   **11.8**

1.0 Reach Tritt Gap (elev. 3,050 feet).   **10.8**

1.4 Follow crest of Ramrock Mountain (elev. 3,200 feet), with views to south.   **10.4**

1.5 Reach Jacks Gap (elev. 3,000 feet).   **10.3**

2.1 Pass through Liss Gap, with large stand of poplar trees.   **9.7**

2.6 Cross abandoned old road.   **9.2**

3.0 Turn in Trail. ■ SOUTHBOUND hikers regain ridgecrest. ■ NORTHBOUND hikers bear around western side of ridge.   **8.8**

S-N

SECTION HIGHLIGHTS

Gooch Gap →

Unpaved USFS 42 leads west 2.7 miles to Suches, by way of Ga. 60, with supplies and post office (0.4 mile to left on Ga. 60). USFS 42 leads 6.1 miles west to Cooper Gap on the A.T. Gooch Gap is a popular area for camping. Water is located about 100 yards north on the Trail, then east about 200 yards down a blue-blazed trail.

USFS 42 →

Until 1949, the A.T. generally followed USFS 42 to Cooper Gap but was relocated at that time to the more remote area away from the increasingly busy road. USFS 42 extends from Ga. 60 at Suches, 1.6 miles north of Woody Gap, about 30 miles west to the Doublehead Gap Road, which connects with Ga. 52 east of Ellijay. The Trail crosses USFS 42 in four locations: Gooch Gap, Cooper Gap, Hightower Gap, and at the foot of Springer Mountain. From Ga. 60, the distance to Springer by this road is approximately 20 miles; to Hightower Gap, 11.9 miles; to Cooper Gap, 8.8 miles; and to Gooch Gap, 2.7 miles. Limited parking is available in the gaps.

Gooch Mountain Shelter →

Constructed in 2001 by the Georgia A.T. Club, the shelter has a loft and picnic table. It accommodates 14 and has bear cables available. A privy is located behind the shelter along a blue-blazed trail. Water is also down a trail behind the shelter at a spring. Tent pads constructed in the area to the side of the shelter offer more privacy to hikers and help to protect the shelter area from overuse. This shelter replaces one built near Gooch Gap in 1960. Funds for the shelter were donated by the family of Kurt vonSeggern, a hiker who died at age 40. His sister, Dolly Hawkins, was the architect for the shelter. Next shelter: south, 7.6 miles (Hawk Mountain); north, 12.4 miles (Woods Hole).

N-S	TRAIL DESCRIPTION	

3.6	Reach **Gooch Gap** and unpaved **USFS 42**. Cross road, and continue.	8.2
3.9	Pass spring along Trail.	7.9
4.6	Reach shallow gap at north end of Horseshoe Ridge.	7.2
5.0	Blue-blazed trail to west leads about 130 yards to **Gooch Mountain Shelter**.	6.8
5.3	Cross Blackwell Creek (elev. 2,600 feet).	6.5
5.8	Reach crest of small ridge.	6.0
5.9	Cross small stream. ■ SOUTHBOUND hikers: *Watch for planned Trail relocation between here and mile 7.1.*	5.9
6.3	Cross Justus Creek on footbridge.	5.5
6.4	Cross old logging road.	5.4
7.1	Reach top of Phyllis Spur (elev. 3,081 feet). ■ NORTHBOUND hikers: *Watch for planned Trail relocation between here and mile 5.9.*	4.7

Gooch Mountain Shelter

SECTION HIGHLIGHTS

USFS 42 →

See mile 3.6/8.2. To the north, USFS 15 leads about 6.0 miles to Gaddistown.

USFS 80 →

Leads 2.7 miles east into a restricted area surrounding U.S. Army Camp Frank D. Merrill and from there about 10.0 miles to Dahlonega. Camp Merrill is home to the 5th Ranger Training Battalion and the mountain phase of the U.S. Army Ranger School, where small unit leaders are instructed in combat techniques and procedures used to move swiftly over all types of terrain, including mountains. The Special Forces camp, which has operated since 1959, was officially designated Camp Frank D. Merrill in honor of the commander, a major general, of "Merrill's Marauders" during Burma operations of World War II. The 2nd Ranger Company was reorganized and redesignated in 1988 as the 5th Ranger Training Battalion. A.T. hikers may encounter Rangers training in the woods above Camp Merrill.

Hightower Gap →

In the late 1920s and early 1930s, Hightower Gap was "the center of hunting and fishing activities" in the Blue Ridge Game Management Area. A 20,000-acre game refuge, as well as a fish hatchery, was located just down USFS 69 from the gap, and a forest ranger station was in or near the gap.

Southern end of section →

USFS 42 passes through Hightower Gap. To the east, it leads about 4.0 miles to Winding Stair Gap and about 7.0 miles to the foot of Springer Mountain. To the west, it leads about 3.0 miles to Cooper Gap. USFS 69 leads west, downhill, about 2.0 miles to Rock Creek Lake, then about 15.0 miles to Ga. 60. No services are available at the Trailhead.

N-S

| | TRAIL DESCRIPTION | |

| 7.4 | Pass through small gap. | 4.4 |

| 7.7 | Reach summit of Justus Mountain (elev. 3,224 feet). | 4.1 |

| 8.3 | Forest roads **USFS 42** and **USFS 80** intersect in Cooper Gap (elev. 2,828 feet). Cross through gap, and ascend in either direction. | 3.5 |

| 8.9 | Summit of Sassafras Mountain (elev. 3,336 feet). ■ SOUTH-BOUND hikers begin 1.0-mile, 663-foot descent. | 2.9 |

| 9.9 | Follow Trail through Horse Gap (2,673 feet). USFS 42 is visible to west. ■ SOUTHBOUND hikers follow gradually climbing ridgecrest. ■ NORTHBOUND hikers begin 1.0-mile, 663-foot ascent of Sassafras Mountain. | 1.9 |

| 11.8 | Reach **Hightower Gap** (elev. 2,854 feet) and **southern end of section** at USFS 42. ■ SOUTHBOUND hikers ascend, skirting north side of Hawk Mountain (see Section Seventeen). ■ NORTHBOUND hikers follow ridgecrest and ascend. | 0.0 |

Turk's-cap Lily on Sassafras Mountain

S-N

Hightower Gap (USFS 42) to Springer Mountain

8.3 MILES

The Appalachian Trail begins (or ends, depending upon one's point of view) at Springer Mountain, and, as the highest point on the Trail south of Woody Gap, it is the highlight of this section. Until 1958, the Trail's southern terminus was Mt. Oglethorpe, about 23 miles farther south, but commercial development necessitated the relocation to a site within the Chattahoochee National Forest. Between Springer and Hightower Gap, the A.T. ascends Hawk Mountain (not crossing its summit), follows the ridgecrest, and descends to the Long Creek/Three Forks area of beautiful mountain streams, waterfalls, majestic trees, and rhododendron "hells."

Road Approaches—Hightower Gap can be accessed by vehicle by way of USFS 42 and USFS 69. Three Forks can also be reached by way of USFS 58. All roads are unpaved and often very rough and muddy. USFS 42 crosses the Trail within 1.0 mile of the Springer Mountain summit but does not lead to the summit.

Maps—ATC Chattahoochee National Forest map (with this guide); USGS Noontootla quadrangle.

Shelters and Campsites—This section has three shelters. Hawk Mountain Shelter is at mile 0.5/7.8; Stover Creek Shelter, at mile 5.5/2.8, and Springer Mountain Shelter, at mile 8.1/0.2. Campsites are available in the area of Three Forks at mile 4.0/4.3 and at Springer Mountain Shelter. A fourth shelter is located 1.5 miles south of Springer on the Approach Trail (see page 214). The Trail corridor in this section lies within the Chattahoochee National Forest, and camping is permitted except where noted otherwise. *Camping is prohibited on the summit of Springer Mountain.*

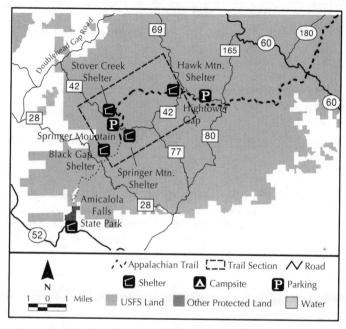

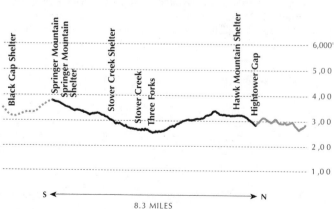

Northern end of section →

USFS 42 passes through Hightower Gap. To the east, it leads about 4 miles to Winding Stair Gap and about 7 miles to the foot of Springer Mountain. To the west, it leads about 3 miles to Cooper Gap. USFS 69 leads west, downhill, about 2 miles to Rock Creek Lake, then about 15 miles to Ga. 60. No services are available at the Trailhead.

Hawk Mountain Shelter →

Built in 1994 by the Georgia A.T. Club, Forest Service, and Upper Loft Designs. Accommodates 12. Bear cables, loft, privy. Water is located at a stream about 400 yards behind the shelter. This is the third shelter erected on Hawk Mountain. The first was built in 1960 by the Forest Service near the summit. In 1979, that shelter was relocated to the small flat area where the present blue-blazed trail leads west to the current shelter. Next shelter: south, 5.4 miles (Stover Creek); north, 7.6 miles (Gooch Mountain).

Hawk Mountain →

For almost fifty years, the Trail crossed the summit of Hawk Mountain (elev. 3,619 feet). In 1979, it was moved off the top to its present location around the north side. A fire tower was located there until the late 1970s, and a firewarden was on duty. In the early years, his cabin could be used as emergency shelter by hikers. Army Rangers from Camp Merrill (see Section Sixteen) use the summit as a base of operations but do not often come in contact with hikers.

Hickory Flats Cemetery →

The area designated "Hickory Flats" was, in the early 1900s, a dispersed community that farmed in "the flats" until the 1920s. The ruins of an old church beside the cemetery could still be seen in 1960. Community members and descendants of those buried here still return frequently to this small private tract to picnic under a shelter and to care for the old cemetery.

N-S

TRAIL DESCRIPTION

0.0 Reach Hightower Gap (elev. 2,854 feet) and **northern**   **8.3**
end of section at USFS 42 and 69. ■ SOUTHBOUND hikers
ascend, skirting north side of Hawk Mountain. ■ NORTH-
BOUND hikers follow ridgecrest and ascend (see Section
Sixteen).

0.5 At turn in Trail, blue-blazed side trail leads west about   **7.8**
0.2 mile to **Hawk Mountain Shelter**.

0.6 Trail crosses a stream as it skirts the north side of **Hawk**   **7.7**
Mountain.

1.2 Ridgecrest. ■ SOUTHBOUND hikers reach ridgecrest below   **7.1**
summit of Hawk Mountain. ■ NORTHBOUND hikers leave
ridgecrest and skirt western side of Hawk Mountain.

2.3 Cross unpaved road. To west is **Hickory Flats Ceme-**   **6.0**
tery.

S-N

SECTION HIGHLIGHTS

Benton MacKaye Trail →

Marked with white, diamond-shaped blazes, it is named for the "father" of the Appalachian Trail. It was intended, in part, to follow the western ridge of the Blue Ridge Mountains, where MacKaye had initially envisioned the A.T. The 288-mile BMT forms a 500-mile "loop" with the A.T., with its southern terminus on Springer Mountain and its northern terminus at Davenport Gap in Tennessee at the eastern end of Great Smoky Mountains National Park. From here, the BMT heads north and west; at mile 69.4 from its Springer terminus, still in Georgia, it intersects with the Pinhoti Trail, which extends southwesterly across Alabama for 300 miles (www.pinhotitrail-alliance.org). The BMT (www.bmta.org) intersects the A.T. three times between here and Springer Mountain: at miles 4.1/4.2, 6.4/1.9, and 7.0/1.3. Between here and mile 4.1/4.2, the BMT and A.T. share the same route.

Duncan Ridge Trail →

Blazed blue, it was built in the 1960s by the Georgia A.T. Club, when the historic (and present) route of the A.T. was threatened with extinction by a proposed extension of the Blue Ridge Parkway from North Carolina into Georgia. Fortunately, that road was never built, thanks to the designation in 1968 of the A.T. as a national scenic trail, giving it more protection under federal law. Until 1980, the DRT was called "Loop Trail in Georgia." Today, it is the Duncan Ridge National Recreation Trail. It extends about 30 miles from Three Forks to the north side of Blood Mountain on the A.T. It can be used as a 60-mile loop trail with the A.T. The DRT and the BMT follow the same path for about 20 miles, from Three Forks to Rhodes Mountain. The portion between Springer Mountain and Rhodes Mountain is managed and maintained by the Benton MacKaye Trail Association; the portion between Rhodes Mountain and Blood Mountain, by the Forest Service and volunteers.

N-S

TRAIL DESCRIPTION

3.2 Junction of three trails. A.T. turns slightly to the east. **Benton MacKaye Trail** (BMT), marked with white, diamond-shaped blazes, and **Duncan Ridge Trail** (DRT), marked with blue blazes, enter from the west. Another blue-blazed trail leads west 0.1 mile to **Long Creek Falls**, a spectacular waterfall, with a beautiful pool suitable for swimming at its base. At one time, there was a grist mill at the site, part of the Hickory Flats-Long Creek community, which was, in part, in the Long Creek Valley. Evidence of home sites has been found in the general area.

5.1

Long Creek Falls

S-N

SECTION HIGHLIGHTS

Three Forks →

Three beautiful mountain streams—Stover, Chester and Long creeks—converge here to form Noontootla Creek. *Noontootla,* a Cherokee word, means "shining water." To the east, USFS 58 leads 2.6 miles to Winding Stair Gap and USFS 42, which leads left to Hightower Gap and right to Springer Mountain. To the west, USFS 58 leads about 5 miles to Doublehead Gap Road. Three Forks is also the southern terminus of the Duncan Ridge Trail. Campsites are available along and near the streams in the area.

Hemlocks →

The magnificent hemlocks along this section of Trail are believed to be the only virgin stand between Georgia and the Great Smoky Mountains National Park. In the 1970s, determined efforts of the Georgia A.T. Club, with the cooperation of the Chattahoochee National Forest, succeeded in routing the Trail along Stover Creek and thus protecting the hemlocks from logging. The hemlocks are currently threatened by the hemlock woody adelgid, however. Efforts are being made to contain the spread of the infestation.

Stover Creek Shelter →

The newest shelter on the Georgia Trail. A shelter was built in 1960 by the Forest Service at Big Stamp Gap on USFS 42; it was relocated in 1977 to a nearby area called Cross Trails. In 1984, it was moved to Stover Creek. In 2006, a new shelter was built at a site farther from the Trail by GATC with grants from L.L.Bean, ATC, and the U.S. Forest Service. (The 1960 shelter, the oldest wooden one on the Georgia A.T., was then demolished and signs removed, to allow the site to return to a natural state.) Accommodates 16. Bear cables, privy north of the shelter, tent pads. Water from the creek. *No tenting near water.* Next shelter: south, 2.8 miles (Springer Mountain); north, 5.4 miles (Hawk Mountain).

Benton MacKaye Trail →
See mile 3.2/5.1.

N-S

	TRAIL DESCRIPTION	

4.0	Reach USFS 42 and an area called **Three Forks**. ■ SOUTH-BOUND hikers cross road and footbridge over Chester Creek. ■ NORTHBOUND hikers cross road and continue along old road bed, paralleling Long Creek.	**4.3**
4.1	**Benton MacKaye Trail** intersects to east. Between here and mile 3.2/5.1, the BMT and A.T. share the same route.	**4.2**
4.5	Cross Stover Creek.	**3.8**
5.0	Trail parallels Stover Creek through stand of **hemlocks**.	**3.3**
5.4	Sharp turn in Trail. ■ SOUTHBOUND hikers turn left, descend steps, and cross Stover Creek. ■ NORTHBOUND hikers turn right and continue along west side of Stover Creek.	**2.9**
5.5	Blue-blazed trail leads 0.2 mile to **Stover Creek Shelter**. ■ SOUTHBOUND hikers make sharp right turn to continue on Trail. ■ NORTHBOUND hikers make sharp left.	**2.8**
5.7	Cross Stover Creek.	**2.6**
6.4	Crest of ridge on Rich Mountain, where A.T. intersects with **Benton MacKaye Trail** to east.	**1.9**
6.7	Cross Davis Creek and small tributary.	**1.6**
7.0	A.T. intersects with **Benton MacKaye Trail** to east.	**1.3**

S-N

SECTION HIGHLIGHTS

USFS 42 →

USFS 42 leads east 2.6 miles to Winding Stair Gap and continues to Hightower Gap. To west, it leads about 7 miles to Doublehead Gap Road and then to Ellijay. This is a popular access point for people seeking to begin a northbound A.T. hike at the nearby summit of Springer Mountain.

Springer Mountain Shelter →

Built in 1993. Accommodates 12. Bear cables; privy behind the shelter. *Camping is prohibited on the summit of Springer, except at designated sites.* Midway along the trail to the shelter, a side trail leads to a large open area with campsites, with a privy nearby. Past the shelter is a spring, and beyond are more campsites/tent pads. Next shelter: south, 1.7 miles on the Approach Trail (Black Gap); north, 2.8 miles (Stover Creek).

Springer Mountain →

The Springer overlook provides an excellent view of the Blue Ridge range from Rich Mountain to the northwest to the Cohuttas beyond. In the rock marking the terminus of the Trail is a bronze plaque depicting a hiker facing north. The plaque was installed by the GATC in 1959 after the terminus was moved from Mt. Oglethorpe (see page 214). On the upper edge of the rock outcrop (above the Trail register box embedded in the rock) is a plaque installed in 1993 by the USFS, identifying Springer Mountain as the southern terminus of the A.T. Historians are not sure where the name Springer came from. Until the mid-1950s, some county residents still called it Penitentiary Mountain, but it is not known why.

Southern end of section →

Nearest road access is by USFS 42 (mile 7.3/1.0 above). No services or accommodations are available at the terminus. Lodging, food, camping, shelter, and road access are located in Amicalola Falls State Park (see Approaches section, next). *Because of misuse and resource damage, camping is prohibited on the Springer Mountain summit area.*

N-S

| TRAIL DESCRIPTION |

7.3 Parking area at **USFS 42**. Parking fee required. ■ South- **1.0**
bound hikers cross parking area toward information
board, continue on path, cross road, and begin climb
toward Springer Mountain summit. ■ Northbound hikers
cross road into parking area, bear to right to eastern end,
and enter woods.

8.1 Southern terminus of the **Benton MacKaye Trail**, just **0.2**
below summit of Springer Mountain. ■ Southbound hik-
ers continue 50 feet and reach blue-blazed trail to east
leading to **Springer Mountain Shelter**. ■ Northbound
hikers descend toward USFS 42.

8.3 Rock overlook on summit of **Springer Mountain** (elev. **0.0**
3,782 feet), southern terminus of the Appalachian Trail
and **southern end of the section.** ■ For southbound hikers, the blue-blazed Amicalola Falls Approach Trail descends south 8.8 miles to Amicalola Falls State Park (see
next section), passing a shelter 1.5 mile beyond the
Springer summit. ■ Northbounders begin gradual descent. The northern terminus of the Appalachian Trail is
more than 2,176 miles away, at Katahdin in Maine's
Baxter State Park.

S-N

Approaches to the Southern Terminus of the A.T.

8.8 MILES

A blue-blazed "approach trail" leads along the northern 8.8 miles of the Amicalola Range between Amicalola Falls State Park and the A.T. The southern terminus of the A.T. was moved from Mt. Oglethorpe to Springer Mountain in 1958. Most of the route that was abandoned was on private land, and development and chicken farming along the ridge intruded on the wilderness experience of the hiker. Springer Mountain was chosen because of its relatively remote location in a national forest and its significance as the apex of the eastern and western ranges of the Blue Ridge Mountains. The approach trail was marked on its present route about 1970.

Road Approaches—The southern terminus of the Approach Trail, at Amicalola Falls State Park, is accessible by car. USFS 42 crosses the A.T. 1.0 mile north of the Springer Mountain summit but does not lead to the summit. Forest Service roads also cross the Approach Trail at miles 2.8/6.0, 3.7/5.1, and 7.3/1.5.

Maps—ATC Chattahoochee National Forest map (with this guide); USGS Nimblewell quadrangle.

Shelters and Campsites—Shelters are at mile 1.5/7.3 and mile 8.7/0.1 below. Springer Mountain Shelter is 0.2 mile north of the summit, on the A.T. (see Section Seventeen). *Camping is prohibited on the Springer Mountain summit area.* The route in this section lies mostly within the Chattahoochee National Forest, and camping is generally permitted. Tent camping in Amicalola Falls State Park is permitted only at designated locations.

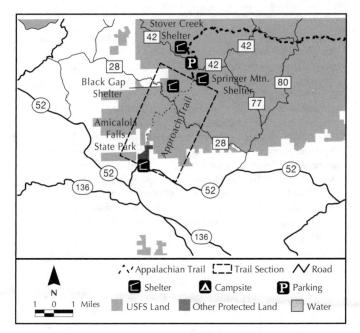

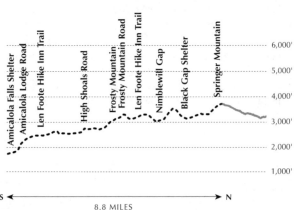

Springer Mountain →

The northern end of the Approach Trail is the rock overlook and hiker plaque on the summit of Springer Mountain (see Section Seventeen). From 1931, when the Georgia Trail was built, until 1958, Mt. Oglethorpe, about 23 miles to the southwest by trail, was the terminus. Much of the route between Amicalola Falls and Oglethorpe was on private land, and development and industrial encroachment made the Trail difficult to maintain and unpleasant to hike. Springer Mountain was chosen as the new terminus because of its remote location within the Chattahoochee National Forest and its significance as the intersection of the eastern and western ranges of the Blue Ridge Mountains. The trail between Amicalola Falls and Springer was retained as an "approach trail," largely because Amicalola Falls State Park was easily accessible by car and offered lodging, camping, and other facilities.

Black Gap Shelter →

The shelter was "reconstructed" in 1993 by the Georgia A.T. Club. Its frame was formerly part of the old Springer Mountain Shelter, which was moved to Black Gap by helicopter, thanks to the Army Rangers at nearby Camp Merrill. A new roof was then installed by the GATC. Water is downhill to the east several hundred yards. Privy, bear cables. Next shelter: south, 7.2 miles (Amicalola Falls); north, 1.2 miles (Springer Mountain).

Nimblewill Gap →

In the gap, USFS 28 leads east 7.4 miles to Nimblewill Church and 10.0 miles to Ga. 52. To the west, it leads down the mountain to Bucktown Creek and the valley below. An old road (USFS 46), impassable by car, leads uphill to the south and west, more or less parallel to the Trail to Frosty Mountain.

N-S

TRAIL DESCRIPTION

Plaque at Springer Mountain terminus

0.0	**Springer Mountain** (elev. 3,782 feet), southern terminus of the A.T. and northern end of the approach trail. ■ SOUTHBOUND hikers leave rocky summit and descend through trees, beginning 8.8-mile, 2,082-foot descent to the trailhead in Amicalola Falls State Park. ■ NORTHBOUND hikers begin gradual descent along ridge.	**8.8**
1.5	In gap (elev. 3,400 feet), **Black Gap Shelter** is located about 300 feet to west.	**7.3**
2.0	Swing around western shoulder of Black Mountain.	**6.8**
2.6	Reach flat ridge.	**6.2**
2.8	Reach **Nimblewill Gap** (elev. 3,100 feet) and USFS 28.	**6.0**
3.1	Cross Woody Knob (elev. 3,400 feet).	**5.7**

S-N

SECTION HIGHLIGHTS

Len Foote Hike Inn →

The Hike Inn is a "no-frills" lodge, offering meals, lodging, hot showers, good views, and a restful atmosphere for registered overnight guests. Day-hikers are welcome to stop and visit, refill water bottles, and enjoy the view. The yellow-blazed trail leads from the approach trail one mile to the lodge and five more miles back to Amicalola Falls State Park, offering an alternative to the blue-blazed Approach Trail. The inn, which opened in 1998, is owned by the Georgia Department of Natural Resources and managed by Appalachian Education and Recreation Services, which is affiliated with the Georgia A.T. Club. Reservations are required, but walk-ins are accepted if space is available. For reservations, call (800) 581-8032. Web site: <www.hike-inn.com>.

Frosty Mountain →

The summit of Frosty Mountain (no views) is the former site of a fire tower, removed in the 1970s. The abandoned fire warden's cabin on the summit was used by hikers for about ten years as a Trail shelter. In 1951–52, the cabin was dismantled by the GATC and rebuilt as a shelter (no longer standing). A spring, unreliable in dry weather, is down an overgrown trail to the east.

High Shoals Road →

High Shoals Church, about 0.5 mile to the west along High Shoals Road, was the center of a substantial community from the mid-1800s until the early 1930s. When the federal government purchased the land in the area for a national forest, people living there sold their property and moved away. The original church was used for the last time in 1934 and later burned down. In the 1960s, former residents, relatives, and friends began to meet in the old cemetery on the site and later in an open shelter. In 1975, they rebuilt the church where it now stands. In 1989, the church was "reconstituted" and today has about 50 members.

Chattahoochee National Forest →

See page 146.

N-S   TRAIL DESCRIPTION

3.4	Side trail (yellow-blazed) intersects on east side of trail (leads east 1.0 mile to **Len Foote Hike Inn** and 6.0 miles to Amicalola Falls State Park).	**5.4**
3.7	Cross USFS 46.	**5.1**
4.0	Cross open, grassy top of **Frosty Mountain** (elev. 3,382 feet).	**4.8**
5.6	Cross unpaved **High Shoals Road**.	**3.2**
7.3	Cross unpaved USFS 46 alongside stream near southern boundary of **Chattahoochee National Forest**.	**1.5**
7.4	Junction with 5-mile trail to **Len Foote Hike Inn.**	**1.4**

Len Foote Hike Inn

Len Foote Hike Inn →

See mile 3.4/5.4. The yellow-blazed trail leads 5.0 miles east to the inn.

Amicalola Lodge →

The Amicalola Lodge and Conference Center, built in 1992, is a 57-room facility featuring a restaurant with panoramic views of the surrounding country. From the paved road crossing the Approach Trail, it is about 0.1 mile uphill to the lodge.

Amicalola Falls →

The 729-foot falls drop from ledge to ledge down the mountain, illustrating the name given to it by the Cherokee Indians, *Um Ma Calo La,* meaning "tumbling (or sliding) waters."

Amicalola Falls Trail Shelter →

This shelter was donated by the "A.T. Gang," a group of hikers in North Georgia. It is maintained by Amicalola Falls State Park.

Amicalola Falls State Park →

The approach trail begins (or ends) behind the visitors center in Amicalola Falls State Park. The park, consisting of 1,020 acres, is one of the most popular in Georgia and boasts the highest waterfall east of the Mississippi River. The park was established in the early 1940s. A lake, which was formed at that time above the falls, was drained in the late 1970s. From its beginning at Mt. Oglethorpe, the A.T. entered the area of the park from the west along Amicalola Ridge, passed above the falls, and continued along what is now USFS 46 as far as Frosty Mountain. The first shelter on the Georgia Trail was built in 1931 along Amicalola Creek, about 0.5 mile north of the falls.

N-S

TRAIL DESCRIPTION

7.6   Cross paved road leading east to **Amicalola Lodge**.   **1.2**

7.7   Junction with wide trail leading east to **Amicalola Lodge**   **1.1**
and west several yards to Hike Inn parking lot. ■ SOUTH-
BOUND hikers cross Len Foote Hike Inn parking lot at top
of Amicalola Falls, descend 604 steps to base of falls, and
pass through picnic area to visitors center just beyond
Amicalola Falls Trail Shelter.

8.8   Visitors center at **Amicalola Falls State Park** (elev. 1,700   **0.0**
feet) and terminus of A.T. Approach Trail. ■ NORTHBOUND
hikers take trail behind visitors center, pass to left of
shelter, walk through picnic-shelters area, ascend 604
steps to top of Amicalola Falls, and cross Len Foote Hike
Inn parking lot before continuing ascent.

Amicalola Falls steps

S-N

Day Hikes and Loop Hikes

Between Davenport Gap and Springer Mountain, the Trail offers hikers a wealth of day-hikes and loop hikes of varying lengths. The following list is only a small selection. For detailed descriptions of trails other than the A.T., contact the district offices of the national forests and parks (see page 19 for World Wide Web sites) or local hiking guidebooks.

Great Smoky Mountains National Park

Note: *The ridges of the Great Smokies are the highest of the Trail, and most hikes start at the foot of the ridge and ascend to the top. Hiking up from most trailheads means an ascent of 2,000-plus feet. Prepare accordingly.*

SECTION 1

Mt. Cammerer Loop—This strenuous, 17-mile loop hike requires two days for most hikers to complete, which means getting an overnight permit from park rangers. Park at the Big Creek Ranger Station near Davenport Gap. Follow the Chestnut Branch Trail 2.0 miles to the A.T. (page 43), turning left and following the white blazes along the ridge for 6.1 miles, ascending Mt. Cammerer, passing Low Gap, to the Cosby Knob Shelter (page 45). Hikers planning an overnight may wish to camp here. From Cosby Knob Shelter, return along the A.T. 0.7 mile to Low Gap (page 43), and turn right (east) on the Low Gap Trail. Low Gap Trail descends 2.5 miles to Lower Walnut Bottoms Campsite at Big Creek. From there, turn left, and follow the Big Creek Trail 5.2 miles down to the parking area at Big Creek Picnic Area. From there, it is another 0.5 mile to Big Creek Ranger Station.

Charlies Bunion Day-hike—A popular, but strenuous, 8.0-mile out-and-back day-hike to the scenic "Bunion" leads from the parking area at Newfound Gap (page 57), past the Boulevard Trail and Icewater Spring Shelter to the short loop trail around Charlies Bunion and Fodder Stack (page 55). This day-hike requires a steep ascent of about 1,000 feet out of Newfound Gap.

Rocky Top Loop—This strenuous 14.7-mile loop leads up to the Trail from scenic Cades Cove and back down again. The 3,500-foot ascent to Rocky Top takes so much out of many hikers that an overnight hike is advisable. As with all overnight trips in the Smokies, it requires that you get a permit in advance. From the parking area in Cades Cove, ascend following the Anthony Creek Trail 1.3 miles to the Russell Field Trail. Turn right, and ascend 3.5 miles to the intersection with the A.T. near Russell Field Shelter, on the open ridgeline of the Smokies (page 73). Turn right, and follow the A.T. north 2.5 miles to the point where the Eagle Creek and Bote Mountain trails intersect with the A.T., near Spence Field Shelter, a good spot to spend the night. From Spence Field (page 71), ascend 1.2 miles to the summit of Rocky Top (page 71), with good views, and return the way you came to the intersection near the shelter. Turn right, and descend 1.7 miles on the Bote Mountain Trail to the Anthony Creek Trail. Turn left, and descend 3.2 miles to the trailhead.

Shuckstack Day-hike—This up-and-back 8-mile day-hike offers a strenuous 2,280-foot climb to a marvelous view from the old fire tower on Shuckstack Mountain. Park in the lot near Fontana Dam (page 83), and follow the white blazes north from the valley of the Little Tennessee River to a viewpoint on Shuckstack that reveals the high ridge of the Smokies, rising to the A.T.'s high point at Clingmans Dome, and the impoundment of the Tennessee Valley Authority's Fontana Lake, filling the river valley.

Nantahala National Forest

Note: Be aware that ascents and descents at Nantahala Gorge, in either direction on the A.T., involve elevation changes of 3,000 feet or more. Plan hikes accordingly, and know your own limits.

SECTION 5

Bartram Trail Loop—Hikers looking for a long loop hike of a week or more may wish to consider combining the A.T. and the Bartram Trail (BT). A 57-mile loop is possible that includes some of the most spectacular sections of the Nantahalas. From Wesser (page 101), climb north out of Nantahala Gorge on the A.T. 8.5 miles to the intersection of the Bartram Trail, near the summit of Cheoah Bald. From there, turn left (west), on the yellow-blazed Bartram Trail, following it 6.5 miles back down into the gorge and crossing the Nantahala Rver near Beechertown. From Beechertown, follow the BT on trails and forest roads up Rattlesnake Knob and along the slopes above the Nantahala Gorge, 11.5 miles to Appletree Campground, near the river. From there, follow the BT another 6.0 miles to Nantahala Lake. From Nantahala Lake, follow the BT east 7.4 miles, ascending to Wayah Bald, where it rejoins the A.T. From there, follow the A.T. north to Wesser (Sections Six and Seven), to complete the loop. The yellow-blazed BT is not as well-marked as the A.T. and includes several road sections. For a guide and maps, contact the N.C. Bartram Trail Society, P. O. Box 144, Scaly Mountain, NC 28775; <info@ncbartramtrail.org>.

SECTION 6

Wesser Bald Loop—A 13.5-mile loop hike is possible by combining the A.T. and the Wesser Creek Trail, for an overnight or a very challenging one-day. From Wesser (page 105), roadwalk along U.S. 19 east 0.9 mile to Wesser Creek Road. Before 1981, the A.T. was routed along the highway here, but it was relocated because of dangerous traffic, so be careful, or arrange for a ride to skip the road-walk. Turn right on Wesser Road, and continue 1.7 miles along the road until you reach a parking area and the beginning of a graded trail, blazed blue, which was the A.T. until the 1980s. After 0.4 mile, reach Wesser Creek. After another 1.3 miles, leave the creek, and ascend steeply toward Wesser Bald, reaching the A.T. in 1.9 miles. From there, it is 0.8 mile south to the lookout tower on Wesser Bald, with fine views of the Nantahala Gorge and the Smokies. From the lookout, follow the A.T. north 6.5 miles, descending past two Trail shelters, to Wesser.

SECTION 8

Siler Bald Day-hikes—A strenuous 3.8-mile, 800-foot, up-and-back day-hike to the open summit of Siler Bald is possible from Wayah Gap (page 119), and a longer, 8.6-mile, 1,130-foot, up-and-back hike is possible to the bald from Winding Stair Gap (page 121).

SECTION 9

Standing Indian Loops—Several popular loop hikes are possible using the A.T. and side trails from Standing Indian Campground (page 125), which is in the middle of a broad bowl of mountains, the rim of which the A.T. follows. A two- or three-day, 24-mile loop is possible starting from the campground and ascending on the Kimsey Creek Trail, 3.7 miles to Deep Gap (page 133). From there, turn left on the A.T., and follow it north, reaching the summit of Standing Indian Mountain in 2.4 miles, an ascent of 2,103 feet from the campground. Carter Gap Shelter is 6.1 miles farther. Follow the A.T. north for 9.6 miles, including the steep climb up Albert Mountain to its lookout tower, passing Big Spring Shelter, to Glassmine Gap. Turn left (west) off the Trail, following the Long Branch Trail 2.0 miles to the campground. Some prefer to start at Deep Gap.

Chattahoochee National Forest

SECTION 12

Rocky Mountain Loop—From Indian Grave Gap (page 161), a popular short loop is to take the A.T. south 1.7 miles, passing the summit of Rocky Mountain, to the intersection of the Rocky Mountain Trail. From there, turn right, and descend 1.0 mile to USFS 283. Turn right, and follow the road 0.8 mile back up to Indian Grave Gap, for a moderate 3.5-mile loop.

SECTION 14

Wolf Laurel Top Day-hike—From the parking area in Tesnatee Gap (page 177), a 4.2-mile, up-and-back day-hike south on the A.T. takes you along scenic cliffs on Cowrock Mountain to a good view from Wolf Laurel Top. Although none of the climbs are more than 600 feet, there are several of them, and they're steep, which can make for a strenuous walk.

SECTION 15

Blood Mountain Loop—Blood Mountain is among the most-visited spots on the southern Trail, so we hesitate to recommend it. But, since you're probably planning to go anyway, consider the following 6.4-mile loop, which can be hiked in a day or as an overnight. From the parking area at the Byron Reece Memorial on U.S. 76, follow the blue-blazed trail south 1.0 mile to the A.T. at Flatrock Gap (page 187). From there, turn right onto the A.T. and ascend to the south 1.4 miles to the rocky summit of Blood Mountain, a 1,400-foot climb from the parking lot. Descend for 1.2 miles on the south side of Blood Mountain, passing designated campsites, to Bird Gap, near the Woods Hole Shelter. At Bird Gap, turn left (east) onto the blue-blazed Freeman Trail, which skirts Blood Mountain for 1.8 miles, rejoining the A.T. at Flatrock Gap. Return on the blue-blazed trail.

Big Cedar Mountain Day-hike—An alternative to the crowds at Blood Mountain is a 2.0-mile, up-and-back day-hike from Woody Gap (page 193). Follow the A.T. north from the gap to "Preaching Rock," a rocky section with good views, 1.0 mile north of the gap, and return.

SECTION 17

Springer Mountain loops—Although not the most spectacular vista, the southern terminus of the Appalachian Trail draws visitors like a magnet and offers a good view to the west. It is also the terminus for the Benton MacKaye Trail (BMT). Two easy loops are possible, one of 4.4 miles and one of 10.0 miles. Begin at Big Stamp Gap, east of the A.T., on USFS 42, and hike south on the BMT, which is marked with white diamond blazes, ascending 1.7 miles to the BMT's southern terminus, at the A.T. just north of the Springer Mountain summit (page 211). Turn left (south) on the A.T., and continue 0.2 mile to the summit. From the summit, hike north on the A.T. (passing the BMT intersection again) for 1.9 miles to another intersection with the BMT. Hikers wishing to do the shorter loop can turn right on the BMT, returning 1.3 miles to Big Stamp Gap. Or, continue on the A.T. for another 3.2 miles, passing the Stover Creek Shelter, then a BMT intersection to the right, until the BMT intersects once more on the right. Turn right on the BMT, and follow it back 4.2 miles to Big Stamp Gap.

Extended Hikes in Alabama, Georgia & North Carolina

Benton MacKaye Trail (BMT)—The BMT, which weaves in and out of Section 17, is a footpath of nearly 300 miles that reconnects with the A.T., and terminates, at Davenport Gap, the northern end of the Trail covered in this guidebook. It passes through some of the most remote backcountry of the three states covered here, crossing eight congressionally designated wilderness areas or areas under study by the Forest Service for such designation. This trail sprang from the desire of several longtime ATC and GATC members to open for hiking Benton MacKaye's originally proposed route for the southern end of the Trail (the western arm of the Blue Ridge), a route soon tagged as impracticable or undesirable in the 1920s. It officially opened as a whole in July 2005, the 25th anniversary of the Benton MacKaye Trail Association, a volunteer, non-profit organization. For detailed information, maps, and a BMT data book, contact the association at P.O. Box 53271, Atlanta, GA 30355, or visit <www.bmta.org>.

Pinhoti Trail—A national recreation trail, the Pinhoti also stems from an early Benton MacKaye proposal: his suggestion at the founding meeting of the ATC in 1925 for a number of extensions off a North Carolina-to-New Hampshire Appalachian Trail "trunk." The Pinhoti Trail intersects the Benton MacKaye Trail 69.4 miles northwest of Springer Mountain and leads southwestward for 320 miles to Bull Gap on Rebecca Mountain in Alabama's Talladega National Forest, southeast of Birmingham. From north to south, it passes such features as the Mountaintown Creek Roadless Area, Civil War fortifications on Rocky Face Mountain, Keown Falls on Johns Mountain, the historic trail town of Cave Spring in Georgia, the 9,200-acre Dugger Mountain Wilderness in Alabama, Cheaha State Park (the location of Mt. Cheaha, Alabama's highest point), the 7,490-acre Cheaha Wilderness, and virgin stands of mountaintop longleaf pine. It officially opened in early 2008. Further information, including trail-route descriptions, can be found on the Internet at <www.pinhotitrailalliance.org>.

Eastern Continental Trail—An informal route of 4,400 miles (including 600 along roads) that connects the Florida, Pinhoti, Benton MacKaye, Appalachian, and International Appalachian trails.

Great Eastern Trail—A work in progress (linking existing trails west of the A.T. from Alabama to the Finger Lakes Trail in New York) of the Great Eastern Trail Association, itself a network of the American Hiking Society and numerous other trail groups. For more information, visit <www.greateasterntrail.org>.

Questions and Answers about the Appalachian Trail

Preparation

What should I carry?

The A.T. is enjoyable to hike, but inexperienced hikers—even those just out for an hour or two—can quickly find themselves deep in the woods, on steep terrain, and in wet, chilly conditions. Carrying a basic "kit" helps hikers cope with such situations.

Packing for a day-hike is relatively simple:

> Map and compass (learn to use them first!)
> Water (at least 2–3 quarts)
> Warm clothing and rain gear
> Food (including extra high-energy snacks)
> Trowel (to bury human waste) and toilet paper
> First-aid kit, with blister treatments
> Whistle (three blasts is the international signal for help)
> Garbage bag (to carry out trash)

On longer hikes, especially in remote or rugged terrain, add:

> Flashlight (with extra batteries and bulb)
> Heavy-duty garbage bag (emergency shelter or to insulate
>   a hypothermia victim)
> Sharp knife
> Fire starter (a candle, for instance) and waterproof matches

If you're backpacking and plan to camp out, we suggest you consult a good "how-to" book for details about what to carry or talk to an experienced hiker. Although we don't have room here to discuss gear in detail, most A.T. backpackers carry the following items, in addition to the day-hike checklist. Some of the items can be shared with a partner to lighten the load:

Shelter (a tent or tarp)
Lightweight pot, cooking utensils
Stove (a small backpacking model, with fuel)
Medium-sized backpack (big "expedition-size" packs
    are usually overkill)
A pack cover or plastic bag (to keep gear dry in rainy weather)
Sleeping pad (to insulate you from the cold ground)
Sleeping bag of appropriate warmth for the season
Food and clothing
Rope or cord (to hang your food at night)
Water filter, iodine tablets, or another method of treating water

Where can I park?

Park in designated areas. Many of them will be indicated in the Trailhead entries for this guidebook and may be marked on Trail maps. If you leave your car overnight unattended, however, you risk theft or vandalism. Many hikers avoid this worry by arranging for a "shuttle" (check <www.appalachiantrail.org> for a list) to drop them off at a Trailhead or arranging to leave their car in the parking lot of a business located near the Trail; ask first, and offer to pay a little something to the business. Some sections of the Trail are served by public transportation. If you decide to park at a Trailhead, hide your property and valuables from sight, or, better yet, leave them at home, so they do not inspire a thief to break in and steal them.

Using the Trail

Where and how do I find water?

Year-round natural water sources are listed in this guidebook; springs and streams are marked on most official A.T. maps. Most (although not all) shelters are near a year-round water source. Some springs and streams dry up during late summer and early fall.

Is the water safe to drink?

Water in the backcountry and in water sources along the A.T. can be contaminated by microorganisms, including *giardia lamblia* and others that cause diarrhea or stomach problems. We recommend that you treat all water, using a filter or purifier or water-treatment tablets, or by boiling it.

Are there rest rooms?
Many A.T. shelters have privies, but usually you will need to "go in the woods." Proper disposal of human (and pet) waste is not only a courtesy to other hikers, but a vital Leave No Trace practice for maintaining healthy water supplies in the backcountry and an enjoyable hiking experience for others. No one should venture onto the A.T. without a trowel, used for digging a "cathole" 6"–8" deep to bury waste. Bury feces at least two hundred feet or seventy paces away from water, trails, or shelters. Use a stick to mix dirt with your waste, which hastens decomposition and discourages animals from digging it up. Used toilet paper should either be buried in your cathole or carried out in a sealed plastic bag. Hygiene products such as sanitary napkins should always be carried out.

Can I wash up in a mountain stream or spring?
Please don't. Carry water from the water source in a bottle or other container, and then wash your dishes, and yourself, at least 70 paces away from streams, springs, and ponds. Don't leave food scraps to rot in water sources, and don't foul them with products such as detergent, toothpaste, and human or animal waste.

Are bikes allowed on the Trail?
Only where the Appalachian Trail shares the route with the C&O Towpath in Maryland, the Virginia Creeper Trail in the vicinity of Damascus, Virginia, roads in towns, and on certain bridges. They are not permitted on most of the Trail.

Can I bring my dog?
Yes, except where dogs are prohibited (in Great Smoky Mountains National Park, Bear Mountain Zoo, and Baxter State Park). Dogs must be leashed on National Park Service lands and on many state park and forest lands. ATC's Web site, <www.appalachiantrail. org>, offers details about hiking with dogs. Although dogs can be wonderful hiking companions, they can create many problems for other hikers and wildlife if you don't control them. If taken, they should not be allowed to run free; leashing at all times is strongly recommended and the law on 40 percent or more of the Trail. Keep dogs out of springs and shelters and away from other hikers, their food, and their gear. Not all dogs can stand the wear and tear of a long hike.

How about horses, llamas, or other pack stock?

Horses are not allowed on the A.T., except where the Appalachian Trail coincides for about three miles with the C&O Canal Towpath in Maryland and on about 50 percent of the A.T. in the Smokies (where, by law, the route is open for horses as a historical use). Llamas and other pack animals are not allowed on the A.T., which is designed, built, and maintained for foot travel. Pack animals would seriously damage the treadway, discourage volunteer maintenance efforts, and make the Trail experience less enjoyable for other hikers.

Are any fees required to hike the A.T.?

No. However, there are entrance fees to some of the national parks the Trail passes through, as well as parking fees and campsite fees in popular areas, to help pay for maintenance costs.

Health and safety

Is the Trail a safe place?

In general, yes. But, like many other popular recreational activities, hiking on the A.T. is not without risk. Don't let the following discussion of potential dangers alarm you or discourage you from enjoying the Trail, but remember not to leave your common sense and intuition behind when you strap on your backpack. Prepare mentally and emotionally.

In an emergency, how do I get help?

Much of the A.T. is within range of cellular phone systems, although signal reception is sometimes not good in gaps, hollows, and valleys; shelters are often located in such areas of poor reception. Emergency numbers are included in this guidebook and on maps. If you don't have a phone or can't get through, the standard call for distress consists of three short calls, audible or visible, repeated at regular intervals. A whistle is particularly good for audible signals. Visible signals may include, in daytime, light flashed with a mirror or smoke puffs; at night, a flashlight or three small bright fires. Anyone recognizing such a signal should acknowledge with two calls—if possible, by the same method—then go to the distressed person to determine the nature of the emergency. Arrange for additional aid, if necessary.

Most of the A.T. is well-enough traveled that, if you are injured, you can expect to be found. However, if an area is remote and the weather is bad, fewer hikers will be on the Trail, especially after dark. As a rule, keep your pack with you, and, even in an emergency, don't leave marked trails and try to "bushwhack" out—you will be harder to find and are more likely to encounter dangerous terrain. If you must leave the Trail, study the guidebook or map carefully for the nearest place where people are likely to be and attempt to move in that direction. If it is necessary to leave a heavy pack behind, be sure to take essentials, in case your rescue is delayed. In bad weather, a night in the open without proper covering could be fatal.

What's the most dangerous aspect of hiking the A.T.?

Perhaps the most serious dangers are hypothermia (see page 234), a fall on slick rocks and logs, or a sprained or broken limb far from the nearest rescue squad or pay phone. Those are also the best arguments for hiking with a partner, who can get help in an emergency.

What sort of first-aid kit should I pack?

A basic kit to take care of bruises, scrapes, skinned knees, and blisters. The following kit weighs about a pound and occupies about a 3" x 6" x 9" space: eight 4" x 4" gauze pads; four 3" x 4" gauze pads; five 2" bandages; ten 1" bandages; six alcohol prep pads; ten large butterfly closures; one triangular bandage (40"); two 3" rolls of gauze; twenty tablets of aspirin-free pain-killer; one 15' roll of 2" adhesive tape; one 3" Ace bandage; one 3" x 4" moleskin or other blister-care products; three safety pins; one small scissors; one tweezers; personal medications as necessary.

Will I encounter snakes?

Poisonous and nonpoisonous snakes are widespread along the Trail in warm weather, but they will usually be passive. Watch where you step and where you put your hands. Please, don't kill snakes! Some are federally protected under the Endangered Species Act.

What other creatures are problems for people?

Allergic reactions to bee stings can be a problem. Ticks, which carry Lyme disease, are also a risk; always check yourself for ticks daily. Poisonous spiders are sometimes found at shelters and campsites. Mosquitoes and blackflies may plague you in some seasons. Porcupines, skunks, raccoons, and squirrels are quite common and occasionally raid shelters and well-established camping areas after dark, looking for food. Mice are permanent residents at most shelters and may carry diseases.

What about bears?
Black bears live along many parts of the Trail and are particularly common in Georgia, the Shenandoah and Great Smoky Mountains national parks, and parts of Pennsylvania and New Jersey. They are always looking for food. Bears that have lost their fear of humans may "bluff charge" to get you to drop food or a backpack. If you encounter a black bear, it will probably run away. If it does not, back away slowly, watching the bear but not making direct eye contact. Do not run away or play dead. If a bear attacks, fight for all you are worth. The best defense against bears is preparing and storing food properly. Cook and eat your meals away from your tent or shelter, so food odors do not linger. Hang your food, cookware, toothpaste, and personal-hygiene items in a sturdy bag from a strong tree branch at least ten feet off the ground, four feet from the tree and branch, and well away from your campsite.

Is poison ivy common along the A.T.?
Yes. It grows plentifully in the wild, particularly south of New England, and can be an annoyance during hiking season. If you have touched poison ivy, wash immediately with strong soap (but not with one containing added oil). If a rash develops in the next day or so, treat it with calamine lotion or Solarcaine. Do not scratch. If blisters become serious or the rash spreads to the eyes, see a doctor.

Will I catch a disease?
The most common illnesses encountered on the A.T. are water-borne, come from ingesting protozoa (such as *giardia lamblia*), and respond well to antibiotics. But, the Lyme-disease bacterium and other tick-borne illnesses are legitimate concerns, too; mosquito-borne illnesses such as the West Nile virus are less common in Trail states. Cases of rabies have been reported in foxes, raccoons, and other small animals; a bite is a serious concern, although instances of hikers being bitten are rare. One

case of the dangerous rodent-borne disease hantavirus has been reported on the A.T.: Avoid sleeping on mouse droppings (use a mat or tent) or handling mice. Treat your water, and wash your hands.

Will I encounter hazardous weather?

Walking in the open means you will be susceptible to sudden changes in the weather, and traveling on foot means that it may be hard to find shelter quickly. Pay attention to the changing skies. Sudden spells of "off-season" cold weather, hail, and even snow are common along many parts of the Trail. Winter-like weather often occurs in late spring or early fall in the southern Appalachians, Vermont, New Hampshire, and Maine. In the northern Appalachians, it can snow during any month of the year.

What are the most serious weather-related dangers?

Hypothermia, lightning, and heat exhaustion are all legitimate concerns. Don't let the fear of them ruin your hike, but take sensible precautions.

Hypothermia—A cold rain can be the most dangerous weather of all, because it can cause hypothermia (or "exposure") even when conditions are well above freezing. Hypothermia occurs when wind and rain chill the body so that its core temperature drops; death occurs if the condition is not caught in time. Avoid hypothermia by dressing in layers of synthetic clothing, eating well, staying hydrated, and knowing when to hole up in a warm sleeping bag in a tent or shelter. Cotton clothing, such as blue jeans, tends to chill you when it gets wet from rain or sweat; if the weather turns bad, cotton clothes increase your risk of hypothermia. Natural wool and artificial fibers such as nylon, polyester, and polypropylene all do a much better job of insulation in cold, wet weather. Remember that, when the wind blows, its "chill" effect can make you much colder than the temperature would lead you to suspect, especially if you're sweaty or wet.

Lightning—The odds of being struck by lightning are low, but an open ridge is no place to be during a thunderstorm. If a storm is coming, immediately leave exposed areas. Boulders, rocky overhangs, and shallow caves offer no protection from lightning, which may actually flow through

TEMPERATURE (¼F)

	40	35	30	25	20	15	10	5	0	-5	-10	-15	-20	-25	-30	-35	-40	-45
5	36	31	25	19	13	7	1	-5	-11	-16	-22	-28	-34	-40	-46	-52	-57	-63
10	34	27	21	15	9	3	-4	-10	-16	-22	-28	-35	-41	-47	-53	-59	-66	-72
15	32	25	19	13	6	0	-7	-13	-19	-26	-32	-39	-45	-51	-58	-64	-71	-77
20	30	24	17	11	4	-2	-9	-15	-22	-29	-35	-42	-48	-55	-61	-68	-74	-81
25	29	23	16	9	3	-4	-11	-17	-24	-31	-37	-44	-51	-58	-64	-71	-78	-84
30	28	22	15	8	1	-5	-12	-19	-26	-33	-39	-46	-53	-60	-67	-73	-80	-87
35	28	21	14	7	0	-7	-14	-21	-27	-34	-41	-48	-55	-62	-69	-76	-82	-89
40	27	20	13	6	-1	-8	-15	-22	-29	-36	-43	-50	-57	-64	-71	-78	-84	-91
45	26	19	12	5	-2	-9	-16	-23	-30	-37	-44	-51	-58	-65	-72	-79	-86	-93
50	26	19	12	4	-3	-10	-17	-24	-31	-38	-45	-52	-60	-67	-74	-81	-88	-95
55	25	18	11	4	-3	-11	-18	-25	-32	-39	-46	-54	-61	-68	-75	-82	-89	-97
60	25	17	10	3	-4	-11	-19	-26	-33	-40	-48	-55	-62	-69	-76	-84	-91	-98

(Left axis: **WIND (mph)**)

30 min. 10 min. 5 minutes

FROSTBITE TIMES

Wind Chill (¼F) = 35.74 + 0.6215T - 35.75($V^{0.16}$) + 0.4275T($V^{0.16}$)
Where, T= Air Temperature (¼F) V= Wind Speed (mph)
National Weather Service and National Oceanic and Atmospheric Administration
Effective 11/01/01

them along the ground after a strike. Tents and convertible automobiles are no good, either. Sheltering in hard-roofed automobiles or large buildings is best, although they are rarely available to the hiker. Avoid tall structures, such as ski lifts, flagpoles, powerline towers, and the tallest trees, solitary rocks, or open hilltops. If you cannot enter a building or car, take shelter in a stand of smaller trees or in the forest. Avoid clearings. If caught in the open, crouch down on your pack or pad, or roll into a ball. If you are in water, get out. Disperse groups, so that not everyone is struck by a single bolt. Do not hold a potential lightning rod, such as a fishing pole or metal hiking pole.

Dehydration—Dry, hot summers are common along the Trail, particularly in the Virginias and the mid-Atlantic. Water may be scarce on humid days, sweat does not evaporate well, and many hikers face the danger of heat stroke and heat exhaustion if they haven't taken proper precautions, such as drinking lots of water. Learn how to protect yourself from heat exhaustion. Dehydration also is common in winter, when sweating may not be as obvious. Drink lots of water all year!

Is crime a problem?

The Appalachian Trail is safer than most places, but a few crimes of violence have occurred. Awareness is one of your best lines of defense. Be aware of what you are doing, where you are, and to whom you are talking. Hikers looking out for each other can be an effective "community watch." Be prudent and cautious without allowing common sense to slip into paranoia. Remember to trust your gut—it's usually right. Other tips include the following:

- Don't hike alone. If you are by yourself and encounter a stranger who makes you feel uncomfortable, say you are with a group that is behind you. Be creative. If in doubt, move on. Even a partner is no guarantee of safety, however; pay attention to your instincts about other people.

- Leave your hiking itinerary and timetable with someone at home, but *don't* post it on an on-line Trail journal. Be sure your contacts and your family know your "Trail name," if you use one of those fanciful aliases common on the A.T. Check in regularly, and establish a procedure to follow if you fail to check in. On short hikes, provide your contacts with the numbers of the land-managing agencies for the area of your hike. On extended hikes, provide ATC's number, (304) 535-6331.

- Be wary of strangers. Be friendly, but cautious. Don't tell strangers your plans (and don't post them in real time on the Internet). Avoid people who act suspiciously, seem hostile, or are intoxicated.

- Don't camp near roads.

- Dress conservatively to avoid unwanted attention.

- Don't carry firearms. They are prohibited on National Park Service lands and in most other areas without a permit, they could be turned against you or result in an accidental shooting, and they are extra weight.

- Eliminate opportunities for theft. Don't bring jewelry. Hide your money. If you must leave your pack, hide it, or leave it with someone trustworthy. Don't leave valuables or equipment (especially in sight) in vehicles parked at Trailheads.

- Use the Trail registers (the notebooks stored at most shelters). Sign in using your given name, leave a note, and report any suspicious activities. If someone needs to locate you, or if a serious crime has been committed along the Trail, the first place authorities will look is in the registers.

- Report any crime or harassment to the local authorities and ATC.

Trail history

Who was Benton MacKaye, and what was his connection to the Appalachian Trail?

He first published the idea. MacKaye (1879–1975) grew up mostly in Shirley Center, Massachusetts, reading the work of American naturalists and poets and taking long walks in the mountains of Massachusetts and Vermont. MacKaye (which is pronounced like "sky") sometimes claimed that the idea for the A.T. was born one day when he was sitting in a tree atop Stratton Mountain in Vermont. After graduating from Harvard, he eventually went to work in the new U.S. Forest Service and began carving out a niche as a profound thinker and an advocate for wilderness. By 1919, his radical ideas had led to him being edged out of the government, and he turned his attention to creating a new discipline that later came to be called "regional planning." His initial 1921 "project in regional planning" was a proposal for a network of work camps and communities in the mountains, all linked by a trail that ran from the highest point in New England to the highest point in the South. He called it "an Appalachian Trail."

Why did he propose it?

MacKaye was convinced that the pace of urban and industrial life along the East Coast was harmful to people. He envisioned the A.T. as a path interspersed with planned wilderness communities where people could go to renew themselves. That idea never gained much traction, but the notion of a two-thousand-mile footpath in the mountains fired the imaginations of hikers and outdoorsmen from Maine to Georgia. Inspired by him, they began building trails and trying to connect them.

What was his connection to the Appalachian Trail Conference?

MacKaye was responsible for convening and organizing the first Appalachian Trail "conference" in Washington, D.C., in 1925. That gathering of hikers, foresters, and public officials embraced the goal of building the Trail. They established the Appalachian Trail Conference, appointed MacKaye as its "field organizer," and named Major William Welch, manager of New York's Harriman Park, as its first chairman.

What happened next?

Some perfunctory scouting of routes took place. A few short sections were marked and connected. New trails were built in New York. Welch designed a logo and Trail markers. Committees met in a few northeastern states and talked about the idea. But, for several years, the idea didn't really go anywhere. MacKaye was much better at inspirational abstract thinking than practical organizing, and it soon became apparent that someone else was going to have to take the lead for the Trail to actually get built.

Who pushed the project forward?

Two men, retired Judge Arthur Perkins of Connecticut and admiralty lawyer Myron Avery of Washington, D.C. Perkins took the idea and ran with it, essentially appointing himself as the acting chairman of ATC in the late 1920s and recruiting Avery to lead the effort in the area around Washington. Both began vigorously proselytizing the idea of the Trail in 1928 and 1929, championing MacKaye's ideas to recruit volunteers, establishing hiking clubs up and down the coast, and actually going out to hike, clear brush, and mark paths themselves. As Perkins' health failed in the early 1930s, Avery took over, devoting incredible time, energy, and willpower to establishing a network of volunteers, developing clubs, working with the government, building the organization of the ATC, and setting the Trail's northern terminus at Katahdin in his native Maine. Avery remained chairman of ATC until 1952.

What was the relationship between MacKaye and Myron Avery?
They were cordial at first, but, by the mid-1930s, as Avery took charge of the Trail project, they quarreled over fundamental issues and visions of what the Trail should be. Avery was more interested in hiking and in connecting the sections of the Trail, while MacKaye was more interested in the Trail's role in promoting wilderness protection.

When was the Trail completed?
In 1937. It fell into disrepair during World War II, when Trail maintainers were unable to work on it, and parts of the route were lost. After the war, a concerted effort was made to restore it, and it was once again declared complete in 1951.

What happened after it was completed?
It's useful to look at the Trail's history in three eras: the era of Trail-building, which lasted until the Trail was completed in 1937; the era of Trail protection, which lasted until 1968, when Congress made the A.T. a national scenic trail; and the era of management and promotion, which has lasted until the present day. The first era was dominated by personalities and focused on getting the thing built and blazed from one end to the other. The second era saw the beginning of growth of the clubs taking care of it and the Conference, the construction of shelters, and a continuing battle to keep the route open over the many hundreds of miles of private property that it crossed. The third era saw an explosion of the number of people hiking the A.T. as the government began buying land along the route to guarantee the permanence of the footpath and volunteers shifted their emphasis to the hard work of managing a part of the national park system. In July 2005, the Conference became the A.T. Conservancy, to better express its work of protecting Trail resources.

How was the original Trail different from today's A.T.?
At first, the goal was simply to blaze a connected route. Often, this meant that the Trail led along old forest roads and other trails. Trail maintainers mostly just cleared brush and painted blazes. Today's Trail has mostly been moved off the old roads and onto new paths dug and reinforced especially for hikers. Today's route, although engineered much more

elaborately, often requires more climbing, because it leads up the sides of many mountains that the old woods roads bypassed.

How do terms like "Trailway," "greenway," "buffer," and "viewshed" fit into this history?

The idea of a "Trailway" was first embraced by ATC in 1937. It meant that there was more to the Appalachian Trail than just the footpath. The "Trailway" referred to an area dedicated to the interests of those on foot, originally a mile on either side. In some cases, that came to mean a "buffer"—a legally protected area around the path that kept the sights and sounds of civilization, logging, and development away from the solitary hiker. In other cases, it meant a great deal more. It evolved into a notion of a "greenway," a broad swath of protected land through which the Trail ran. Crucial to the idea of a greenway was that of the "viewshed," the countryside visible from the Trail's high points. In the years since the A.T. became a national scenic trail, the Conservancy has worked to influence the development of surrounding areas so that the views from the Trail remain scenic, even when those views are of areas well outside the boundaries of the public Trail lands themselves.

When did Trail protection begin?

The notion of a protected zone was first formalized in an October 15, 1938, agreement between the National Park Service and the U.S. Forest Service for the promotion of an Appalachian Trailway through the relevant national parks and forests, extending one mile on each side of the Trail. Within this zone, no new parallel roads would be built or any other incompatible development allowed. Timber cutting would not be permitted within 200 feet of the Trail. Similar agreements, creating a zone one-quarter-mile in width, were signed with most states through which the Trail passes.

How were Trail lands identified?

Much of the Trail was already in national forests or national parks and state and local parks, but large portions were on private property, with the agreement of the property owners. In 1970, supplemental agreements under the 1968 National Trails Systems Act—among the National Park Service, the U.S. Forest Service, and the Appalachian Trail Conservancy—established the specific responsibilities of those organizations for initial mapping, selection of rights-of-way, relocations, maintenance, development, acquisition of land, and protection of a permanent Trail. Agreements also were signed between the Park Service and the various states, encouraging them to acquire and protect a right-of-way.

Why has complete protection taken so long?

Getting federal money appropriated was difficult, and not all property owners were willing to sell, which occasionally raised the specter of the government's threatening to condemn land for the Trail—always a politically unpopular action. Slow progress of federal efforts and lack of initiative by some states led Congress to strengthen the National Trails System Act in an amendment known as the Appalachian Trail Bill, which was signed by President Jimmy Carter on March 21, 1978. The new legislation emphasized the need for protecting the Trail, including acquiring a corridor, and authorized $90 million for that purpose. More money was appropriated during the Reagan, Bush, and Clinton administrations. Today, more than 99 percent of the Trail runs across public lands.

What is the relationship between the A.T. and the government, the Conservancy, and the clubs?

In 1984, the Interior Department delegated the responsibility for managing the A.T. corridor lands outside established parks and forests to the ATC. The Conservancy and its affiliated clubs retain primary responsibility for maintaining the footpath, too. A more comprehensive, 10-year agreement was signed in 1994 and renewed in November 2004.

Trail geology

Lynn S. Fichter, Professor, Department of Geology and Environmental Science, James Madison University

Why aren't the Appalachians as high as other American mountain systems?

In a word: erosion. The modern Appalachians are not even true "mountains" in the geologic sense, but the incompletely eroded remnants of an ancient, 30,000-foot-high mountain range, the Alleghanian, that formed about 300 million years ago. In contrast, the modern Appalachians are from 3,000 to 6,000 feet high. During the continental collision that formed the Alleghanian mountains, the ancient rocks we know as today's Appalachians were folded and faulted while deep underground.

So, what are we seeing when we look at today's Appalachians?
We see five geologic divisions (called *provinces*) that run roughly parallel to the Atlantic coast. Each province contains rocks that formed at different times in geologic history. They are, from east to west, the coastal plain, Piedmont, Blue Ridge, Ridge and Valley Province, and Allegheny Plateau.

What caused them to form?
The Appalachian rocks you see on and from the Trail are the result of the opening and closing of ocean basins. In the opening phase, a huge land mass called a supercontinent rifts into continent-sized fragments. As the continents spread apart, an ocean basin opens. The land and undersea areas along the edges of the new continent are called *divergent continental margins* (DCMs). Today's Atlantic seaboard is just such a margin, while the great valleys west of the Trail contain the remnants of an ancient DCM that formed about 500 million years ago.

What happens when an ocean basin starts to close?
When an ocean basin begins to close, and continents converge together, *subduction zones* form in the basin, where one part of the ocean floor is forced under another part, or under a continental plate, forming mountains. Such a zone under the edge of a continent builds mountains like today's Andes, at the ocean's edge. Such a zone in midocean forms a *volcanic arc* of islands, like those of modern-day Japan. As the ocean basin continues to close, eventually the volcanic arc collides with a continent, building more mountains. Finally, mountains build when the ocean basin closes completely and two continental plates collide, creating the next supercontinent.

What are the geologic events recorded in the Appalachians?
The Appalachian mountains give us a geological record stretching back 1.8 billion years and containing the closing half of one cycle, which built

an ancient supercontinent (called "Rodinia"), then a full cycle that built a more recent supercontinent ("Pangaea"), and finally the opening half of a third cycle that has produced the modern-day Atlantic seaboard.

What was the first Appalachian mountain-building event?

The *Grenville orogeny*, one billion years ago, is the oldest of which we have a geologic record. The ocean floor was pushed under the North American continent, building Andean-sized mountains, followed by the continent-to-continent collision that created the Rodinia supercontinent. On the Trail, you spend much of your time crossing rocks formed during the Grenville orogeny (mountain-building event).

What were the other mountain-building events?

For half a billion years, eastern North America lay in the center of a supercontinent. But, about 600 million years ago, that continent rifted apart to form what geologists call the "proto-Atlantic" (or Iapitus) ocean and a divergent continental margin. The rocks left over from that are preserved today in the great valleys west of the Trail. During the closing phase of the cycle, there were three more orogenies: the *Taconic* (a volcanic arc collision), the *Acadian* (a volcanic arc/microcontinent collision), and the *Alleghanian* (when what is now Africa collided with eastern North America, closed the proto-Atlantic, and formed Pangaea). The modern Atlantic Ocean and its present-day divergent continental margin began forming 200 million years ago.

How high were the ancient mountains?

During the Grenville and Alleghanian orogenies, Andean- and Himalayan-sized mountains formed. During the smaller Taconic and Acadian orogenies, mountains formed that were the size of today's Alps or Rockies—14,000 to 15,000 feet high.

How are each the five Appalachian provinces different?

- The *coastal plain* is the newest and youngest. There are no mountain-built structures or rocks here, just sediment brought down to the coast from inland. The A.T. never descends to the coastal plain.

- The *Piedmont* is mostly "exotic," meaning that it contains volcanic arcs and fragments of ocean floor brought to North America from other places in the world. They are severely deformed, metamorphosed, and eroded down to their deep roots. The Trail in New Hampshire and Maine is actually part of this region, although it crosses some of the Trail's highest mountains that might not appear at first to fit the definition of "piedmont" (foothills).

- The *Blue Ridge* contains the eroded roots of the Grenville mountains, which once covered the eastern part of the continent from Texas to Quebec. Long sections of the Trail follow the Blue Ridge.

- The *Ridge and Valley Province* is made of folded and faulted sedimentary rocks and contains rocks from the proto-Atlantic, as well as sediments eroded from the Taconic and Acadian mountains. The Trail in the mid-Atlantic enters this province.

- Finally, farthest west, the *Allegheny Plateau* is made of sedimentary rocks and contains virtually a complete sedimentary record of everything since the proto-Atlantic began forming.

Why does so much of the Trail follow the Blue Ridge?

The Blue Ridge acts like a backbone for the Appalachian region and thus for the Trail. Not only is it the central province, its rocks are the oldest and stand the highest, primarily because they are still gently rising. Looking east into the Piedmont, we see the eroded remains of the Taconic and Acadian mountains. Looking west into the Ridge and Valley Province, we see the sediments eroded from those mountains that were deposited in deep basins existing there at the time. All this must be in the geological imagination, of course; none of what we see today resembles the ancient landscapes in topography, vegetation, or climate.

Why are there so many long, folded ridges today?

The modern landscape is largely the result of the Alleghenian orogeny, which folded and faulted all the previous rocks and shuffled them like a deck of cards. Virtually no rocks exposed today are where they originally formed, except for the Allegheny Plateau, west of the A.T. During the Alleghanian orogeny, Africa rode up over the edge of North America, peeled the rocks off in layers thousands of feet thick and shoved them dozens of miles inland from their original locations. The faults and folds all run parallel to each other, and, where they bring soft rocks to the surface, erosion is easy and valleys form. The ridges are made of more erosion-resistant rocks.

What rocks are those divisions made of?

In places in Virginia, core rocks are overlain by 600-million-year-old basalt lava flows (dark green) ejected when the proto-Atlantic ocean opened. In the Smokies, many of the rocks began as sedimentary rocks of about the same age as the lava flows, moved westward from the Piedmont regions during the Alleghanian orogeny, and metamorphosed by heat and pressure. East of the Blue Ridge, and in northern New England, the rocks are all igneous and metamorphic. They include lava flows associated with several ancient volcanic arcs or rocks deposited on the sides of the volcanic arcs. Looking west from the Blue Ridge, the rocks are all sedimentary. The Roanoke Valley, Shenandoah/Page valleys, and the Great Valley of Maryland and Pennsylvania, for example, are underlain largely by limestones of the proto-Atlantic continental margin. The far mountain ridges west of the Shenandoah and Great Valley are mostly sandstones and shales from the Taconic and Acadian orogenies. All of those rocks are *thrust faulted;* that is, they consist of a series of "sheets"—a mile or more thick—that have been shoved over each other and stacked.

Were the Appalachians affected by the Ice Age?

Repeatedly. The Trail's lowest point is just southwest of where it crosses the Hudson River, a scant 124 feet above sea level. Ice Age glaciers carved the Hudson River Valley, the only fjord on the Trail. From the Delaware Water Gap north, you enter glacial country from the Ice Age that ended about 20,000 years ago, and, the farther north you go, the more glacial evidence you can see. New England mountains are typically scraped nearly bare on top, with swampy, fertile valleys where soil was deposited when the ice melted. Large *erratics*, boulders that the glaciers carried miles from the rock formations they were broken away from, appear regularly in this region. *Cirques* carved by growing glaciers, rubble hills (*terminal moraines*) formed where glaciers stopped advancing, and long, gravely mounds (*eskers*) formed by deposits from melting ice are other features. The Trail runs along some rocky ridges where the scratches and scrapes of moving ice are still visible.

Wildlife along the A.T.

How "wild" is the A.T.?

The well-known plaque at Springer Mountain in Georgia describes the A.T. as "a footpath for those who seek fellowship with the wilderness." What does that mean? The Trail will indeed take you deep into some of the wildest and most remote woodlands of the eastern United States. But, true "wilderness," in the sense of untouched wild country, is rare, even on the A.T. Much of the land that the Trail follows was once farmland—even the steep, stony, remote slopes—and nearly all of it has been logged at some time during the last four centuries. Except for bears, bobcats, and coyotes, most large natural predators have been exterminated.

In the twentieth century, much of the formerly settled land was incorporated into state and national parks and forests. On that land, forests and wildlife have returned. As you walk through what seems like primeval wilderness, you're likely to run across old stone walls or abandoned logging roads or the foundations of nineteenth-century homesteads. The federal government has designated some of those areas as protected wilderness areas, which strictly limits the ways in which they can be used. Today, the mountains teem with creatures of all sorts, from microbes to moose. To the casual hiker who knows only the woods of a suburban park, it can seem very wild indeed.

One good way to look at the "wilderness" of the A.T. is as a series of long, skinny islands of wildness, surrounded by a sea of populated valleys inhabited by working farms and suburban communities. In the vast national forests of the South and the spreading timberlands of northern New England, those "islands" are somewhat broader. But, even in its wildest places, the A.T. hiker is rarely more than a strenuous day's walk from the nearest highway or community.

What large animals might I see?

Moose, the largest animal that hikers encounter along the Trail (often weighing in at more than 1,000 pounds), inhabit deep woodlands and wetlands from Massachusetts north, especially in New Hampshire and

Maine. White-tailed deer can be found along the entire length of the Trail. Elk have been reintroduced to Pennsylvania, North Carolina, and Tennessee. Black bears have been spotted in all Trail states and are especially common in Georgia, North Carolina, Tennessee, Virginia, Pennsylvania, and New Jersey. Wild boars live in the Great Smoky Mountains National Park. Bobcats and coyotes are stealthy residents along most of the route of the Trail, although they're rarely seen. Fishers, otters, and beavers are occasionally reported by hikers.

What small animals might I see?

By far the most familiar will be mice, chipmunks, rabbits, and squirrels, but foxes, raccoons, opossums, skunks, groundhogs, porcupines, bats, weasels, shrews, minks, and muskrats are also common. Tree frogs and bullfrogs inhabit wet areas in warm weather, lizards scurry along rocks and fallen logs, snakes (both venomous and not) are common south of New England, and streams and ponds are home to salamanders, bass, trout, bream, sunfish, and crayfish.

Which animals are dangerous?

Few A.T. hikers encounter aggressive animals, but any wild animal will fight if cornered or handled roughly—even timid animals such as deer can be quite dangerous in those circumstances. The large wild animals most likely to be aggressive include moose (during rutting season) and black bears (especially mother bears with cubs). Mountain lions, which have stalked people in western states, have long been rumored to have returned to the Appalachians, but so far scientists have not been able to confirm any sightings in mountains that the A.T. traverses.

When disturbed or stepped on, many other creatures will strike back aggressively, inflicting painful wounds or poisonous stings. Those include timber rattlesnakes and copperheads, hornets, wasps, yellow jackets, Africanized bees, and black widow and brown recluse spiders. Foxes, bats, raccoons, and other small animals susceptible to rabies may bite when suffering from infection. Mice, although not aggressive, may transmit diseases, and biting insects such as mosquitoes and ticks can infect hikers with bacteria. Hikers in more populated sections of the Trail also might encounter aggressive dogs.

What rare or endangered animal species might I see?

Birders might spot rare species such as the Bicknell's thrush, hermit thrush, gray-cheeked thrush, northern raven, olive-sided flycatcher, black-billed cuckoo, spruce grouse, bay-breasted warbler, cerulean warbler, blackburnian warbler, magnolia warbler, blackpoll warbler, alder flycatcher, rusty blackbird, Swainson's warbler, yellow-bellied sapsucker, winter wren, redbreasted nuthatch, sharp-shinned hawk, northern saw-whet owl, golden eagle, peregrine falcon, merlin, bald eagle, and Cooper's hawk.

Harder to find, but also present, are the Carolina northern flying squirrel, Virginia northern flying squirrel, rock vole, Allegheny wood rat, eastern wood rat, water shrew, and fence lizard. The black bear and eastern timber rattlesnake, although not uncommon along the Trail, are on the rare-species list. You may also find a number of rare crustaceans, reptiles, and amphibians, including the zig-zag salamander, northern cricket frog, triangle floater mussel, Jefferson salamander, Appalachian brook crayfish, wood turtle, broadhead skink, pigmy salamander, shovelnose salamander, Shenandoah salamander, Weller's salamander, and squawfoot mussel.

What birds will I see in the Appalachians that I might not see at my backyard feeder?

Birds with summer ranges normally far to the north of where most A.T. hikers live are often found in the mountains, where the altitude makes the climate resemble that of Canada. Insect-eating birds such as whippoorwills, flycatchers, and swallows rarely show up in backyards but are common along the Trail. The songs of deep-woods birds such as the ovenbird, kinglet, veery, pewee, and red-eyed vireo will provide an ongoing chorus for summer hikers. Pileated woodpeckers hammer deliberately on dead trees. Large game birds, such as wild turkey, ruffed grouse, and spruce grouse, forage on the forest floor and surprise hikers as they burst into flight. Many hikers linger to admire the soaring acrobatics of ravens, vultures, hawks, eagles, and falcons on the thermals and updrafts along the rocky crests of the mountains.

Trees and wild plants along the A.T.

How old are the Appalachian forests?

The forests of the Appalachians have been logged heavily for more than three centuries. Photographs from the late nineteenth and early twentieth centuries show many areas almost completely stripped of trees. Many Trail areas were open farmland or pastureland in the 1700s and early 1800s. Lumber is still harvested in national forests and privately owned timberlands along the Trail. Although today's mountains are heavily forested again, it is mostly "second-growth" timber, except in a few isolated coves of "old-growth" forest that date back to precolonial times.

Forest that has grown back from burning or clearing through successive stages to the point at which it reaches a fairly steady state, with dominant full-grown trees, is known as a "climax forest." Several different climax forests appear along the A.T., and they are not mutually exclusive—different types can be found on the same mountain. The kind you encounter will depend on where you are, on what type of soil is underfoot, and the climate. The climate often depends on how high the mountains are—the higher they are, the more "northern" (or boreal) the climate.

What kinds of forests will I encounter along the Trail?

- The *mixed deciduous forest* (also called the *southern hardwood forest*) dominates the foothills of the southern mountains and Trail lands south of New England. Various kinds of broad-leafed trees are dominant, and the understory of small trees and shrubs is profuse. Oak and hickory are the most common large trees, with maple and beech evident in more northerly sections; some sproutings of chestnut (a species that dominated until a blight devastated it early in the twentieth century) can be found as well. Understory trees such as redbud, dogwood, striped maple, and American holly are common, as are shrubs such as witch hazel, pawpaw, and mountain pepperbush.

- The *southern Appalachian forest,* found above the foothills from Georgia to central Virginia, contains more tree species than any other forest in North America and actually takes in a range of different forest types that can vary dramatically according to elevation. Climax hardwood forests of basswood, birch, maple, beech, tuliptree, ash, and magnolia can be found in some coves, while, above about 4,000 feet, the climax forests are typically spruce, fir, and hemlock, particularly on the wetter western slopes. Old-growth forest can be found in isolated parts of the Great Smoky Mountains National Park. Oak forests often predominate on the eastern faces of the mountains, which typically do not receive as much moisture. Pine and oak may mix on some slopes. At higher elevations, the understory is less varied: Shrubs of mountain laurel and rhododendron form nearly impenetrable thickets that are densest where conditions are wettest.

- The *transition forest* tends to be wetter and more northerly than the mixed deciduous forest. Hikers marveling at the colors of a New England fall are admiring the transition forest. It extends across the hillsides and lowlands of the north and reaches down into the high country of the southern Appalachians. It appears as a mosaic of spruce, fir, hemlock, pine, birch, maple, basswood, and beech forests. The substory of transition forest tends to be more open, with ferns and shrubs of elderberry, hazel, and bush honeysuckle, and often a thick carpet of evergreen needles covers the ground under the trees. Conifers tend to predominate at the higher elevations.

- The northern, or *boreal forest,* is the largest North American forest. Most of it is in Canada and Alaska, but A.T. hikers encounter it while traversing the highest ridges of the southern Appalachians and the coniferous uplands of northern New England. Pines and hemlocks characterize its southern reaches, while dwarfed spruces and firs (known as *krummholz* or *taiga*) grow at treeline in New Hampshire and Maine, just as they grow at the borders of the arctic lands farther north. In between is a spruce-fir climax forest. Evergreens such as white pine, red pine, white spruce, balsam fir, black spruce, and jack pine predominate, but hardwoods such as aspen and birch are mixed in as well. The ground of the boreal forest is typically thin and muddy, with little in the way of an understory, and it includes sphagnum bogs surrounded by a wide variety of aquatic plants, ferns, subalpine plants, blueberry bushes, and mountain maple and ash shrubs.

What wildflowers can I look for, and when will I see them?
Among the small joys of hiking the Trail are the wildflowers that grow along the way. Some poke their heads out of the forest duff in late winter and are gone by the time the spreading canopy of late-spring trees blocks out the sun. Some cluster near the edges of clearings in midsummer, while others hide in the deep shade. And, still others blossom amid the falling leaves and early snows of the Appalachian fall.

Winter/early spring—First to bloom in swampy areas most years is the maroon-colored cowl that shelters the tiny, foul-smelling flowers of skunk cabbage, which may appear while snow is still on the ground. In March and April, along the high, dry ridges, the delicate starbursts of bloodroot appear, along with the corncob-like clusters of squaw root on fallen oak trees; the graceful, lily-like dogtooth violet; the white bunches of early saxifrage; fanlike, purple clusters of dwarf iris in southern sections; the pink-purple flowers and liver-shaped leaves of hepatica; the delicate, white rue anemone; the bee-buzzing carpets of fringed phacelia in the South; and the waxy, pink trailing arbutus farther north.

Spring/early summer—During May and June, as the tree canopy shades the forest floor, the variety of wildflowers blooming along the A.T. becomes too extensive to keep track of. The bubblegum scent and orange blooms of flame azalea shrubs burst out in the southern Appalachians, along with the white and pink blossoms of its close relatives, mountain laurel and rhododendron. The garlicky wild leek, or ramp, flowers in early summer. Hikers may spot the green tubes of jack-in-the-pulpit, dove-like red clusters of wild columbine, vessel-like orchid blossoms of pink lady's-slipper, spade-leaved trillium, bright blue of viper's bugloss, the blue-violet of spiderwort in sunny clearings, black cohosh's delicate cone of tiny blooms, and, in the cold bogs of the northern states, the white blossoms of Labrador tea and the pink pentagons of bog laurel.

Late summer—The heat of July and August in the Appalachians coaxes blossoms from a number of mountain shrubs, shade plants, and meadow plants. The wintergreen shrub blooms white in oak forests, the white starbursts of tall meadow rue appear near open fields, the white petals of the bug-trapping sundew appear in wet areas, mountain cranberry's small bell-like pink blossoms appear in New England, the white-and-yellow sunbursts of oxeye daisy grow along hedgerows, and the greenish-white clusters of wild sarsaparilla appear in the dry, open woods. In the mid-Atlantic states, the understory becomes a waist-deep sea of wood nettle, the delicate white flowers of which belie unpleasant stinging hairs that bristle from the stems and leaves. The succulent stalks of jewel-weed, which has a pale yellow flower, often sprout nearby, and their juice can help ease the sting and itch of the nettles and poison ivy.

Fall and early winter—Certain wildflowers continue blooming late into the fall along the A.T., disappearing from the woods about the same time hikers do. Goldenrod spreads across open fields in September, about the time the leaves start changing color. The intricate white discs of Queen Anne's lace adorn ditches and roadsides until late in the year. Other common fall wildflowers include aster, wood sorrel, monkshood, and butter-and-eggs.

Can I eat wild plants I find?
You could eat certain plants, but, in keeping with the principles of Leave No Trace, you shouldn't. Leave the wild blueberries and raspberries and blackberries of summer for the birds and bears. Resist the temptation to spice up your noodles with ramps in the spring. "Chicken of the woods" mushrooms should stay in the woods. Wild watercress belongs in a stream, not a salad. Rather than brewing your own ginseng or sassafras tea from wild roots, visit the supermarket in town. Many edible plants along the A.T. are rare and endangered, and harvesting them is illegal. Even when the flora are plentiful, remember that the fauna of the Appalachians have no option other than to forage for it; you do.

What rare or endangered plant species might I see?
Most of the federally listed plant species (threatened or endangered) along the Appalachian Trail are found in the high country of the southern Appalachians or the alpine environments of northern New England. There are too many to list here, but typical of those in the southern Appalachians is the spreading avens, a plant with fan-shaped leaves and small, yellow flowers that grows in rock crevices. Although bluets are common along the A.T., a subspecies called Roan Mountain bluet is found in only nine

sites there—the only known sites in the world. Gray's lily is found only on the high balds near Roan Mountain. Although goldenrod is plentiful along the Trail and sometimes considered something of a pest, one rare subspecies, the Blue Ridge goldenrod, is known to exist only on one cliff in North Carolina. Similarly, many of the plants at and above treeline in New England, such as Robbins cinquefoil, are extremely vulnerable to damage from hikers wandering off the A.T. Below treeline, plants such as the small whorled pogonia, an orchid, are threatened by development. Please don't pick the flowers along the A.T.—they might be the only ones of a kind.

The how and why of Trail construction

Who decides which route the Trail takes?

A local Trail-maintaining club, in consultation with the Appalachian Trail Conservancy and the government agency responsible for managing the land in question, determines the route that the footpath follows over a section. According to the National Trails System Act that authorized federal protection of the A.T., the goal is to expose the walker to "the maximum outdoor recreation potential and … enjoyment of the nationally significant scenic, historic, natural, or cultural qualities of the area." In plain language, that means routing the Trail in such a way that walkers have the chance to encounter and appreciate the wildlife, geography, and geology, as well as the historical and natural context of the Appalachians, while merging with, exploring, and harmonizing with the mountain environment.

How is today's A.T. different from the original Trail?

When the A.T. was first built, the main goal was a continuous, marked route, which often meant connecting existing footpaths and woods roads. Long sections of "roadwalks" linked the footpaths. Where no existing routes were available, Trail builders marked out new ones, cleared brush, and painted blazes. But, that was about it, and, for many years, when few people knew about or hiked the Trail, it was enough. Beginning in the 1960s, two things happened: The A.T. became a part of the national park system, and the numbers of people using it began skyrocketing. With increased use, mud and erosion became problems.

As the Trail was moved away from existing footpaths and roads and onto new paths planned and built especially for the A.T. on federal land, Trail builders began "hardening" the path and designing it to stand up to heavier use.

What causes the Trail to deteriorate?

Erosion can damage the footpath quickly. The mineral soil of the footpath is made of very fine particles bound together by clay that, once broken from the ground by boots and hiking poles, is easily washed away by fast-flowing water. (Water moving at two miles per hour has sixty-four times more ability to carry soil particles than water moving at one mile per hour.) Trail builders work to separate water from the treadway. Where that is not possible, they try to slow it down. Since water in rivulets or ruts flows faster than water flowing across the Trail in sheets, trail builders try to channel water off the part that hikers walk on. Where they can't, they slant the path outward so that water will stay "thin" and flow slowly off the sides in a sheet, rather than becoming "thick" and channeling down the middle of the Trail.

Why are parts of the Trail routed over narrow log walkways?

Believe it or not, it's not to keep your feet dry. The goal is to protect the land, not your nice, new boots. Bog bridges, also called "puncheon," allow the Trail to take hikers into an important part of the mountain environment without turning such ecologically sensitive swamp areas into hopeless quagmires, disrupting plant and animal life there. The Trail is supposed to "wear lightly on the land," and this is one way to do so. Walkways may be built on piles driven into the ground, or they may "float" on boggy ground; in both cases, the wetlands are disturbed much less than they would be by mud holes that widen every time a hiker tries to skirt the edges.

Why does the Trail zigzag up steep mountains?

When it was first marked, the Trail often climbed steep slopes by the most direct route, and older parts of today's Trail still tend to have the steepest sections. But, water runs faster down a steeper trail and erodes it more quickly. In recent years, many sections have been rerouted so that the Trail ascends by way of "sidehill" that slants up a mountainside and "switchbacks" that zigzag across its steepest faces. Again, it isn't done to make the Trail easier for hikers, although that's sometimes the effect, but rather to make the footpath itself more durable and less subject to erosion.

How does the Trail cross creeks and rivers?

Bridges take the Trail across all its major river crossings, except for the Kennebec River in Maine (where hikers ferry across in canoes). Most, such as the Bear Mountain Bridge across the Hudson in New York, are highway bridges; a few others, such as the James River Foot Bridge in Virginia, are built especially for foot travelers. A few large creeks require fording, but most are crossed by footbridges or stepping stones. Small streams may require fording when spring floods submerge the rocks and stepping stones that lead across them.

Why are there so many logs and rock barriers in the path?

Unless the logs result from a "blowdown" (a fallen tree) or the rocks from a rockslide, they're probably water-diversion devices, such as waterbars or check dams that have been added to older, eroding sections of the Trail. Avoid stepping on them, if possible: Not only can they be slippery (particularly the logs), but they will last longer if you step over them.

Why is the Trail so rocky?

As you may have read in the section of this guide devoted to geology, the Appalachians are the product of erosion, which tends to strip away soil and leave rocks on the surface. Since rocky sections offer a durable surface and often provide spectacular views for hikers, Trail designers don't hesitate to route the footpath along them. This is particularly true from central Virginia through Connecticut and eastern New Hampshire through Maine; many older sections of the Trail are routed along ridge-lines. Typically, the A.T. will climb a ridge on smoother "sidehill" Trail and then follow a rocky ridgeline for some distance, before descending again.

Summary of Distances

Miles from Davenport Gap, Tenn.		Miles from Springer Mountain
0.0	Davenport Gap, Tenn. 32/N.C. 284; northern park boundary	235.9
0.9	Davenport Gap Shelter	235.0
5.2	Mt. Cammerer Side Trail (5,000')	230.7
8.0	Cosby Knob Shelter	227.9
11.9	Snake Den Ridge Trail	224.0
13.8	Mt. Guyot Side Trail	222.1
14.5	Guyot Spur (6,360')	221.4
15.7	Tri-Corner Knob Shelter	220.2
16.7	Mt. Chapman	219.2
18.2	Mt. Sequoyah	217.7
20.9	Pecks Corner Shelter (0.5m E)	215.0
25.5	Porters Gap, the Sawteeth	210.4
27.4	Charlies Bunion	207.5
28.3	Icewater Spring Shelter	207.6
28.6	Boulevard Trail to Mt. LeConte	207.3
31.3	Newfound Gap, U.S. 441 (5,045')	204.6
33.0	Indian Gap	202.9
35.8	Mt. Collins Shelter (0.5m W)	200.1
38.0	Mt. Love	197.9
39.2	Clingmans Dome (6,643')	196.7
42.1	Double Spring Gap Shelter (5,507')	193.8
43.6	Silers Bald	192.3
43.8	Silers Bald Shelter	192.1
46.5	Buckeye Gap (4,817')	189.4
49.3	Derrick Knob Shelter	186.6
50.4	Sugar Tree Gap (4,435')	185.5
52.8	Mineral Gap (5,030')	183.1

Miles from Davenport Gap, Tenn.		Miles from Springer Mountain
53.5	Beechnut Gap	182.4
54.4	Rocky Top	181.5
55.6	Eagle Creek Trail to Spence Field Shelter (0.2m E), Bote Mountain Trail	180.3
58.5	Russell Field Shelter	177.4
60.7	Devil's Tater Patch (4,775')	173.2
61.0	Mollies Ridge Shelter	174.9
64.1	Doe Knob (4,520')	171.8
66.4	Birch Spring Campsite	169.5
67.6	Shuckstack Mountain	168.3
71.6	Little Tennessee River, Fontana Dam, Southern park boundary	164.3
72.0	Fontana Dam Visitors Center	163.9
72.3	Fontana Dam Shelter	163.6
73.4	N.C. 28	162.5
76.1	Walker Gap (3,450')	159.8
78.9	Cable Gap Shelter	157.0
79.8	Yellow Creek Gap, Yellow Creek Mountain Road (2,980')	156.1
82.2	Cody Gap	153.7
84.8	Brown Fork Gap	151.1
85.0	Brown Fork Gap Shelter	150.9
87.4	Stecoah Gap, N.C. 143 (3,165') (Sweetwater Creek Road)	148.5
90.5	Locust Cove Gap	145.4
92.9	Cheoah Bald (5,062')	143.0
94.1	Sassafras Gap Shelter	141.8
95.0	Swim Bald	140.9

Miles from Davenport Gap, Tenn.		Miles from Springer Mountain
97.9	Grassy Gap (3,050')	138.0
101.0	U.S. 19, U.S. 74, Nantahala River (1,740'); Wesser, N.C.	134.9
101.8	A. Rufus Morgan Shelter	134.1
106.7	Wesser Creek Trail, Wesser Bald Shelter	129.2
107.5	Wesser Bald (4,627')	128.4
108.9	Tellico Gap, N.C. 1365 (3,850')	127.0
110.6	Side trail to Rocky Bald Lookout	125.3
111.8	Copper Ridge Bald Lookout (5,150')	124.1
112.5	Cold Spring Shelter	123.4
113.7	Burningtown Gap, N.C. 1397 (4,250')	122.2
117.3	Wayah Shelter	118.6
117.8	Campsite	118.1
118.2	Wayah Bald (5,342')	117.7
120.1	Wine Spring	115.8
122.4	Wayah Gap, N.C. 1310 (4,130')	113.5
124.6	Siler Bald Shelter (0.5m E)	111.3
126.3	Panther Gap	109.6
127.2	Swinging Lick Gap	108.7
127.4	Campsite	108.5
128.3	Winding Stair Gap, U.S. 64	107.6
131.4	Wallace Gap, Old U.S. 64	104.5
132.1	Rock Gap Shelter	103.8
134.6	Glassmine Gap	101.3
137.4	Big Spring Shelter	98.5
138.0	Albert Mountain (5,220')	97.9

Miles from Davenport Gap, Tenn.		Miles from Springer Mountain
138.3	Bear Pen Trail, USFS 67	97.6
139.6	Mooney Gap, USFS 83	96.3
140.5	Betty Creek Gap (4,300′)	95.4
144.2	Carter Gap Shelter	91.7
144.6	Timber Ridge Trail	91.3
147.4	Beech Gap (4,460′)	88.5
150.3	Lower Trail Ridge Trail, Standing Indian Mountain (5,498′)	85.6
151.8	Standing Indian Shelter	84.1
152.7	Deep Gap, USFS 71 (4,340′)	83.2
155.7	Chunky Gal Trail	80.2
156.0	Whiteoak Stamp	79.9
156.7	Muskrat Creek Shelter (4,600′)	79.2
157.6	Sassafras Gap	78.3
159.5	Bly Gap (3,880′)	76.4
159.6	North Carolina–Georgia Line	76.3
161.7	Campsite	73.2
162.6	Blue Ridge Gap (3,020′)	73.3
163.2	As Knob	72.7
163.9	Plumorchard Gap Shelter (0.2m E)	72.0
166.6	Cowart Gap	69.3
167.3	Campsite	68.6
168.4	Dicks Creek Gap, U.S. 76	67.5
170.6	Powell Mountain (3,850′)	65.3
171.9	Deep Gap Shelter (0.3m E)	64.0
172.8	Kelly Knob (4,276′)	63.1
173.8	Addis Gap (3,304′)	62.1
175.8	Swag of the Blue Ridge	60.1

Miles from Davenport Gap, Tenn.		Miles from Springer Mountain
179.4	Tray Mountain Shelter (0.2m W)	56.5
179.8	Tray Mountain (4,430')	56.1
180.6	Tray Gap, Tray Mountain Road (USFS 79)	55.3
181.4	Cheese Factory Campsite	54.5
181.7	Tray Mountain Road (USFS 79)	54.2
182.4	Indian Grave Gap (3,113')	53.5
183.7	Rocky Mountain (4,017')	52.2
185.0	Unicoi Gap, Ga. 75 (2,949')	50.9
186.4	Blue Mountain (4,025')	49.5
187.2	Blue Mountain Shelter	48.7
188.1	Campsite	47.8
189.4	Chattahoochee Gap (3,500')	46.5
190.6	Cold Springs Gap	45.3
194.4	Low Gap Shelter (3,050')	41.5
195.2	Sheep Rock Top	40.7
196.9	Poor Mountain	39.0
198.8	Hogpen Gap, Ga. 348 (3,450')	37.1
199.0	Whitley Gap Shelter (1.2m E)	36.9
199.7	Tesnatee Gap, Ga. 348 (3,138')	36.2
200.5	Cowrock Mountain (3,842')	35.4
201.0	Baggs Creek Gap	34.9
203.7	Levelland Mountain (3,942')	32.2
205.2	Neels Gap, U.S. 19/129	30.7
206.2	Trail to Byron Reece Memorial	29.7
207.6	Blood Mountain Shelter (4,461')	28.3
208.4	Slaughter Creek Campsite	27.5
208.9	Wood's Hole Shelter (0.4m W)	27.0

Miles from Davenport Gap, Tenn.		Miles from Springer Mountain
210.7	Burnett Field Mountain	25.2
213.5	Dan Gap	22.4
214.8	Big Cedar Mountain (3,737')	21.1
215.8	Woody Gap, Ga. 60 (3,150')	20.1
217.2	Ramrock Mountain	18.7
219.4	Gooch Gap, USFS 42 (2,784')	16.5
220.8	Gooch Mountain Shelter (0.1m W)	15.1
222.1	Justus Creek (2,550')	13.8
224.1	Cooper Gap, USFS 42/80	11.8
227.6	Hightower Gap, USFS 42/69	8.3
228.1	Hawk Mountain Shelter (0.2m W)	7.8
229.9	Logging Road	6.0
231.6	Three Forks, USFS 58 (2,530')	4.3
233.1	Stover Creek Shelter	2.8
234.9	USFS 42	1.0
235.7	Springer Mountain Shelter (0.2m E)	0.2
235.9	Springer Mountain (3,782')	0.0

Index